THE SILENCED MAJORITY

Our Nick,

Democracy Now!

THE SILENCED MAJORITY
STORIES OF UPRISINGS, OCCUPATIONS, RESISTANCE, AND HOPE

AMY GOODMAN
AND
DENIS MOYNIHAN

Haymarket Books
Chicago, Illinois

© 2012 Amy Goodman and Denis Moynihan

Published by
Haymarket Books
P.O. Box 180165, Chicago, IL 60618
773-583-7884
info@haymarketbooks.org
www.haymarketbooks.org

ISBN: 978-1-60846-231-5

Trade distribution:
In the U.S. through Consortium Book Sales and Distribution, www.cbsd.com
In the UK, Turnaround Publisher Services, www.turnaround-uk.com
In Canada, Publishers Group Canada, www.pgcbooks.ca
In Australia, Palgrave Macmillan, www.palgravemacmillan.com.au
All other countries, Publishers Group Worldwide, www.pgw.com

Special discounts are available for bulk purchases by organizations and institutions. Please contact Haymarket Books for more information at 773-583-7884 or
info@haymarketbooks.org.

This book was published with the generous support of the Wallace Global Fund
and the Lannan Foundation.

Author photograph by David Belisle courtesy of *Democracy Now!*

Printed in Canada by union labor.

Library of Congress CIP Data is available.

1 3 5 7 9 10 8 6 4 2

MIX
Paper from
responsible sources
FSC® C103567

This book is dedicated to our parents,
Patricia Moynihan, the late Michael Moynihan
and the late George and Dorrie Goodman

TABLE OF CONTENTS

Acknowledgments

This book exists only thanks to the contributions and support of so many.

First, the remarkable team at *Democracy Now!*, who work day and night to give voice to the Silenced Majority. Julie Crosby, Brenda Murad, and Karen Ranucci have for many years committed themselves tirelessly, and without them our work would be impossible.

Our daily, global, grassroots news hour is produced by a remarkable team, including *Democracy Now!*'s award-winning journalist and cohost Juan Gonzalez, our incredible team of producers: Mike Burke, Renee Feltz, Aaron Maté, Steve Martinez, Nermeen Shaikh, Deena Guzder, Hany Massoud, Robby Karran, Sam Alcoff, and Amy Littlefield; and the team who pulls together the broadcast each morning, including Mike DiFilippo, Miguel Nogueira, Becca Staley, Hugh Gran, John Wallach, Vesta Goodarz, Jon Randolph, Kieran Krug-Meadows, Rah Campenni, Carlo de Jesus, Ahmed Abdel Kouddous, Jon Gerberg and Manal Khan; and the crew who helps keep the whole operation running smoothly, among whom are Neil Shibata, Isis Phillips, Angie Karran, Miriam Barnard, Rob Young, Wayne Neale, Jessica Lee, Simin Farkhondeh, Diana Sands, Sumner Rieland and Brendan Allen.

Democracy Now!'s Spanish language team, in addition to putting out our daily headlines in text and audio for the world, also does a very careful translation of the column, along with an audio version of it. Spanning many countries, this amazing group includes Clara Ibarra, Maria Eva Blotta, Mercedes Camps, Alléne Hébert, César Gamboa, Fernanda Gómez, Andres Conteris, Oscar Benitez, Daniella Méndez, Marcela Schenck, Gonzalo Giuria, Rossana Spinelli, Fernanda Gerpe, and the inimitable Chuck Scurich.

Also, we continue to be inspired by the very talented journalists who have worked with us and moved on to continue as friends as they pursue their work around the world, including Sharif Abdel Kouddous, Anjali Kamat, Nicole Salazar, Ana Nogueira, Elizabeth Press, John Hamilton, Jaisal Noor, Ryan Devereaux, Frank Lopez, Julie Drizin, Dan Coughlin, Rick Rowley, Jacquie Soohen and Jeremy Scahill. Allan Nairn remains a constant inspiration as both friend and journalist.

We thank Patrick Lannan, Andy Tuch, Laurie Betlach, Randall Wallace, Janet MacGillivray Wallace, Irma Weiss, Diana Cohn, Israel and Edith Taub, Len Goodman, Edith Penty, Roy Singham and the Thoughtworkers.

At King Features, Glenn Mott, the ever-patient Chris Richcreek, and Amy Anderson, and the talented team at Haymarket Books, especially Anthony Arnove, Julie Fain, Sarah Macaraeg, and Eric Kerl.

Also deep appreciation for the support of Elisabeth Benjamin, Caren Spruch, Maria Carrion, and their little and not-so-little ones, Ceci, Rory, Sara, Aliza, Gabriela, and Estrella.

Loving thanks to our family members, as always, who provide constant support, including the Goodman brothers, Dan, David and Steve, along with sisters-in-law Sue Minter and Ruth Levine, and all the incredible nieces and nephews: Jasper, Ariel, Eli, Sarah and Anna. Also the Moynihan brothers Tim, Sean and Mike, sister Deirdre, sisters-in-law Mary, Kate, and Amy, the nieces and nephews Quinn, Liam, Maren, Nora, Evan, Maeve and Fergus, and, for her support, caring, and tolerance for frequent absences, Denis' fiancée, Trish Schoch.

July 17, 2012

Foreword by Michael Moore

I first met Amy Goodman in the first month of the First Palestinian Intifada. It's where I usually go to meet people. You throw an intifada—I'm there! And so is Amy. In fact, if you're in the middle of any sort of rebellion, revolution, uprising or you're just getting the familiar everyday ass-whoopin' by forces that seem much greater than yours, that is where you'll find the fearless Amy Goodman. It's safe to say that she lives by the promise Tom Joad made to his mother at the end of Steinbeck's *Grapes of Wrath*:

> "I'll be ever'where. . . . Wherever there's a fight so hungry people can eat, I'll be there. Wherever there's a cop beatin' up a guy, I'll be there."

If there's one thing you can trust, it's that Amy Goodman will always be there.

The weeks we spent together in the West Bank and Gaza were, to say the least, quite harrowing, and yet they had a profound impact on both of us. It was just after Christmas 1987, and the Palestinian people had decided to rise up and resist their Israeli minders with protests, civil disobedience, and stones. Stones! Ah, remember the days of stones? Such an innocent time it was back then.

Ralph Nader had asked a group of us, mostly writers and journalists, to go over to the Occupied Territories and bring back to the American public the truth about what was really going on. Little did we know that we would be witnessing the first weeks of what, sadly, is now a twenty-five-year-long resistance.

Here's the dominant image in my head of Amy Goodman during that month in Palestine: When the Israeli soldiers started firing their rubber bullets at us and a group of unarmed Palestinians, we would all run the other way (i.e., away from the bullets) and Amy Goodman would be running the opposite way—straight into melee. She appeared as if she were invincible, and while I do not want to imply she's some sort of superhero with supernatural powers, I will say that I'm glad she's on our side and leave it at that!

Two years later, in 1990, Amy Goodman and fellow journalist Allan Nairn traveled to East Timor to cover their independence movement. And it was there that she personally witnessed the murder and massacre of 270 Timorese civilians by the Indonesian army. And for bearing witness to this horrific event, she and Allan were beaten by the army officials. I cannot imagine what it would be like to be present while 270 people are being killed. But there was Amy, again, on the front lines, searching out the truth, and at great personal risk.

Amy is a serious journalist who has won many of the nation's top journalism honors, including the George Polk Award, the Alfred I. duPont–Columbia University Award, and the Robert F. Kennedy Journalism Award, among others.

Amy's daily television and radio show, *Democracy Now!*, is currently in its sixteenth year. How on earth she and her remarkable team pull this together, day after day, is beyond me. (When I did a weekly TV show I wanted to throw myself into the East River at the end of every week.) I have been on her show many times and I have seen backstage the incredible, professional operation they have over there in downtown Manhattan. I don't know if they give tours like they do at NBC, but I would put the *Democracy Now!* headquarters on any intelligent tourist's must-see list.

This book, produced in cooperation with the incomparable Denis Moynihan, contains many of Amy's commentaries and columns over the past years. It is fascinating reading, a true chronicle of our times, and a real head shaker as you read it and wonder: "How is it we're still here?"

Back in early 1988, as we traveled the back roads of the West Bank, going from one village to another, there was much that we saw that would make even the most committed among us give up hope, beset with the knowledge that true justice seemed like a faraway destination. After all, this was a struggle between a massive military machine that had nuclear weapons and children with slingshots. Who wins that fight? Well, there was a day a long, long time ago that an oppressed people had a young boy with a slingshot, and that boy used that slingshot, and for that his people would be free. So, we didn't leave Palestine in total despair. In fact, we were deeply inspired by the will and determination of the people we met, people who had nothing, people who were in it for the long haul and had no intention of giving up. It was a good lesson for us to learn.

It would be another two years before I would release my first film, *Roger & Me*, and it would be eight more years before *Democracy Now!* would go on the air. We became committed to doing our best with the slingshots we have.

Journalism for (and by) the 99 Percent

> *The media conglomerates are not the only industry whose own-*
> *ers have become monopolistic in the American economy. But*
> *media products are unique in one vital respect. They do not*
> *manufacture nuts and bolts: they manufacture a social and po-*
> *litical world.*
>
> —Ben Bagdikian, *The New Media Monopoly*

Media coverage of the Occupy Wall Street movement and of the Arab Spring challenged much of the traditional corporate media around the world. Whether broadcasting from Tahrir Square, under the yoke of a U.S.-backed military dictatorship, or from Liberty Square, being beaten and harassed by the NYPD, a vibrant independent media emerged, a media that let people speak for themselves.

We need a media that covers grassroots movements, that seeks to understand and explain the complex forces that shape our society, a media that empowers people with information to make sound decisions on the most vital issues of the day: war and peace, life and death. Instead, the media system in the United States, increasingly concentrated in the hands of fewer and fewer multinational corporations, spews a relentless stream of base "reality" shows (which depict anything but reality), hollow excuses for local news that highlight car accidents and convenience store robberies larded with ads, and the obsessive coverage of traffic, sports, and extreme weather (never linked to another two words: *climate change*). Perhaps most harmful of all, we get the same small circle of pundits who know so little about so much, explaining the world to us and getting it so wrong.

The corporate media came late to Occupy Wall Street, offered superficial, often derogatory coverage, and, with a few exceptions, still haven't gotten it right. *Democracy Now!* was on the story before it began. Justin Wedes, one of the organizers, told our team the day before OWS started, "More than having any specific demand per se, I think the purpose of September seventeenth, for many of us who are helping to organize it and people who are coming out, is to begin a conversation, as citizens, as people affected by this financial system in collapse, as to how we're going to fix it, as to what we're going to do in order to make it work for us again."

As the protest unfolded on its first day, organizer Lorenzo Serna told *Democracy Now!*, "The idea is to have an encampment . . . this isn't a one-day event. We're hoping that people come prepared to stay as long as they can and that we're there to support each other." Another participant explained, "I came because I'm upset with the fact that the bailout of Wall Street didn't help any of the people holding mortgages. All of the money went to Wall Street, and none of it went to Main Street."

The gross disparity in coverage between independent, noncommercial news organizations like *Democracy Now!* and most of the corporate entities was part of the problem that drove the OWS movement in the first place. Among the grievances against corporations detailed in the first major statement of OWS, the September 29, 2011, Declaration of the Occupation of New York City, was "They purposely keep people misinformed and fearful through their control of the media."

True to OWS's accusations, corporate media descended on Zuccotti Park, complaining that the movement had no identifiable leaders and no clear, concise list of demands. Freshly hired by CNN, Erin Burnett, known for her fawning interviews with corporate CEOs at her prior position on the financial channel CNBC, produced, for her first show on CNN, a mocking segment called "Seriously?!" She opened with a clichéd video montage, mischaracterizing protesters as dirty, unemployed layabouts seeking handouts who were universally ignorant of the very financial industry they were protesting:

ERIN BURNETT: Seriously, it's a mixed bag. But they were happy to take some time from their books, banjos, bongos, sports drinks, catered lunch. Yes, there was catered lunch, designer yoga clothing—that's a little lemon logo— computers, lots of MacBooks, and phones to help us get to the bottom of it. This is unemployed software developer Dan. . . . So do you know that taxpayers actually made money on the Wall Street bailout?

DAN: I was unaware of that.

ERIN BURNETT: They did. They made—not on GM, but they did on the Wall Street part of the bailout.

DAN: Okay.

ERIN BURNETT: Does that make you feel any differently?

DAN: Well, I would have to do more research about it, but um—

ERIN BURNETT: If I were right it might?

DAN: Oh, sure.

[END VIDEO CLIP]

ERIN BURNETT: Seriously?! That's all it would take to put an end to the unrest?

Well, as promised we did go double-check the numbers on the bank bailout and this is what we found. Yes, the bank bailouts made money for American taxpayers, right now to the tune of $10 billion, anticipated that it will be $20 billion. Those are seriously the numbers. This was the big issue, so we solved it.

Burnett ambushed one person, asking about what is likely the largest and most complex emergency financial program in the history of money, claiming that the purported revenue from the U.S. Treasury's TARP should mollify the OWS protesters. Jump over to nonprofit investigative news organization ProPublica's detailed reportage on the bailout, and you see that the $10 billion to $20 billion in reported revenue from TARP is dwarfed by the hundreds of billions still outstanding, likely never to be recovered. Burnett's coverage was sadly typical.

Skeptical of the corporate media, people have developed their own. The decade that preceded OWS saw the rapid maturation of the digital media sector. In late 1999, media activists set up an independent media center and website to cover the World Trade Organization protest in Seattle, Washington. Days after going live, Indymedia.org was getting more hits than CNN.com, exposing police violence denied by the mainstream news. In the lead-up to the invasion of Iraq in 2002–2003, when the public was being force-fed pro-war propaganda through the mainstream media (weapons of mass destruction? mushroom clouds?), millions turned to the Internet as an alternative source of information, and people around the globe used it to organize the largest antiwar protests in history. On February 15, 2003, millions rocked the globe for peace. During major protests in New York City in 2004, against President George W. Bush and the Republican National Convention, technology activists deployed a program that allowed protesters to coordinate actions, TXTMob, which later evolved into Twitter.

Justin Wedes explained media strategy as we walked through Liberty Square, the name given by OWS to Zuccotti Park in lower Manhattan: "Throughout this process, we understood the importance of having an independent media center—in other words, of creating our own media. We could never rely on the mainstream media to depict us fairly. And we wanted to be the most go-to, responsible, accurate depictors of what is happening in this space. So, from day one, we set up an Indymedia Center, which includes a live stream."

The live video streams of OWS advanced independent media strategy by making the unfiltered activity of the occupation available in real time to a global audience. The way the protest was organized, how the General Assembly operated and how working groups were established, was all streamed live, serving as an organizing template for solidarity occupations that began sprouting around the world. GlobalRevolution.tv, a group formed at OWS to videostream the events there and to aggregate live video feeds from around the world, was co-founded by Vlad Teichberg, a Muscovite whose parents were forced out of the Soviet Union in the early 1980s. Teichberg was a derivatives trader on Wall Street until 2001, when he saw both the negative effects of globalization pushed by his industry and the rightward political shift in the United States following 9/11. He quit and became an activist opposing corporate power.

Teichberg told *Democracy Now!* that the media center "allows many people to work together to push out the message of what is being done, why it's being done. . . . About a week and a week and a half into the protests, we finally broke through the mainstream media wall. At least the event was no longer boycotted or blocked. And, you know, the rest was history."

The live video stream, along with increased interest in the story from mainstream journalists, and the near ubiquity of cell phone cameras and social media, allowed for another aspect of the protests to become widely and instantly publicized: the police crackdown. Thousands of arrests have been made since OWS started, in New York and around the country, including those of an extraordinary number of journalists. Josh Stearns of the media policy group Free Press started documenting the stories and amassed a list of close to sixty journalists arrested at the time of this writing.

In New York City, the volume of the arrests, and the police harassment and intimidation of journalists, led a consortium of news outlets and professional organizations, including the *New York Times*, the Associated Press, Reuters, and Dow Jones, to appeal for action from Mayor Michael Bloomberg and Police Commissioner Raymond Kelly.

During the November 15, 2011, early-morning raid on Zuccotti Park, BuzzFeed's Rosie Gray told the police she was press and was told back, "Not tonight." In mid-December, police raided the Brooklyn building to which Global Revolution TV moved after the shutdown of Liberty Square, arresting Teichberg and five other volunteers. Other occupants of the building, which the city's Department of Buildings abruptly deemed "imminently perilous to life," were not arrested.

Arrests of reporters, as Stearns' data show, are not limited to New York City, and present a serious threat to journalism. Targeting of journalists is by no means a new phenomenon. What seems to be accelerating, along with the technological ease with which both the press and the public can record, stream, post, and otherwise publish events as they occur, is police interference, through intimidation, forced relocation away from sites of newsworthy events, assault, destruction of equipment or the erasure of digital media, and arrest.

Three years earlier, two colleagues and one of us (Amy) were violently arrested while covering the 2008 Republican National Convention in St. Paul, Minnesota. The police pulled the battery from my coworker Nicole Salazar's video camera as they pinned her to the ground, bloodying her face. After Sharif Abdel Kouddous and I were handcuffed, a U.S. Secret Service agent tore our press credentials from our necks, declaring, "You won't be needing these anymore." More than forty journalists were arrested there that week. St. Paul Police Chief John Harrington offered no apologies. Rather, he suggested we could "embed" with the mobile field force. He was referring to the Pentagon system of embedding reporters with the troops in Iraq and Afghanistan, which has brought the media to an all-time low.

Embed with the police? Rather than do that, we sued and, after three years, won a settlement, which included, in addition to a monetary penalty, the requirement that the St. Paul police receive training in how to conduct themselves while being covered by the press. The court ordered that the course curriculum meet the approval of the three journalists who had been arrested, along with that of the American Civil Liberties Union and the Center for Constitutional

Rights. While enormously time-consuming, the lawsuit was one of the only available means by which to hold the authorities accountable.

At the heart of the Occupy Wall Street movement is the critique that wealth and opportunity are not equitably distributed, and our media system, largely controlled by corporations, contributes to that status quo. The Internet has created a seismic disruption to the balance of power in the media. It is getting easier and easier to post your thoughts, photos, or videos. Yet the Wild West of the Web is being tamed. Small Internet service providers are being driven out of business, with corporations like Comcast, Time Warner, Verizon, and AT&T dominating the market. Privacy, security, and the freedom to publish without fear of censorship are dwindling with each merger, with each effort by corporate lobbyists to further restrict the open Internet in favor of a narrow profit advantage.

While fighting to preserve a free Internet, journalists, press organizations, and the public must not give up on the older legacy media institutions. Television is still how most Americans get their news. We have a public television system in the United States that is a shadow of public broadcasting abroad, forever hobbled by congressional threats to "zero out" its budget. Groups like the Prometheus Radio Project fought for over a decade to win an opening for potentially thousands of new, low-power FM community radio stations to open. To take advantage of that, groups will have to organize and do the hard legwork to submit applications to the Federal Communications Commission. Public access television stations around the country are under attack from cable companies, who want to defund and shutter them, which will require time and organizing to combat.

The "crisis in journalism," which has been blamed on the Internet's disruption of traditional advertising business models, is also traceable to the very corporate behavior that many of the Occupiers are protesting. Leveraged buyouts of media properties have left newspapers with massive debt, forcing layoffs of journalists and support staff. By stripping away the profit motive, by removing the Wall Street bankers from the picture, solid, disciplined, nonprofit journalism is possible.

When the police raided Zuccotti Park on November 15, 2011, and evicted the entire occupation, they destroyed the 5,000-plus-book OWS People's Library, along with the tent that housed it, which had been donated by legendary rocker and National Book Award winner Patti Smith. The *Democracy Now!*

team managed to get behind police lines to document the raid. Amid the rubble, we found one tattered book that escaped the library's destruction: Aldous Huxley's *Brave New World Revisited*, published in 1958.

Huxley wrote in the book: "Big Business, made possible by advancing technology and the consequent ruin of Little Business, is controlled by the State—that is to say, by a small group of party leaders and the soldiers, policemen and civil servants who carry out their orders. In a capitalist democracy, such as the United States, it is controlled by what Professor C. Wright Mills has called the Power Elite." Huxley goes on, "This Power Elite directly employs several millions of the country's working force in its factories, offices and stores, controls many millions more by lending them the money to buy its products, and, through its ownership of the media of mass communication, influences the thoughts, the feelings and the actions of virtually everybody."

To avoid Huxley's grim vision, to turn the tide against it, we need a strong, independent media, a media that serves the interest of the silenced majority.

OBAMA'S WARS:
A TRAGEDY IN THREE ACTS

ACT I
THE WARS ABROAD

September 16, 2009

Let Us Not Become the Evil We Deplore

On September 14, 2001, the U.S. House of Representatives considered House Joint Resolution 64, "To authorize the use of United States Armed Forces against those responsible for the recent attacks launched against the United States." The wounds of 9/11 were raw, and the lust for vengeance seemed universal. The House vote was remarkable, relative to the extreme partisanship now in evidence in Congress, since 420 House members voted in favor of the resolution. More remarkable, though, was the one lone vote in opposition, cast by Barbara Lee of San Francisco. Lee opened her statement on the resolution, "I rise today with a heavy heart, one that is filled with sorrow for the families and loved ones who were killed and injured in New York, Virginia and Pennsylvania." Her emotions were palpable as she spoke from the House floor.

"September 11 changed the world. Our deepest fears now haunt us. Yet I am convinced that military action will not prevent further acts of international terrorism against the United States. . . . We must not rush to judgment. Far too many innocent people have already died. Our country is in mourning. If we rush to launch a counterattack, we run too great a risk that women, children and other noncombatants will be caught in the crossfire."

The Senate also passed the resolution, 98–0, and sent it on to President George W. Bush. What he did with the authorization, and the Iraq War authorization a year later, has become, arguably, the greatest foreign policy catastrophe in United States history. What President Barack Obama will do with Afghanistan is the question now.

On October 7, the U.S. enters its ninth year of occupation of Afghanistan—equal to the time the United States was involved in World War I, World War II, and the Korean War combined. Obama campaigned on his opposition to the war in Iraq, but pledged at the same time to escalate the war in Afghanistan. On his first Friday in office, Commander in Chief Obama's military fired three Hellfire missiles from an unmanned drone into Pakistan, reportedly killing twenty-two people, mostly civilians, including women and children. He has increased U.S. troops in Afghanistan by more than 20,000, to a total numbering 61,000. This does not count the private contractors in Afghanistan, who now outnumber the troops. The new U.S. military commander in Afghanistan, Gen. Stanley McChrystal, is expected to ask for even more troops. This past August was the deadliest month yet for U.S. troops in Afghanistan, with fifty-one killed, and 2009 is by far the deadliest year, with 200 U.S. troops killed so far. These statistics don't count the soldiers who commit suicide after returning home, nor those injured, and certainly don't include the number of Afghans killed. The attacks also are increasing in sophistication, according to recent reports. So it may be no surprise that more comparisons are now being made between Afghanistan and Vietnam.

When asked about the comparison, Obama recently told the *New York Times*: "You have to learn lessons from history. On the other hand, each historical moment is different. You never step into the same river twice. And so Afghanistan is not Vietnam.... The dangers of overreach and not having clear goals and not having strong support from the American people, those are all issues that I think about all the time."

According to a recent CNN / Opinion Research poll, 57 percent of those asked oppose the U.S. war in Afghanistan, reportedly the highest level of opposition since the war began in 2001. Among those polled, 75 percent of Democrats opposed the war, which might explain statements recently from key congressional Democrats against sending more troops to Afghanistan. House Speaker Nancy Pelosi said last Thursday, "I don't think there's a great deal of support for sending more troops to Afghanistan in the country or in the Congress," echoing Sen. Russ Feingold, D-Wis., and Sen. Carl Levin, D-Mich., the chairman of the Senate Armed Services Committee.

Obama said in his health care speech before the joint session of Congress, "The plan I'm proposing will cost around $900 billion over ten years—less than we have spent on the Iraq and Afghanistan wars."

President Lyndon Johnson escalated the war in Vietnam and ultimately decided not to run for re-election. But he also passed Medicare, the revered, single-payer health insurance program for seniors. Barbara Lee presciently compared the invasion of Afghanistan to Vietnam in her speech back in 2001 and closed by quoting the Rev. Nathan Baxter, dean of the National Cathedral: "As we act, let us not become the evil that we deplore."

November 4, 2009

The Tortured Logic Continues

"Extraordinary rendition" is White House–speak for kidnapping. Just ask Maher Arar. He's a Canadian citizen who was "rendered" by the U.S. to Syria, where he was tortured for almost a year.

Just this week, the U.S. Court of Appeals for the Second Circuit, in New York City, dismissed Arar's case against the government officials (including FBI Director Robert Mueller, former Homeland Security Secretary Tom Ridge and former Attorney General John Ashcroft) who allegedly conspired to have him kidnapped and tortured. Arar is safe now, recovering in Canada with his family. But the decision sends a signal to the Obama administration that there will be no judicial intervention to halt the cruel excesses of the Bush-era "Global War on Terror," including extraordinary rendition, torture, and the use of the "state secrets privilege" to hide these crimes.

Arar's life-altering odyssey is one of the best known and best investigated of those victimized by U.S. extraordinary rendition. After vacationing with his family in Tunisia, Arar attempted to fly home to Canada. On September 26, 2002, while changing planes at JFK Airport, Arar was pulled aside for questioning. He was fingerprinted and searched by the FBI and the New York Police Department. He asked for a lawyer and was told he had no rights. He was then taken to another location and subjected to two days of aggressive interrogations, with no access to phone, food, or a lawyer. He was asked about his membership with various terrorist groups, about Osama bin Laden, Iraq, Palestine, and more. Shackled, he was then moved to a maximum-security federal detention center in Brooklyn, strip-searched and threatened with deportation to Syria.

Arar was born in Syria and told his captors that if he returned there, he would be tortured. As Arar's lawyers would later argue, however, that is exactly what they hoped would happen. Arar was eventually allowed a call—he got through to his mother-in-law, who got him a lawyer—and a visit from a Canadian Consulate official. For nearly two weeks, the U.S. authorities held the Syria threat over his head. Still, he denied any involvement with terrorism. So in the middle of the night, over a weekend, without normal immigration proceedings—without telling his lawyer or the Canadian Consulate—he was dragged in chains to a private jet contracted by the CIA and flown to Jordan, where he was then handed over to the Syrians.

For ten months and ten days, Maher was held in a dark, damp, cold cell, measuring six feet by three feet by seven feet high, the size of a grave. He was beaten repeatedly with a thick electrical cable all over his body, punched, made to listen to the torture of others, denied food, and threatened with electrical shock and an array of more horrors. To stop the torture, he falsely confessed to attending terrorist training in Afghanistan. Then, after nearly a year, he was abruptly released to Canada, forty pounds lighter and emotionally destroyed.

The Canadian government, under conservative Prime Minister Stephen Harper, investigated, found its own culpability in relaying unreliable information to the FBI, and settled with Arar, giving him an apology and $10 million. The U.S. government has offered no apology and has kept Arar on a terrorist watch list. He is not allowed to enter the U.S. Two years ago, he had to testify before Congress via video conference.

He said: "These past few years have been a nightmare for me. Since my return to Canada, my physical pain has slowly healed, but the cognitive and psychological scars from my ordeal remain with me on a daily basis. I still have nightmares and recurring flashbacks. I am not the same person that I was. I also hope to convey how fragile our human rights have become and how easily they can be taken from us by the same governments that have sworn to protect them."

Given the excesses of the Bush administration and Barack Obama's promise of change, it has surprised many that these policies are continuing, and that Congress and the courts have not closed this chapter of U.S. history. President Obama has never once condemned extraordinary rendition. Arar's lawyer, Maria LaHood of the Center for Constitutional Rights, calls the court decision against Arar "an outrage." In his dissent, Judge Guido Calabresi wrote, "I believe that when the history of this distinguished court is written, today's majority decision will be viewed with dismay." Given the torture that Arar suffered, his response was remarkably measured: "If anything, this decision is a loss to all Americans and to the rule of law."

April 1, 2010

The Obscenity of War

President Barack Obama has just returned from his first trip as commander in chief to Afghanistan. The U.S.-led invasion and occupation of that country are now in their ninth year, amid increasing comparisons to Vietnam.

Daniel Ellsberg, whom Henry Kissinger once called "the most dangerous man in America," leaked the Pentagon Papers in 1971. Ellsberg, who was a top Pentagon analyst, photocopied this secret, 7,000-page history of the U.S. role in Vietnam and released it to the press, helping to end the Vietnam War.

"President Obama is taking every symbolic step he can to nominate this as Obama's war," Ellsberg told me recently. He cites the "Eikenberry memos," written by U.S. Ambassador to Afghanistan Karl Eikenberry, which were leaked, then printed last January by the *New York Times*.

Ellsberg said: "Eikenberry's cables read like a summary of the Pentagon Papers of Afghanistan. . . . Just change the place names from 'Saigon' to 'Kabul' . . . and they read almost exactly the same."

The Eikenberry memos recommend policies opposite those of Gens. David Petraeus and Stanley McChrystal, who advocated for the surge and a counterinsurgency campaign in Afghanistan. Eikenberry wrote that President Hamid Karzai is "not an adequate strategic partner," and that "sending additional forces will delay the day when Afghans will take over, and make it difficult, if not impossible, to bring our people home on a reasonable timetable." Petraeus and McChrystal prevailed. The military will launch a major campaign in June in Afghanistan's second-largest city, Kandahar. Meanwhile, with shocking candor, McChrystal said in a video conference this week, regarding the number of civilians killed by the U.S. military, "We have shot an amazing number of people, but to my knowledge, none has ever proven to be a threat." U.S. troop fatalities, meanwhile, are occurring now at twice the rate of one year ago.

Tavis Smiley has a PBS special this week on one of the most powerful, and overlooked, speeches given by the Rev. Martin Luther King Jr. The address was made on April 4, 1967, exactly one year to the day before King was assassinated. The civil rights leader titled his speech "Beyond Vietnam," and controversially called the U.S. government "the greatest purveyor of violence in the world today." The press vilified King. *Time* magazine called the speech "demagogic slander that sounded like a script for Radio Hanoi." Smiley told me: "Most Americans, I think, know the 'I Have a Dream' speech. Some Americans know the 'Mountaintop' speech given the night before he was assassinated in Memphis. But most Americans do not know this 'Beyond Vietnam' speech." Smiley added, "If you replace the words Iraq for Vietnam, Afghanistan for Vietnam, Pakistan for Vietnam, this speech is so relevant today."

Like King, Obama is a recipient of the Nobel Peace Prize. In his acceptance speech, Obama mentioned King six times, yet defended his war in Afghanistan. Princeton University professor Cornel West, interviewed by Smiley, said of Obama's Nobel speech, "It upset me when I heard my dear brother Barack Obama criticize Martin on the global stage, saying that Martin Luther King Jr.'s insights were not useful for a commander in chief, because evil exists, as if Martin Luther King Jr. didn't know about evil."

In early March, Rep. Dennis Kucinich, D-Ohio, offered a resolution to end the war in Afghanistan, saying: "We now have about 1,000 U.S. troops who have perished in the conflict. We have many innocent civilians who have lost their lives. We have a corrupt central government in Afghanistan that is basically stealing U.S. tax dollars." The resolution was defeated by a vote of 356–65. A *Washington Post* poll of 1,000 people released this week found that President Obama enjoys a 53 percent approval rating on his handling of the war in Afghanistan.

The public is unlikely to oppose something that gets less and less coverage. While the press is focused on the salacious details of Republican National Committee spending on lavish trips, especially one outing to a Los Angeles strip club, the cost to the U.S. taxpayer for the war in Afghanistan is estimated now to be more than $260 billion. The cost in lives lost, in people maimed, is incalculable. The real obscenity is war. Ellsberg hopes that the Eikenberry memos will be just the first of many leaks, and that a new wave of Pentagon Papers will educate the public about the urgent need to end Obama's war.

June 16, 2010

Broken Promises, Broken Laws, Broken Lives

Federal authorities are investigating whether officials of the government south of the border participated in a citizen's kidnapping and torture—Canadian authorities, that is, investigating the possible role of U.S. officials in the "extraordinary rendition" of Canadian citizen Maher Arar. "Extraordinary rendition" is White House–speak for arresting someone and secretly sending him to another country, where he is likely to be tortured. Arar revealed that, for the past four years, the Royal Canadian Mounted Police (RCMP) has been investigating possible roles of U.S. and Syrian officials in his rendition and torture. This announcement follows the U.S. Supreme Court's decision that it will not consider Arar's case, ending his pursuit of justice through U.S. courts.

Arar is the Canadian citizen seized by U.S. officials while changing planes in New York, heading home from a family vacation in September 2002. He was secretly sent to Syria by the Bush administration, where he was held for almost a year in a gravelike cell. He was repeatedly tortured, then returned home to Canada, without charge, a broken man. In 2004, the Center for Constitutional Rights filed suit in U.S. federal court on Arar's behalf as he recovered in Canada. While his legal case came to an end this week, his fight against impunity continues.

Ontario Justice Dennis O'Connor headed the Canadian government's inquiry into Arar's arrest, removal to Syria, and subsequent torture. From 2004 to 2006, O'Connor interviewed scores of people and reviewed thousands of documents. The inquiry completely exonerated Arar. The conservative Canadian Prime Minister Stephen Harper apologized, and Arar was awarded $11.5 million in reparations and legal fees. Now, we learn, the RCMP, the Canadian equivalent of the FBI, is conducting an investigation that could lead to criminal charges. Arar told me: "They've been collecting evidence. They've been interviewing people both in Canada and internationally ... their focus is on the Syrian torturers, as well as those American officials who were complicit in my torture."

If the RCMP charges U.S. officials with complicity in the abduction and torture of Arar, it would put the strong extradition treaty between the U.S. and Canada to the test. In the meantime, the Center for Constitutional Rights is encouraging people to contact the White House and their representatives in Congress to demand redress for Arar, including an apology, his removal from the terrorist watch list, financial damages, an investigation, and assurances that no one else will suffer a similar fate.

Sen. Patrick Leahy of Vermont, who chairs the powerful Judiciary Committee, expressed his disappointment with this week's Supreme Court decision, saying the Arar case "remains a stain on this nation's legacy as a human-rights leader around the world ... the United States has continued to deny culpability in this case." Back in a January 2007 hearing, Leahy fumed at then Attorney General Alberto Gonzales: "We knew damn well, if he went to Canada, he wouldn't be tortured. He'd be held. He'd be investigated. We also knew damn well, if he went to Syria, he'd be tortured."

The Obama administration continues controversial Bush-era policies, with detention without charge at Guantánamo and the Bagram air base, and with, as Leahy has noted, reliance on "state secrets" privilege to dodge legal actions to expose and punish torture. On the same day as this week's Supreme Court announcement, another court in Washington, D.C., acquitted twenty-four anti-torture activists who were arrested at the U.S. Capitol on January 21, 2010, the day by which President Barack Obama originally pledged Guantánamo would be closed. Their banner read "Broken Promises, Broken Laws, Broken Lives." Several were arrested inside the Capitol Rotunda while conducting a funeral service for three Guantánamo prisoners who may have been tortured to death. The U.S. government claims they committed suicide.

Maher Arar has completed his Ph.D. in Canada and founded an online news magazine, Prism-Magazine.com. He has been focusing on the case of Canadian citizen Omar Khadr, who was arrested in Afghanistan as a child and has grown to adulthood in the Guantánamo prison. Arar, married with two children, told me, "The struggle for justice and struggle against oppression has become a way of life for me, and I can never go back to just a simple 9-to-5 engineer anymore."

September 8, 2010

September 11: A Day Without War

The ninth anniversary of the September 11 attacks on the United States should serve as a moment to reflect on tolerance. It should be a day of peace. Yet the rising anti-Muslim fervor here, together with the continuing U.S. military occupation of Iraq and the escalating war in Afghanistan (and Pakistan), all fuel the belief that the U.S. really is at war with Islam.

September 11, 2001, united the world against terrorism. Everyone, it seemed, was with the United States, standing in solidarity with the victims, with the families who lost loved ones. The day will be remembered for generations to come, for the notorious act of coordinated mass murder. But that was not the first September 11 to be associated with terror:

September 11, 1973, Chile: Democratically elected President Salvadore Allende died in a CIA-backed military coup that ushered in a reign of terror under dictator Augusto Pinochet, in which thousands of Chileans were killed.

September 11, 1977, South Africa: Anti-apartheid leader Stephen Biko was being beaten in a police van. He died the next day.

September 11, 1990, Guatemala: Guatemalan anthropologist Myrna Mack was murdered by the U.S.-backed military.

September 9–13, 1971, New York: The Attica prison uprising occurred, during which New York state troopers killed thirty-nine prisoners and guards and wounded hundreds of others.

September 11, 1988, Haiti: During a mass led by Father Jean-Bertrand Aristide at the St. Jean Bosco Church in Port-au-Prince, right-wing militiamen attacked, killing at least thirteen worshippers and injuring at least seventy-seven. Aristide would later be twice elected president, only to be ousted in U.S.-supported coups d'etat.

If anything, September 11 is a day to remember the victims of terror, all victims of terror, and to work for peace, like the group September 11th Families for Peaceful Tomorrows. Formed by those who lost loved ones on 9/11/2001, their mission could serve as a national call to action: "[T]o turn our grief into action for peace. By developing and advocating nonviolent options and actions in the pursuit of justice, we hope to break the cycles of violence engendered by war and terrorism. Acknowledging our common experience with all people affected by violence throughout the world, we work to create a safer and more peaceful world for everyone."

Our *Democracy Now!* news studio was blocks from the twin towers in New York City. We were broadcasting live as they fell. In the days that followed, thousands of fliers went up everywhere, picturing the missing, with phone numbers of family members to call if you recognized someone. These reminded me of the placards carried by the Mothers of the Plaza de Mayo in Argentina. Those are the women, wearing white headscarves, who courageously marched, week after week, carrying pictures of their missing children who disappeared during the military dictatorship there.

I am reminded, as well, by the steady stream of pictures of young people in the military killed in Iraq and in Afghanistan, and now, with increasing frequency (although pictured less in the news), who kill themselves after multiple combat deployments.

For each of the U.S. or NATO casualties, there are literally hundreds of victims in Iraq and Afghanistan whose pictures will never be shown, whose names we will never know.

While angry mobs continue attempts to thwart the building of an Islamic community center in lower Manhattan (in a vacant, long-ignored, damaged building more than two blocks away), an evangelical "minister" in Florida is organizing a September 11 "International Burn the Koran Day." Gen. David Petraeus has stated that the burning, which has sparked protests around the globe, "could endanger troops." He is right. But so does blowing up innocent civilians and their homes.

As in Vietnam in the 1960s, Afghanistan has a dedicated, indigenous, armed resistance, and a deeply corrupt group in Kabul masquerading as a central government. The war is bleeding over into a neighboring country, Pakistan, just as the Vietnam War spread into Cambodia and Laos.

Right after September 11, 2001, as thousands gathered in parks around New York City, holding impromptu candlelit vigils, a sticker appeared on signs, placards, and benches. It read, "Our grief is not a cry for war."

This September 11, that message is still—painfully, regrettably—timely.

Let's make September 11 a day without war.

September 22, 2010

Torture in Iraq Continues, Unabated

Combat operations in Iraq are over, if you believe President Barack Obama's rhetoric. But torture in Iraq's prisons, first exposed during the Abu Ghraib scandal, is thriving, increasingly distant from any scrutiny or accountability. After arresting tens of thousands of Iraqis, often without charge, and holding many for years without trial, the United States has handed over control of Iraqi prisons, and 10,000 prisoners, to the Iraqi government. Meet the new boss, same as the old boss.

After landing in London late Saturday night, we traveled to the small suburb of Kilburn to speak with Rabiha al-Qassab, an Iraqi refugee who was granted political asylum in Britain after her brother was executed by Saddam Hussein. Her husband, sixty-eight-year-old Ramze Shihab Ahmed, was a general in the Iraqi army under Saddam, fought in the Iran–Iraq War, and was part of a failed plot to overthrow the Iraqi dictator. The couple was living peacefully for years in London, until September 2009.

It was then that Ramze Ahmed learned his son, Omar, had been arrested in Mosul, Iraq. Ahmed returned to Iraq to find him and was arrested himself.

For months, Rabiha didn't know what had become of her husband. Then, on March 28, her cell phone rang. "I don't know the voice," she told me.

"I said, 'Who are you?' He said he is very sick ... he said, 'Me, Ramze, Ramze. Call embassy.' And they took the mobile, and they stop talking."

Ramze Ahmed was being held in a secret prison at the old Muthanna Airport in Baghdad. A recent report from Amnesty International, titled "New Order, Same Abuses," describes Muthanna as "one of the harshest" prisons in Iraq, the scene of extensive torture and under the control of Iraqi Prime Minister Nouri al-Maliki.

As Rabiha showed me family photos, a piece of paper with English and Arabic words slipped out. Rabiha explained that in order to describe in English what happened to her husband, she had to consult a dictionary, since she had never used several of the English words: "Rape." "Stick." "Torture." She wept as she described his account of being sodomized with a stick, suffocated repeatedly with plastic bags placed over his head, and shocked with electricity.

Not surprisingly, as detailed in the Amnesty report, the Iraqi government said that Ramze Shihab Ahmed had confessed to links to al-Qaida in Iraq. In a January 2010 press conference organized by the Iraqi Ministry of Defense, videotapes were played showing nine others confessing to crimes, including Ahmed's son, Omar, who, showing signs of beatings, confessed to "the killing of several Christians in Mosul and the detonation of a bomb in a village near Mosul."

Malcolm Smart, director of Amnesty International's Middle East and North Africa program, told me in London, "there's a culture of abuse [in Iraq] that has taken root. It was certainly there during the days of Saddam Hussein, but what we wanted to see from 2003 was a turning of the page, and that hasn't happened. So we see secret prisons, people being tortured and ill-treated, being forced to make confessions . . . the perpetrators are not being held to account. They're not being identified."

After that brief, interrupted phone call that Rabiha received from her husband, she did call the British government, and its embassy in Iraq tracked Ahmed down in al-Rusafa prison in Baghdad. Normally with a cane, they found him in a wheelchair. Rabiha has a photo of him taken by the British representative.

Amnesty reports that there are an estimated 30,000 prisoners in Iraq (200 remaining under U.S. control). The condition and treatment of the Iraqi prisoners is considered by the U.S. to be, Smart says, "an Iraqi issue." But with the U.S. continuing to pour billions of dollars into its ongoing military presence there, and to fund the Iraqi government, the treatment of prisoners is clearly a U.S. issue as well. Amnesty has launched a grassroots campaign to spur further action to secure Ahmed's release.

Meanwhile, Rabiha al-Qassab, isolated and alone in north London, spends time feeding the ducks in a local park, which her husband used to do.

She told me: "I talk with the ducks. I say, 'You remember the man who gave you the food? He is in a prison. Ask God to help him.'"

October 27, 2010

War Should Be an Election Issue

Just days away from crucial midterm elections, WikiLeaks, the whistle-blower website, unveiled the largest classified military leak in history. Almost 400,000 secret Pentagon documents relating to the U.S. invasion and occupation of Iraq were made available online. The documents, in excruciating detail, portray the daily torrent of violence, murder, rape, and torture to which Iraqis have been subjected since George W. Bush declared "Mission Accomplished." The WikiLeaks release, dubbed "The Iraq War Logs," has been topping the headlines in Europe. But in the U.S., it barely warranted a mention on the agenda-setting Sunday talk shows.

First, the documents themselves. I spoke with Julian Assange, the founder and editor in chief of WikiLeaks.org. He explained: "These documents cover the periods of 2004 to the beginning of 2010. It is the most accurate description of a war to have ever been released . . . each casualty, where it happened, when it happened and who was involved, according to internal U.S. military reporting."

David Leigh, investigations editor at the *Guardian* of London, told me the leak "represents the raw material of history . . . what the unvarnished version does is confirm what many of us feared and what many journalists have attempted to report over the years, that Iraq became a bloodbath, a real bloodbath of unnecessary killings, of civilian slaughter, of torture and of people being beaten to death."

The reports, in bland bureaucratic language and rife with military jargon, are grisly in detail. Go to the website and search the hundreds of thousands of records. Words like "rape," "murder," "execution," "kidnapping," and "decapitation" return anywhere from hundreds to thousands of reports, documenting not only the scale and regularity of the violence, but, ultimately, a new total for civilian deaths in Iraq.

The British-based Iraq Body Count, which maintains a carefully researched database on just the documented deaths in Iraq, estimates that the Iraq War Logs document an additional 15,000 heretofore unrecorded civilian deaths, bringing the total, from when the invasion began, to more than 150,000 deaths, 80 percent of which are civilian.

In one case, in February 2007, two Iraqi men were attempting to surrender, under attack by a U.S. helicopter gunship. The logs reveal that the crew members called back to their base and were told, "They cannot surrender to aircraft and are still valid targets." The two were killed. The helicopter unit was the same one that, months later, attacked a group of civilians in Baghdad, killing all of the men, including two Reuters employees, and injuring two children. That case, also documented in the Iraq War Logs, was the subject of another high-profile WikiLeaks release, which it called "Collateral Murder." The Apache helicopter's own video of the violent assault, with the accompanying military radio audio, revealed soldiers laughing and cursing as they slaughtered the civilians, and made headlines globally.

Imagine if the military operations were not subject to such secrecy, if the February murder of the two men with their arms raised, trying to surrender, had become public. If there was an investigation, and appropriate punitive action was taken. Perhaps Reuters videographer Namir Noor-Eldeen, twenty-two years old, and his driver, Saeed Chmagh, the father of four, would be alive today, along with the civilians they were unlucky enough to be walking with that fateful July day. That's why transparency matters.

Sunday's network talk shows barely raised the issue of the largest intelligence leak in U.S. history. When asked, they say the midterm elections are their main focus. Fine, but war is an election issue. It should be raised in every debate, discussed on every talk show.

I see the media as a huge kitchen table, stretching across the globe, that we all sit around, debating and discussing the most important issues of the day: war and peace, life and death. Anything less than that is a disservice to the servicemen and -women of this country. They can't have these debates on military bases. They rely on us in civilian society to have the discussions that determine whether they live or die, whether they are sent to kill or be killed. Anything less than that is a disservice to a democratic society.

January 12, 2012

Guantánamo at Ten:
The Prisoner and the Prosecutor

Ten years ago, Omar Deghayes and Morris Davis would have struck anyone as an odd pair. While they have never met, they now share a profound connection, cemented through their time at the notorious U.S. military prison at Guantánamo Bay, Cuba. Deghayes was a prisoner there. Air Force Col. Morris Davis was chief prosecutor of the military commissions there from 2005 to 2007.

Deghayes was arrested in Pakistan and handed over to the U.S. military. He told me: "There was a payment made for every person who was handed to the Americans. . . . We were chained, head covered, then sent to Bagram [Afghanistan]—we were tortured in Bagram—and then from Bagram to Guantánamo."

At Guantánamo, Deghayes, one of close to 800 men who have been sent there since January 2002, received the standard treatment: "People were subjected to beatings, daily fear . . . without being convicted of any crime."

While Deghayes and his fellow inmates were suffering in their cages, the Bush administration was erecting a controversial legal framework to prosecute the Guantánamo prisoners. It labeled those rounded up "enemy combatants," argued they had no protections under the U.S. Constitution, nor under the Geneva Conventions, no rights whatsoever. Guantánamo became a legal black hole.

When I asked Col. Davis if he felt that torture was used at Guantánamo, he said: "I don't think there's any doubt. I would say that there was torture. Susan Crawford, a Dick Cheney protégé, said there was torture. John McCain has said waterboarding was torture, and we've admitted we've waterboarded. There have been at least five judges in federal court and military courts that have said detainees were tortured."

Chained, kept in cages in orange jumpsuits, subjected to harsh interrogations and humiliations, with their Muslim faith vilified, the prisoners at Guantánamo began to fight back, through the time-honored tradition of nonviolent noncooperation. They began a hunger strike. In response, examples were made of Deghayes and the other protesters. He recalled: "After beating me in the cell, they dragged me outside, and then one of the guards, while another officer was standing, observing what was happening, [tried] to gouge my eyes out.... I lost sight in both of my eyes. Slowly, I regained my sight in one of the eyes. The other eye has completely gotten worse. And they went to do the same thing to the next cell and the next cell and the next cell . . . to frighten everyone else from campaigning or from objecting to any policies."

Deghayes now has sight in one eye. His right eye remains shut. After his release from Guantánamo, he was sent back to Britain. He is suing the British government for its collaboration in his imprisonment and torture.

Col. Morris Davis, disgusted with the military tribunal process, resigned his position in 2007, and in 2008 retired from the military. He went to work at the Congressional Research Service. After penning an opinion piece critical of the Obama administration's embrace of the military tribunals, which was published in the *Wall Street Journal* in 2009, Davis was fired.

Deghayes notes that the hundreds of men who have left Guantánamo this past decade have been released because of pressure on governments from grassroots campaigning. That is why more than 350 separate protests were held this week, on Guantánamo's tenth anniversary. One hundred seventy-one men remain imprisoned there, more than half of whom have been cleared for release, but languish nevertheless.

To make matters worse, in what Col. Davis called a "complete act of cowardice," President Barack Obama signed the National Defense Authorization Act, giving the U.S. government the power to detain anyone, without charge, for an indefinite period of time. Davis explained that it "is not a dramatic departure from what the policy has been for the last few years, but now it's law."

One could imagine an "Occupy Guantánamo" movement, but that would be redundant: The United States has occupied Guantánamo since 1903. Since the U.S. has maintained a crushing embargo against Cuba for more than half a century, presumably because it doesn't like Cuban policies, you'd think the U.S. would exhibit model behavior on its little slice of Cuba. It does just the opposite. Which is why grassroots movements are so important. With the U.S. presidential race heating up, be assured that the Republican and Democratic parties see eye to eye on Guantánamo.

February 16, 2012

The Afghan War's Nine Lives

Eight youths, tending their flock of sheep in the snowy fields of Afghanistan, were exterminated last week by a NATO airstrike. They were in the Najrab district of Kapisa province in eastern Afghanistan. Most were reportedly between the ages of six and fourteen. They had sought shelter near a large boulder, and had built a fire to stay warm. At first, NATO officials claimed they were armed men. The Afghan government condemned the bombing and released photos of some of the victims. By Wednesday, NATO offered, in a press release, "deep regret to the families and loved ones of several Afghan youths who died during an air engagement in Kapisa province Feb. 8." Those eight killed were not that different in age from Lance Cpl. Osbrany Montes de Oca, twenty, of North Arlington, New Jersey. He was killed two days later, February 10, while on duty in Afghanistan's Helmand province. These nine young, wasted lives will be the latest footnote in the longest war in United States history, a war that is being perpetuated, according to one brave, whistle-blowing U.S. Army officer, through a "pattern of overt and substantive deception" by "many of America's most senior military leaders in Afghanistan."

Those are the words written by Lt. Col. Daniel Davis in his eighty-four-page report, "Dereliction of Duty II: Senior Military Leaders' Loss of Integrity Wounds Afghan War Effort." A draft of that report, dated January 27, 2012, was obtained by *Rolling Stone* magazine. It has not been approved by the U.S. Army Public Affairs office for release, even though Davis writes that its contents are not classified. He has submitted a classified version to members of Congress. Davis, a seventeen-year Army veteran with four combat tours behind him, spent a year in Afghanistan with the Army's Rapid Equipping Force, traveling more than 9,000 miles to most operational sectors of the U.S. occupation and learning firsthand what the troops said they needed most.

In a piece he wrote in *Armed Forces Journal* (*AFJ*) titled "Truth, lies and Afghanistan," Davis wrote of his experience, "What I saw bore no resemblance to rosy official statements by U.S. military leaders about conditions on the ground." Speaking out is strongly discouraged in the U.S. military, especially against one's superiors. His whistle-blowing was picked up by the *New York*

Times and *Rolling Stone*, whose reporter, Michael Hastings, told me, "The fact is that you have a 17-year Army veteran who's done four tours—two in Afghanistan and two in Iraq—who has decided to risk his entire career—he has two and a half more years left before he gets a pension—because he feels that he has a moral obligation to do so."

Davis interviewed more than 250 people—U.S. military personnel and Afghan nationals—in his recent year in the war zone. He compared what he learned from them with optimistic projections from the likes of David Petraeus, former head of the military's CENTCOM and of the U.S. military in Afghanistan, and now head of the CIA, who told Congress on March 15, 2011, that "the momentum achieved by the Taliban in Afghanistan since 2005 has been arrested in much of the country, and reversed in a number of important areas."

In his *AFJ* piece, Davis wrote, "Instead, I witnessed the absence of success on virtually every level . . . insurgents controlled virtually every piece of land beyond eyeshot of a U.S. or International Security Assistance Force (ISAF) base."

His observations concur with the death of Osbrany Montes de Oca. His girlfriend, Maria Samaniego, told the New York *Daily News*, "He was walking out of the base and he was immediately shot."

The number of U.S. military deaths in Afghanistan approaches 2,000, which is about the number of civilians killed there annually. Nic Lee, the director of the independent Afghanistan NGO Safety Office, wrote in his year-end report for 2011, "The year was remarkable for being the one in which the US/NATO leadership finally acknowledged the unwinnable nature of its war with the Taliban."

Defense Secretary Leon Panetta recently remarked, "Hopefully by the mid- to latter part of 2013 we'll be able to make a transition from a combat role to a training, advise and assist role." Petraeus countered, saying the U.S. remains committed to ending the combat mission by the end of 2014. Meanwhile, images surface of U.S. Marines urinating on Afghan corpses, or posing with a Nazi SS flag, and the drumbeat continues, death by death. Lt. Col. Davis wrote, "When having to decide whether to continue a war, alter its aims or to close off a campaign that cannot be won at an acceptable price, our senior leaders have an obligation to tell Congress and the American people the unvarnished truth."

March 15, 2012

Terror, Trauma, and the Endless Afghan War

We may never know what drove a U.S. Army staff sergeant to head out into the Afghan night and allegedly murder at least sixteen civilians in their homes, among them nine children and three women. The massacre near Belambai, in Kandahar, Afghanistan, has shocked the world and intensified the calls for an end to the longest war in U.S. history. The attack has been called tragic, which it surely is. But when Afghans attack U.S. forces, they are called "terrorists." That is, perhaps, the inconsistency at the core of U.S. policy, that democracy can be delivered through the barrel of a gun, that terrorism can be fought by terrorizing a nation.

"I did it," the alleged mass murderer said as he returned to the forward operating base outside Kandahar, that southern city called the "heartland of the Taliban." He is said to have left the base at 3 a.m. and walked to three nearby homes, methodically killing those inside. One farmer, Abdul Samad, was away at the time. His wife, four sons, and four daughters were killed. Some of the victims had been stabbed, some set on fire. Samad told the *New York Times*, "Our government told us to come back to the village, and then they let the Americans kill us."

The massacre follows massive protests against the U.S. military's burning of copies of the Koran, which followed the video showing U.S. Marines urinating on the corpses of Afghans. Two years earlier, the notorious "kill team" of U.S. soldiers that murdered Afghan civilians for sport, posing for gruesome photos with the corpses and cutting off fingers and other body parts as trophies, also was based near Kandahar.

In response, Defense Secretary Leon Panetta rolled out a string of cliches, reminding us that "war is hell." Panetta visited Camp Leatherneck in Helmand province, near Kandahar, this week on a previously scheduled trip that coincidentally fell days after the massacre. The 200 Marines invited to hear him speak were forced to leave their weapons outside the tent. NBC News reported that such instructions were "highly unusual," as Marines are said to always have weapons on hand in a war zone. Earlier, upon his arrival, a stolen truck raced across the landing strip toward his plane, and the driver leapt out of the cab, on fire, in an apparent attack.

The violence doesn't just happen in the war zone. Back in the U.S., the wounds of war are manifesting in increasingly cruel ways.

The thirty-eight-year-old staff sergeant who allegedly committed the massacre was from Joint Base Lewis-McChord (JBLM), a sprawling military facility near Tacoma, Washington, that has been described by *Stars and Stripes* newspaper as "the most troubled base in the military" and, more recently, as "on the brink." The year 2011 marked a record for soldier suicides there. The base also was the home for the "kill team."

The *Seattle Times* reported earlier this month that 285 patients at JBLM's Madigan Army Medical Center had their post-traumatic stress disorder diagnoses inexplicably reversed by a forensic psychiatric screening team. The reversals are now under investigation due to concerns they were partly motivated by a desire to avoid paying those who qualify for medical benefits.

Kevin Baker was also a staff sergeant in the U.S. Army, stationed at Fort Lewis. After two deployments to Iraq, he refused a third after being denied a PTSD diagnosis. He began organizing to bring the troops home. He told me: "If a soldier is wounded on a battlefield in combat, and they're bleeding to death, and an officer orders that person to not receive medical attention, costing that servicemember their life, that officer would be found guilty of dereliction of duty and possibly murder. But when that happens in the U.S., when that happens for soldiers that are going to seek help, and officers are ordering not a clear diagnosis for PTSD and essentially denying them that metaphoric tourniquet, real psychological help, and the soldier ends up suffering internally to the point of taking their own life or somebody else's life, then these officers and this military and the Pentagon has to be held responsible for these atrocities."

While too late to save Abdul Samad's family, Baker's group, March Forward!—along with Iraq Veterans Against the War's "Operation Recovery," which seeks to ban the deployment of troops already suffering from PTSD—may well help end the disastrous, terrorizing occupation of Afghanistan.

OBAMA'S WARS:
A TRAGEDY IN THREE ACTS

ACT II
THE WAR ON VETERANS
AND SOLDIERS

May 23, 2012

Memorial Day: Honor the Dead, Heal the Wounded, Stop the Wars

Gen. John Allen, commander, U.S. Forces Afghanistan, spoke Wednesday at the Pentagon, four stars on each shoulder, his chest bedecked with medals. Allen said the NATO summit in Chicago, which left him feeling "heartened," "was a powerful signal of international support for the Afghan-led process of reconciliation." Unlike Allen, many decorated U.S. military veterans left the streets of Chicago after the NATO summit without their medals. They marched on the paramilitarized convention center where the generals and heads of state had gathered and threw their medals at the high fence surrounding the summit. They were joined by women from Afghans for Peace, and an American mother whose son killed himself after his second deployment to Iraq.

Leading thousands of protesters in a peaceful march against NATO's wars, each veteran climbed to the makeshift stage outside the fenced summit, made a brief statement, and threw his or her medals at the gate.

As taps was played, veterans folded an American flag that had flown over NATO military operations in Bosnia, Kosovo, Serbia, Afghanistan, and Libya and handed it to Mary Kirkland. Her son, Derrick, joined the Army in January 2007, since he was not earning enough to support his wife and child as a cook at an IHOP restaurant. During his second deployment, Mary told me, "he ended up putting a shotgun in his mouth over there in Iraq, and one of his buddies stopped him." He was transferred to Germany then back to his home base of Fort Lewis, Washington.

"He came back on a Monday after two failed suicide attempts in a three-week period. They kept him overnight at Madigan Army Medical Center at Fort Lewis. He met with a psychiatrist the next day who deemed him to be low to moderate risk for suicide." Five days later, on Friday, March 19, 2010, he hanged himself. Said his mother, "Derrick was not killed in action; he was killed because of failed mental health care at Fort Lewis."

On stage, Lance Cpl. Scott Olsen declared: "Today I have with me my Global War on Terror Medal, Operation Iraqi Freedom Medal, National Defense Medal, and Marine Corps Good Conduct Medal. These medals, once upon a time, made me feel good about what I was doing. . . . I came back to reality, and I don't want these anymore." Like the riot police flanking the stage, many on horseback, Olsen also wore a helmet. He is recovering from a fractured skull after being shot in the head at close range by a beanbag projectile. He wasn't shot in Iraq but by Oakland, California, police at Occupy Oakland last fall, where he was protesting.

On stage with the veterans were three Afghan women, holding the flag of Afghanistan. Just before they marched, I asked one of them, Suraia Sahar, why she was there. "I'm representing Afghans for Peace. And we're here to protest NATO and call on all NATO representatives to end this inhumane, illegal, barbaric war against our home country and our people. . . . It's the first time an Afghan-led peace movement is now working side by side with a veteran-led peace movement. And so, this is the beginning of something new, something better: reconciliation and peace."

The night before the protest and the summit, Allen threw out the first pitch at the "Crosstown Classic" baseball game between the Chicago White Sox and the Chicago Cubs. Members of the teams joked that Allen could join them in the dugout, if he would only quit his day job. I dare say, the members of the Iraq Veterans Against the War wish he would.

After the march and the return of the medals, I caught up with Kirkland's mourning mother as she embraced her new family: those who were protesting the wars that had taken the life of her son. I asked if she had any message for President Obama and the NATO generals. This quiet, soft-spoken woman from Indiana didn't hesitate: "Honor the dead, heal the wounded, stop the wars."

• •

May 16, 2012

Veterans Say No to NATO

This week, NATO, the North Atlantic Treaty Organization, is holding the largest meeting in its sixty-three-year history there. Protests and rallies will confront the two-day summit, facing off against a massive armed police and military presence. The NATO gathering has been designated a "National Special Security Event" by the Department of Homeland Security, empowering the U.S. Secret Service to control much of central Chicago, and to employ unprecedented authority to suppress the public's First Amendment right to dissent.

The focus of the summit will be Afghanistan. "Operation Enduring Freedom," as the Afghanistan War was named by the Bush administration and continues to be called by the Obama administration, is officially a NATO operation. As the generals and government bureaucrats from around the world prepare to meet in Chicago, the number of NATO soldiers killed in Afghanistan since 2001 topped 3,000. First Lt. Alejo R. Thompson of Yuma, Arizona, was killed on May 11 this year, at the age of thirty. He joined the military in 2000 and served in both Iraq and Afghanistan. Shortly after his death, the Associated Press reported that Thompson would be receiving the Purple Heart medal posthumously and is "in line for a Bronze Star." On Wednesday, President Barack Obama awarded, also posthumously, the Medal of Honor to Leslie H. Sabo Jr., killed in action in Cambodia in 1970.

While the president and the Pentagon are handing out posthumous medals, a number of veterans of Iraq and Afghanistan will be marching, in military formation, to McCormick Place in Chicago to hand their service medals back. Aaron Hughes left the University of Illinois in 2003 to join the military, and was deployed to Iraq and Kuwait. He served in the Illinois National Guard from 2000 to 2006. Since leaving active duty, Hughes has become a field organizer with the group Iraq Veterans Against the War (IVAW). He explained why he is returning his medals:

> Because every day in this country, 18 veterans are committing suicide. Seventeen percent of the individuals that are in combat in Afghanistan, my brothers and sisters, are on psychotropic medication. Twenty to 50 percent of the individuals that are getting deployed to Afghanistan are already diagnosed with post-traumatic stress disorder, military sexual trauma or a traumatic brain injury. Currently one-third of the women in the military are sexually assaulted.

IVAW's Operation Recovery seeks increased support for veterans, and to stop the redeployment of traumatized troops. Hughes elaborated:

The only type of help that [veterans] can get is some type of medication like trazodone, Seroquel, Klonopin, medication that's practically paralyzing, medication that doesn't allow them to conduct themselves in any type of regular way. And that's the standard operating procedures. Those are the same medications that service members are getting redeployed with and conducting military operations on.

Another veteran—of the anti-war movement of the 1960s—and now a law professor at Northwestern University, longtime Chicago activist Bernardine Dohrn, also will be in the streets. She calls NATO the "militarized arm of the global 1 percent," and criticizes Chicago mayor and former Obama White House Chief of Staff Rahm Emanuel for misappropriating funds for the summit: "Suddenly we don't have money here for community mental-health clinics. We don't have money for public libraries or for schools. We don't have money for public transportation. But somehow we have the millions of dollars necessary ... to hold this event right here in the city of Chicago."

Occupy Chicago, part of the Occupy Wall Street movement, has been focused on the NATO protests. The unprecedented police mobilization, which will include, in addition to the Chicago police, at least the Secret Service, federal agents, and the Illinois National Guard, also may include extensive surveillance and infiltration. Documents obtained through Freedom of Information requests by the activist legal organization Partnership for Civil Justice (PCJ) indicate what the group calls "a mass intelligence network including fusion centers, saturated with 'anti-terrorism' funding, that mobilizes thousands of local and federal officers and agents to investigate and monitor the social-justice movement." PCJ says the documents clearly refute Department of Homeland Security claims that there was never a centralized, federal coordination of crackdowns on the Occupy Wall Street movement.

Aaron Hughes and the other vets understand armed security, having provided it themselves in the past. He told me the message he'll carry to the military and the police deployed across Chicago: "Don't stand with the global 1 percent. Don't stand with these generals that continuously abuse their own service members and then talk about building democracy and promoting freedom."

October 28, 2009

The War Condolences Obama Hasn't Sent

U.S. Army Reserve Spc. Chancellor Keesling died in Iraq on June 19, 2009, from "a non-combat related incident," according to the Pentagon. Keesling had killed himself. He was just one in what is turning out to be a record year for suicides in the U.S. military.

In August, President Barack Obama addressed the Veterans of Foreign Wars convention, saying, "[T]here is nothing more sobering than signing a letter of condolence to the family of [a] serviceman or -woman who has given their life for our country." To their surprise, Jannett and Gregg Keesling, Chance's parents, won't be getting such a letter. Obama does not write condolence letters to loved ones of those who commit suicide in the theater of combat. (After making inquiries, the Keeslings discovered that this was not because of an oversight. Instead, it's because of a longstanding U.S. policy to deny presidential condolence letters to the families of soldiers who take their own lives.)

Jannett told me: "Chancellor was recruited right out of high school, and this was something he was passionate about, joining the military. I wanted him to go to college, but he said that he wanted to be a soldier." Gregg added: "We had doubts about him joining. . . . When the war broke out in 2003, when many of us were trying to retreat, Chancy decided, 'This is my duty.' . . . But once he did his first tour . . . his marriage broke up during that deployment."

Chance was very troubled during his first tour of duty in Iraq, although he performed admirably by all accounts. At one point he was put on a suicide watch and had his ammunition taken away for a week. After Iraq, Chance declined a $27,000 reenlistment bonus and transitioned to the U.S. Army Reserves, hoping to avoid another deployment. He sought and was receiving treatment at a Veterans Affairs facility. Gregg said, "We sat down as a family, and we said, 'President Obama is going to be elected, and President Obama will end this war, and you won't have to go.'" But then his son's orders to deploy came again.

Current laws prevent transfer of mental health information from active-duty military to the reserves, so Chance's commanders did not know of his previous struggles. Last June, troubled again, he sent his parents a dire email, mentioning suicide. Jannett recalled: "I spoke to Chancellor the night before he died for about four minutes. And as always, he wore a really tough exterior. . . . But what he did tell me that night is that he was going to have a very long, difficult day. His conversation was quite brief. Normally he would say that he loves me, and he would say goodbye. But this time he simply hung up."

The next morning, Gregg said, Chance "locked himself in the latrine and took his own life, with his M-4 . . . our grief is deep. The letter won't stop [our pain]—we'll still be hollow inside for the rest of our lives, but the acknowledgment from the president that our son gave his life in service to the causes of the United States is important to us."

The Pentagon admits to a mounting suicide crisis in its ranks. Numbers of acknowledged suicides have steadily climbed, from fewer than 100 in 2005, by one report, to nearly 200 in 2008, with a like number among Iraq and Afghanistan veterans. Gregg Keesling said that when he and Jannett went to Dover Air Force Base to greet Chance's coffin, a master sergeant encouraged him to speak out, saying: "I'm greeting a suicide body almost every day. There's something going on."

The Keeslings credit Maj. Gen. Mark Graham with helping them through their grief, and working to reduce the stigma of suicide within the military. One of Graham's sons committed suicide in 2003, while studying as an Army ROTC cadet in college. His other son, also in the Army, deployed to Iraq months later and was killed by a bomb not long thereafter. But the GI Rights Hotline, which advises active-duty soldiers on options for leaving the military, says outside psychological professionals can help suicidal soldiers obtain a medical discharge: "The military wants to know whether the patient can perform their duties without causing trouble, embarrassment or expense. His or her welfare is distinctly less important."

The United States is engaged in two intractable, massive military occupations, with no end in sight. Obama should certainly write letters of condolence to the Keeslings and to others whose loved ones have found that the only sure way to end the living hell of war, or to escape the horror of its aftermath, is to kill themselves. But an immediate withdrawal from the wars Obama inherited is the only way to stem the bleeding.

December 29, 2010

"The Comeback Kid"
and the Kids Who Won't

President Barack Obama signed a slew of bills into law during the lame-duck session of Congress and was dubbed the "Comeback Kid" amid a flurry of fawning press reports. In the hail of this surprise bipartisanship, though, the one issue over which Democrats and Republicans always agree, war, was completely ignored. The war in Afghanistan is now the longest war in U.S. history, and 2010 has seen the highest number of U.S. and NATO soldiers killed.

As of this writing, 497 of the reported 709 coalition fatalities in 2010 were U.S. soldiers. The website iCasualties.org has carefully tracked the names of these dead. There is no comprehensive list of the Afghans killed. But one thing is clear: Those 497 U.S. soldiers, under the command of the "Comeback Kid," won't be coming back.

On December 3, Commander in Chief Obama made a surprise visit to his troops in Afghanistan, greeting them and speaking at Bagram Air Base. Bagram is the air base built by the Soviet Union during that country's failed invasion and occupation of Afghanistan. Now run by U.S. forces, it is also the site of a notorious detention facility. On December 10, 2002, almost eight years to the day before Obama spoke there, a young Afghan man named Dilawar was beaten to death at Bagram. The ordeal of his wrongful arrest, torture, and murder was documented in the Oscar-winning documentary by Alex Gibney, *Taxi to the Dark Side*. Dilawar was not the only one tortured and killed there by the U.S. military.

Obama told the troops: "We said we were going to break the Taliban's momentum, and that's what you're doing. You're going on the offense, tired of playing defense, targeting their leaders, pushing them out of their strongholds. Today we can be proud that there are fewer areas under Taliban control, and more Afghans have a chance to build a more hopeful future."

Facts on the ground contradict his rosy assessment from many different directions. Maps made by the United Nations, showing the risk-level assessments of Afghanistan, were leaked to the *Wall Street Journal*. The maps described the risk to U.N. operations in every district of Afghanistan, rating them as "very high risk," "high risk," "medium risk," and "low risk." The *Journal* reported that, between March and October 2010, the U.N. found that southern Afghanistan remained at "very high risk," while sixteen districts were upgraded to "high risk." Areas deemed "low risk" shrank considerably.

And then there are the comments of NATO spokesman Brig. Gen. Joseph Blotz: "There is no end to the fighting season. . . . We will see more violence in 2011."

Long before WikiLeaks released the trove of U.S. diplomatic cables, two key documents were leaked to the *New York Times.* The "Eikenberry cables," as they are known, were two memos from Gen. Karl Eikenberry, the U.S. ambassador in Afghanistan, to Secretary of State Hillary Clinton, urging a different approach to the Afghan War, with a focus on providing development aid instead of a troop surge. Eikenberry wrote of the risk that "we will become more deeply engaged here with no way to extricate ourselves, short of allowing the country to descend again into lawlessness and chaos."

A looming problem for the Obama administration, larger than a fraying international coalition, is the increasing opposition to the war among the public here at home. A recent *Washington Post* / ABC News poll found that 60 percent believe the war has not been worth fighting, up from 41 percent in 2007. As Congress reconvenes, with knives sharpened to push for what will surely be controversial budget cuts, the close to $6 billion spent monthly on the war in Afghanistan will increasingly become the subject of debate.

As Nobel Prize–winning economist Joseph Stiglitz repeatedly points out, the cost of war extends far beyond the immediate expenditures, with decades of decreased productivity among the many traumatized veterans, the care for the thousands of disabled veterans, and the families destroyed by the death or disability of loved ones. He says the wars in Iraq and Afghanistan will ultimately cost between $3 trillion and $5 trillion.

One of the main reasons Barack Obama is president today is that by openly opposing the U.S. war in Iraq, he won first the Democratic nomination and then the general election. If he took the same approach with the war in Afghanistan, by calling on U.S. troops to come back home, then he might truly become the "Comeback President" in 2012 as well.

May 4, 2011

Accomplish the Mission: Bring the Troops Home

On May 1, the U.S. president addressed the nation, announcing a military victory. May 1, 2003, that is, when President George W. Bush, in his form-fitting flight suit, strode onto the deck of the aircraft carrier USS *Lincoln*. Under the banner announcing "Mission Accomplished," he declared that "major combat operations in Iraq have ended."

That was eight years to the day before President Barack Obama, without flight suit or swagger, made the surprise announcement that Osama bin Laden had been killed in a U.S. military operation (in a wealthy suburb of Pakistan, notably, not Afghanistan).

The U.S. war in Afghanistan has become the longest war in U.S. history. News outlets now summarily report that "The Taliban have begun their annual spring offensive," as if it were the release of a spring line of clothes. The fact is, this season has all the markings of the most violent of the war, or as the brave reporter Anand Gopal told me Tuesday from Kabul: "Every year has been more violent than the year before that, so it's just continuing that trend. And I suspect the same to be said for the summer. It will likely be the most violent summer since 2001."

Let's go back to that fateful year. Just after the September 11 attacks, Congress voted to grant President Bush war authorization. The resolution passed the Senate 98–0, and passed the House 420–1. The sole vote against the invasion of Afghanistan was cast by California Congresswoman Barbara Lee. Her floor speech in opposition to House Joint Resolution 64 that September 14 should be required reading: "I rise today with a heavy heart, one that is filled with sorrow for the families and loved ones who were killed and injured in New York, Virginia and Pennsylvania.... September 11 changed the world. Our deepest fears now haunt us. Yet I am convinced that military action will not prevent further acts of international terrorism against the United States.... We must not rush to judgment. Far too many innocent people have already died. Our country is in mourning. If we rush to launch a counterattack, we run too great a risk that women, children and other noncombatants will be caught in the crossfire.... As a member of the clergy so eloquently said, 'As we act, let us not become the evil that we deplore.'"

Ten years after her courageous speech, Lee, whose anti-war stance is increasingly becoming the new normal, wants a repeal of that war resolution: "That resolution was a blank check. . . . It was not targeted toward al-Qaida or any country. It said the president is authorized to use force against any nation, organization or individual he or she deems responsible or connected to 9/11. It wasn't a declaration of war, yet we've been in the longest war in American history now, 10 years, and it's open-ended."

Lee acknowledges that Obama "did commit to begin a significant withdrawal in July." But what does troop withdrawal mean with the presence of military contractors in war? Right now, the 100,000 contractors (called "mercenaries" by many) outnumber U.S. troops deployed in Afghanistan.

Gopal says, "The U.S. is really a fundamental force for instability in Afghanistan . . . allying with local actors—warlords, commanders, government officials—who've really been creating a nightmare for Afghans, especially in the countryside, [and with] the night raids, breaking into people's homes, airstrikes, just the daily life under occupation."

Filmmaker Robert Greenwald has partnered with anti-war veterans to produce *Rethink Afghanistan*, a series of films about the war, online at RethinkAfghanistan.com. In response to bin Laden's death, they have launched a new petition to press the White House to bring the troops home. Lee supports it: "I can't overstate how important this is for our democracy—every poll has shown that over 65, 70 percent of the public now is war-weary. And they understand that we need to bring our young men and women out of harm's way. They've performed valiantly and well. They've done everything we've asked them to do, and now it's time to bring them home."

July 13, 2011

Soldier Suicides and the Politics of Presidential Condolences

President Barack Obama just announced a reversal of a longstanding policy that denied presidential condolence letters to the family members of soldiers who commit suicide. Relatives of soldiers killed in action receive letters from the president. Official silence, however, has long stigmatized those who die of self-inflicted wounds. The change marks a long-overdue shift in the recognition of the epidemic of soldier and veteran suicides in this country and the toll of the hidden wounds of war.

The denial of condolence letters was brought to national prominence when Gregg and Jannett Keesling spoke about the suicide of their son, Chancellor Keesling. Chance Keesling joined the Army in 2003. After active duty in Iraq, he moved to the Army Reserves, and was called back for a second deployment in April 2009. The years of war had taken a toll on the twenty-five-year-old. As his father, Gregg, told me: "He was trained for the rebuilding of Iraq. He was a combat engineer. He operated big equipment and loved to run the big equipment. Finally, he was retrained as a tactical gunner sitting on top of a Humvee. Because there was really very little rebuilding going on."

When Chance came home, he sought mental-health treatment from Veterans Affairs. His marriage had failed, and he knew he needed to heal. He turned down the Army's offer of a $27,000 bonus to redeploy. Ultimately, he was sent back to Iraq anyway. Two months after being redeployed there, Chance took his gun into a latrine and shot himself. The Pentagon reported his death was due to "a non-combat related incident." Adding insult to the injury, the VA, five months after his death, sent Chance a letter that his parents received, asking him to complete his "Post Deployment Adjustment."

Kevin and Joyce Lucey understand. Their son, Jeffrey, participated in the invasion of Iraq in 2003. Afterward, back home in Massachusetts, he showed signs of post-traumatic stress disorder (PTSD). He and his family found it next to impossible to get needed services from the VA. Jeffrey turned to self-medication with alcohol. He would dress in camouflage and walk the neighborhood, gun in hand. He totaled the family car. One night following his twenty-third birthday,

Jeffrey curled up in his father's lap, distraught. As Kevin recalled to me this week: "That night he asked if he could sit in my lap, and we rocked for about 45 minutes and then he went to his room. The following day on June 22, he once again was in my lap as I was cutting him down from the beams." Jeffrey hanged himself in the Luceys' basement. On his bed were the dog tags taken from Iraqi soldiers whom he said he had killed.

Since Jeffrey was technically a veteran and not active duty, his suicide is among the suspected thousands. Kevin Lucey summarized, in frustration: "The formal count of suicides that you hear is tremendously underestimated. . . . Jeff's suicide is among the uncounted, the unknown, the unacknowledged. We have heard of presidential study commissions being established almost every year. How often do you have to study a suicide epidemic?"

There is no system for keeping track of veteran suicides. Some epidemiological studies by the Centers for Disease Control and Prevention and others suggest that the suicide rate among veterans is seven to eight times higher than in the general population. One report, from 2005 and limited to sixteen states, found that veteran suicides comprised 20 percent of the total, an extraordinary finding given that veterans make up less than 1 percent of the population. PTSD is now thought to afflict up to 30 percent of close to 2 million active-duty soldiers and veterans of the Iraq and Afghanistan wars. Unemployment among young male veterans is now more than 22 percent.

Take one base: Fort Hood, Texas. Maj. Nidal Hasan faces the death penalty for allegedly murdering thirteen people there in November 2009, a horrific attack heavily spotlighted by the media. Less well known is the epidemic of suicides at the base. Twenty-two people took their own lives there in 2010 alone.

Neither the Luceys nor the Keeslings will get a presidential condolence letter, despite the policy change. The Keeslings won't get it because the decision is not retroactive. The Luceys wouldn't anyway because it narrowly applies only to those suicides by active-duty soldiers deployed in what is considered an active combat zone.

Sadly, those with PTSD can leave the war zone, but the war zone never leaves them. Some see suicide as their only escape. They, too, are casualties of war.

October 14, 2009

Lt. Choi Won't Lie for His Country

Lt. Dan Choi doesn't want to lie. Choi, an Iraq War veteran and a graduate of West Point, declared last March 19 on *The Rachel Maddow Show*, "I am gay." Under the military's "Don't Ask, Don't Tell" regulations, those three words are enough to get Choi kicked out of the military. Choi has become a vocal advocate for repealing the policy, having spoken before tens of thousands of lesbian, gay, bisexual, and transgender (LGBT) people and their allies at last Sunday's National Equality March in Washington, D.C.

Shortly after Choi's public admission to being gay, the Department of the Army sent him a letter stating, in part, that "you admitted publicly that you are a homosexual which constitutes homosexual conduct. . . . Your actions negatively affected the good order and discipline of the New York Army National Guard." Since Don't Ask, Don't Tell was signed into law by President Bill Clinton in 1993, 13,500 soldiers, sailors, and Marines have been discharged from the military for similar alleged behavior. Choi could receive an "other than honorable" discharge, losing the health, retirement, educational, and other benefits to which combat veterans are entitled. While Congress acts to remove the restrictions on health insurance for people with "pre-existing conditions," Choi's pre-existing conditions, being gay and being honest about it, may be enough to keep him out of the Veterans Affairs health care system for life.

The night before Sunday's march, President Barack Obama spoke to the Human Rights Campaign, the largest and wealthiest gay-advocacy group: "We should not be punishing patriotic Americans who have stepped forward to serve this country. . . . I will end 'Don't Ask, Don't Tell.'" He laid out no timetable, however.

After receiving the letter from the Army, Choi wrote an open letter to his commander in chief, Obama. He said: "I have personally served for a decade under Don't Ask, Don't Tell: an immoral law and policy that forces American soldiers to deceive and lie about their sexual orientation. Worse, it forces others to tolerate deception and lying." U.S. troops in Afghanistan are serving side by side with NATO forces that include openly gay and lesbian troops.

Longtime gay-rights activist Urvashi Vaid, author of *Virtual Equality: The*

Mainstreaming of Gay and Lesbian Liberation, is opposed to war and militarism, but told me, "The military is a large employer, and has to commit to not being discriminatory." She, too, was at the march Sunday, whose turnout surprised many of the mainstream gay organizations, as they hadn't actively organized it. She said: "First, it's a generational shift in the LGBT movement. There is a new wave of activism coming up. And it's gay and straight. That's a second big change . . . the third shift that's happening in the LGBT movement is that it's much more of a multi-issue agenda that is being carried by the people who are marching." In addition to Don't Ask, Don't Tell, the LGBT movement is also intent on repealing the Clinton-era Defense of Marriage Act, and on achieving marriage equality. This will be a hard fight, Vaid predicts, based on grassroots activism in every congressional district. Challenging discriminatory laws couldn't be more timely: On the day before Obama's speech to the Human Rights Campaign, a gay man in New York City was taunted with anti-gay slurs and savagely beaten by two men. He is currently in a coma.

Lt. Dan Choi is still technically a serving officer. Obama could halt proceedings against Choi. Activists contend Obama could stop active enforcement of Don't Ask, Don't Tell through an executive order. Presidential or congressional action may not come in time to save Choi's military career. If he loses his health benefits, he has a plan. Choi got a message from an Iraqi doctor whose hospital Choi helped to rebuild while he was there. He said the doctor is "in South Baghdad right now. And he's seen some of the Internet, YouTube and CNN interviews and other appearances, and he said: 'Brother, I know that you're gay, but you're still my brother, and you're my friend. And if your country, that sent you to my country, if America, that sent you to Iraq, will discharge you such that you can't get medical benefits, you can come to my hospital any day. You can come in, and I will give you treatment.'"

Choi ended, "I hope that our country can learn from that Iraqi doctor."

August 4, 2010

Why Did Obama Fire Dan Choi?

"As we mark the end of America's combat mission in Iraq," President Barack Obama said this week, "a grateful America must pay tribute to all who served there." He should have added "unless you're gay," because, despite his rhetoric, weeks earlier the commander in chief fired one of those Iraq vets: Lt. Dan Choi.

Choi was an Iraq War veteran, a graduate of West Point and a trained Arabic linguist. I ran into Choi the day after he received his official discharge. We were at the Netroots Nation conference in Las Vegas, a gathering of thousands of bloggers, activists, and journalists.

Though Choi had known the discharge was coming, he was still shaken to the core. He took out his phone and showed me the letter he was emailed.

Choi announced he was gay on national television in March of 2009. He knew the stakes. I asked why he did it. "I came back from Iraq," he told me, "and I decided that it's not worth it—I could have died at any moment in the area that I was, in the 'Triangle of Death.' Why should I be afraid of the truth of who I am?"

He went on: "I've wanted to go back to Iraq and to Afghanistan, but then I thought, 'If I die in Afghanistan or Iraq, then would my boyfriend be notified? Or would he have to hear about it through *Democracy Now!* or CNN—who would be the one telling him?' And the fact of the matter is 'Don't Ask, Don't Tell' forces our families into the closet and into nonexistence, and that is no way to support our troops or the families that allow them to continue to serve."

Obama promised during his presidential campaign to repeal the law that allows soldiers like Choi to be fired for being openly gay, the so-called Don't Ask, Don't Tell policy. The brainchild of the Clinton administration, it has led to the firing of close to 14,000 members of the military.

Obama has instructed Defense Secretary Robert Gates to conduct a survey among members of the military and their families about the potential impact of repealing Don't Ask, Don't Tell. Sounds reasonable? Not according to Choi.

"I think it's absolutely insulting that we are having a survey right now, in this day and age. That the commander in chief [was] the first racial minority to achieve that rank and that position was a signifying moment for all of us, whether we're racial minorities, whether we're sexual minorities, whether we're

American citizens or not even yet American citizens, it was an absolute moment of vindication for a lot of people." Choi, also a proud Korean-American, continued, "Nobody ever polls the soldiers on whether we should go to war or not. Nobody ever says, 'What do you think about your commander in chief being African-American?'"

It's difficult to think of Dan Choi as lucky, since the West Point graduate wanted to make the military his career, but being honorably discharged, he gets to keep his benefits. He says that's not true of many of his peers. "A lot of people have given up quite a hefty sum of benefits, including your medical benefits, your right to go to a VA hospital without paying, if your disability rating is like mine—I'm something like 50 percent disabled from my time in service—I stood to lose all of that as well as scholarship moneys, GI bill and a home loan through the VA programs."

At the Netroots Nation conference, Democratic leaders tried to convince their progressive base that the Democratic Party truly did represent change. When Senate Majority Leader Harry Reid took the stage, the moderator handed him Lt. Choi's West Point ring and said Choi wanted him to keep it. Choi then joined Reid on the stage. Holding the ring, Reid asked Choi, speaking of the repeal of Don't Ask, Don't Tell, "When we get it passed, you'll take it back, right?" Choi responded, "I sure will, but I'm going to hold you accountable."

OBAMA'S WARS:
A TRAGEDY IN THREE ACTS

ACT III
THE WAR ON THE PUBLIC TREASURY

June 30, 2010

We Can't Afford War

"General Petraeus is a military man constantly at war with the facts," began the MoveOn.org attack ad against Gen. David Petraeus back in 2007, after he had delivered a report to Congress on the status of the war in Iraq. George W. Bush was president, and MoveOn was accusing Petraeus of "cooking the books for the White House." The campaign asked "General Petraeus or General Betray Us?" on a full-page ad in the *Washington Post*. MoveOn took tremendous heat for the campaign, but stood its ground.

Three years later, Barack Obama is president, Petraeus has become his man in Afghanistan, and MoveOn pulls the critical Web content. Why? Because Bush's first war, Afghanistan, has become Obama's war, a quagmire. The U.S. will eventually negotiate its withdrawal from Afghanistan. The only difference between now and then will be the number of dead, on all sides, and the amount of (borrowed) money that will be spent.

Petraeus' confirmation to become the military commander in Afghanistan was never in question. He replaces Gen. Stanley McChrystal, who resigned shortly after his macho criticisms of his civilian leadership became public in a recent *Rolling Stone* magazine article.

The statistics for Afghanistan, Obama's Vietnam, are surging. June, with at least 100 U.S. deaths, is the highest number reported since the invasion in 2001. 2010 is on pace to be the year with the highest U.S. fatalities. Similar fates have befallen soldiers from the other, so-called coalition countries. Petraeus is becoming commander not only of the U.S. military in Afghanistan, but of all forces, as the invasion and occupation of Afghanistan is run by NATO.

U.S. troops, expected to rise to 98,000 this year, far outnumber those from other nations. Public and political support in many of those countries is waning.

Journalist Michael Hastings, who wrote the *Rolling Stone* piece, was in Paris with McChrystal to profile him. What didn't get as much attention was Hastings' description of why McChrystal was there:

"He's in France to sell his new war strategy to our NATO allies—to keep up the fiction, in essence, that we actually have allies. Since McChrystal took over a year ago, the Afghan war has become the exclusive property of the United

States. Opposition to the war has already toppled the Dutch government, forced the resignation of Germany's president and sparked both Canada and the Netherlands to announce the withdrawal of their 4,500 troops. McChrystal is in Paris to keep the French, who have lost more than 40 soldiers in Afghanistan, from going all wobbly on him."

The whistle-blower website WikiLeaks.org, which received international attention after releasing leaked video from a U.S. attack helicopter showing the indiscriminate slaughter of civilians and a Reuters cameraman and his driver in Baghdad, has just posted a confidential CIA memo detailing possible public relations strategies to counter waning public support for the Afghan War. The agency memo reads: "If domestic politics forces the Dutch to depart, politicians elsewhere might cite a precedent for 'listening to the voters.' French and German leaders have over the past two years taken steps to preempt an upsurge of opposition but their vulnerability may be higher now."

I just returned from Toronto, covering the G-20 summit and the protests. The gathered leaders pledged, among other things, to reduce government deficits by 50 percent by 2013. In the U.S., that means cutting $800 billion, or about 20 percent of the budget. Two Nobel Prize–winning economists have weighed in with grave predictions. Joseph Stiglitz said, "There are many cases where these kinds of austerity measures have led to. . . recessions into depressions." And Paul Krugman wrote: "Who will pay the price for this triumph of orthodoxy? The answer is, tens of millions of unemployed workers, many of whom will go jobless for years, and some of whom will never work again."

In order to make the cuts promised, Obama would have to raise taxes and cut social programs such as Social Security and Medicare. Or he could cut the war budget. I say "war budget" because it is not to be confused with a defense budget. Cities and states across the country are facing devastating budget crises. Pensions are being wiped out. Foreclosures are continuing at record levels. A true defense budget would shore up our schools, our roads, our towns, our social safety net. The U.S. House of Representatives is under pressure to pass a $33 billion Afghan War supplemental this week.

We can't afford war.

July 21, 2010

Deficit Doves

Getting out of the red is the new black. Deficit hawks have swooped down on the U.S. budget. This week, they attacked unemployment benefits.

Ultimately, they are going after Social Security and Medicare/Medicaid, the venerable programs once considered untouchable "third rails" of U.S. politics. These have been replaced by a new third rail, the defense budget. To really deal with annual deficits and a surging national debt, we are going to need to cut military spending.

We need some deficit doves.

First, let's call it what it is: the war budget. The government formed the Department of War in 1789, and only in 1949 renamed it the Department of Defense. The war budget President Barack Obama recently sent to Congress, for fiscal year 2011, is $548.9 billion, with an additional $33 billion, which is the 2010 supplemental that is currently being debated in Congress, and $159.3 billion more "to support ongoing overseas contingency operations, including funds to execute the President's new strategy in Afghanistan and Pakistan." Recall, "overseas contingency operations" is how the Obama administration rebranded the "global war on terror."

This is just the publicly available war budget. There is also a "black budget," kept secret, for clandestine operations that former Director of National Intelligence Dennis Blair revealed was about $75 billion. As the *Washington Post* exposed this week, the post-9/11 security state has grown into a massive, unmanageable and largely privatized "enterprise."

Over 2,000 for-profit firms and over 850,000 people with top-secret clearance are engaged in military and intelligence activities, ostensibly for the U.S. government, with seemingly little or no oversight.

Rep. Alan Grayson, D-Fla., has submitted a bill, H.R. 5353, called "The War Is Making You Poor Act." Grayson, with a few Republicans and a number of progressive Democratic co-sponsors, wants to force Commander in Chief Obama to run his two wars with "only" the $548.9 billion base budget. The $159.3 billion saved would be turned into a tax break, making the first $35,000 of income tax-free, and anything left over would be directed to paying down the national debt. The bill is in committee now and may generate genuine bipartisan support. Grayson, when introducing the bill, highlighted a fact worth repeating: The U.S. war budget is greater than the military spending of every other nation on Earth, combined.

Meanwhile, at the National Peace Conference to be held in Albany, New York, this weekend, people are targeting the military budget. Students are organizing around the connection between war expenditures and education budgets that are being slashed, sparking protests at campuses nationwide. Another effort, called "Bring Our War Dollars Home," promotes action at the city council and statehouse level, along with grassroots campaigns to pressure members of Congress to stop funding war.

The cost of the Iraq War was estimated by Nobel Prize–winning economist Joseph Stiglitz, with his colleague Linda Bilmes, at $3 trillion, calculating not only hard, current costs, but also the cost to society of caring for wounded veterans, and the long-term costs of having so many families disrupted by caring for their injured loved ones, or having a breadwinner killed in action. And that's just Iraq. As of May, the monthly cost of the war in Afghanistan surpassed, for the first time, the cost of war in Iraq.

Stiglitz was one of the many economists who said the economic stimulus package (at $787 billion) was too small. He argues that deficit spending, when done wisely, creates long-term returns for an economy.

Conversely, he wrote recently, "Deficits to finance wars or give-aways to the financial sector . . . impos[e] a burden on future generations."

Economist Dean Baker of the Center for Economic and Policy Research says President Obama's Deficit Commission, formally the National Commission on Fiscal Responsibility and Reform, is a major cause for concern. The co-chairs are former Republican Sen. Alan Simpson and Democrat Erskine Bowles, who is on the board of Morgan Stanley, one of the bailed-out Wall Street firms. Baker told me: "Both are on record saying they want to cut Social Security. This should have people very, very worried. That isn't a balanced commission."

March 2, 2011

The Battle of the Budgets:
New Fronts in the Afghan and Iraq Wars

Wisconsin, Indiana, Ohio, Idaho . . . these are the latest fronts in the battle of budgets, with the larger fight over a potential shutdown of the U.S. government looming. These fights, radiating out from the occupation of the Wisconsin capitol building, are occurring against the backdrop of the two wars waged by the U.S. in Iraq and Afghanistan. No discussion or debate over budgets, over wages and pensions, over deficits, should happen without a clear presentation of the costs of these wars—and the incalculable benefits that ending them would bring.

First, the cost of war. The U.S. is spending about $2 billion a week in Afghanistan alone. That's about $104 billion a year—and that is not including Iraq. Compare that with the state budget shortfalls. According to a recent report by the nonpartisan Center on Budget and Policy Priorities, "some 45 states and the District of Columbia are projecting budget shortfalls totalling $125bn for fiscal year 2012."

The math is simple: the money should be poured back into the states, rather than into a state of war.

President Barack Obama shows no signs that he is going to end either the occupation of Iraq or the ongoing war in Afghanistan. Quite the opposite: he campaigned with the promise to expand the war in Afghanistan, and that is one campaign promise he has kept. So how is Obama's war going? Not well.

This has been the deadliest period for civilians in Afghanistan since the U.S.-led invasion began in October 2001. Sixty-five civilians were reportedly killed recently in Kunar, near Pakistan, where mounting civilian casualties lead to increasing popular support for the Taliban. 2010 was the deadliest year for U.S. soldiers as well, with 711 U.S. and allied deaths in Afghanistan. Soldier deaths remain high in 2011, with the fighting expected to intensify as the weather warms.

The *Washington Post* recently reported that Obama's controversial CIA-run drone program, in which unmanned aerial drones are sent over rural Pakistan to launch Hellfire missiles at "suspected militants," has killed at least 581 people, of whom only two were on a U.S. list of people suspected of being "high-level militants." Ample evidence exists that the drone strikes, which have increased in number dramatically under Obama's leadership, kill civilians, not to mention Pakistani civilian support for the United States.

Meanwhile, in Iraq, the democracy that the neocons in Washington expected to deliver through the barrel of a gun with their "shock and awe" may be coming finally—not with the help of the U.S., but, rather, inspired by the peaceful, popular uprisings in Tunisia and Egypt. However, Human Rights Watch has just reported that as people protest and dissidents organize, "the rights of Iraq's most vulnerable citizens, especially women and detainees, are routinely violated with impunity."

Protests have erupted in another Tahrir Square, in Baghdad (yes, it means "liberation" in Iraq and Egypt), against corruption, and demanding jobs and better public services. Iraqi government forces killed twenty-nine people over the weekend; and 300 people, including human-rights workers and journalists, have been rounded up.

Yet, the U.S. continues to pour money and troops into these endless wars. *Rolling Stone*'s Michael Hastings, whose reporting exposed the crass behavior of Gen. Stanley McChrystal, has just exposed what he calls an illegal operation run by Lt. Gen. William Caldwell in Afghanistan, in which a U.S. Army "psy-ops" operation was mounted against U.S. senators and other visiting dignitaries in order to win support and more funding. One of Hastings' military sources quoted Caldwell as saying: "How do we get these guys to give us more people?...What do I have to plant inside their heads?"

The recently retired special inspector general (SIGAR) for Afghanistan reconstruction, Arnold Fields, just reported that $11.4 billion is at risk due to inadequate planning. Another group, the U.S. Commission on Wartime Contracting, "concludes that the United States has wasted tens of billions of the nearly $200 billion that has been spent on contracts and grants since 2002 to support military, reconstruction and other U.S. operations in Iraq and Afghanistan."

Which brings us back to those teachers, nurses, police officers, and firefighters in Wisconsin. Mahlon Mitchell, president of the Professional Fire Fighters of Wisconsin, told me in the capitol rotunda in Madison why the unionized firefighters were there, even though their union was one not targeted by Gov. Scott Walker's bill: "This is about an attack on the middle class."

By shutting down the attacks on the people of Iraq and Afghanistan, we can prevent these attacks on the poor and middle class here at home.

July 27, 2011

War Is a Racket

"War is a racket," wrote retired U.S. Marine Maj. Gen. Smedley D. Butler, in 1935. That statement, which is also the title of his short book on war profiteering, rings true today. One courageous civil servant just won a battle to hold war profiteers accountable. Her name is Bunnatine "Bunny" Greenhouse. She blew the whistle when her employer, the U.S. Army Corps of Engineers, gave a no-bid $7 billion contract to the Halliburton subsidiary Kellogg Brown and Root (KBR) as the invasion of Iraq was about to commence. She was doing her job, trying to ensure a competitive bidding process would save the U.S. government money. For that, she was forced out of her senior position, demoted, and harassed.

Just this week, after waging a legal battle for more than half a decade, Bunny Greenhouse won. The U.S. Army Corps of Engineers settled with Greenhouse for $970,000, representing full restitution for lost wages, compensatory damages, and attorneys' fees.

Her "offense" was to challenge a no-bid, $7 billion-plus contract to KBR. It was weeks before the expected invasion of Iraq, in 2003, and Bush military planners predicted Saddam Hussein would blow up Iraqi oilfields, as happened with the U.S. invasion in 1991. The project, dubbed "Restore Iraqi Oil," or RIO, was created so that oilfield fires would be extinguished. KBR was owned then by Halliburton, whose CEO until 2000 was none other than then Vice President Dick Cheney. KBR was the only company invited to bid.

Bunny Greenhouse told her superiors that the process was illegal. She was overridden. She said the decision to grant the contract to KBR came from the Office of the Secretary of Defense, run by VP Cheney's close friend, Donald Rumsfeld.

As Bunny Greenhouse told a congressional committee, "I can unequivocally state that the abuse related to contracts awarded to KBR represents the most blatant and improper contract abuse I have witnessed during the course of my professional career."

The oilfields were not set ablaze. Nevertheless, KBR was allowed to retool its $7 billion no-bid contract, to provide gasoline and other logistical support to the occupation forces. The contract was so-called cost-plus, which means KBR was not on the hook to provide services at a set price. Rather, it could charge its cost, plus a fixed percentage as profit. The more KBR charged, the more profit it made.

As the chief procurement officer, Greenhouse's signature was required on all contracts valued at more than $10 million. Soon after testifying about the egregious RIO contract, she was demoted and stripped of her top-secret clearance and began receiving the lowest performance ratings. Before blowing the whistle, she had received the highest ratings. Ultimately, she left work, facing an unbearably hostile workplace.

After years of litigation, attorney Michael Kohn, president of the National Whistleblowers Center, brought the case to a settlement. He said: "Bunny Greenhouse risked her job and career when she objected to the gross waste of federal taxpayer dollars and illegal contracting practices at the Army Corps of Engineers. She had the courage to stand alone and challenge powerful special interests. She exposed a corrupt contracting environment where casual and clubby contracting practices were the norm. Her courage led to sweeping legal reforms that will forever halt the gross abuse she had the courage to expose."

The National Whistleblowers Center's executive director, Stephen Kohn (brother of Michael Kohn), told me: "Federal employees have a very, very hard time blowing the whistle. So whenever the government is forced to pay full damages for all back pay, all compensatory damages, all attorneys' fees, that's a major victory. I hope it's a turning point. The case was hard-fought. It should never have had to been filed. Bunny did the right thing."

According to Nobel Prize–winning economist Joe Stiglitz, the cost of the wars in Iraq and Afghanistan alone will exceed $5 trillion. With a cost like this, why isn't war central to the debate over the national debt?

Two-time Congressional Medal of Honor winner Maj. Gen. Smedley Butler had it right seventy-five years ago when he said of war: "It is possibly the oldest, easily the most profitable, surely the most vicious [racket].... It is the only one in which the profits are reckoned in dollars and the losses in lives.... It is conducted for the benefit of the very few, at the expense of the very many."

As President Barack Obama and Congress claim it is Medicare, Medicaid, and Social Security that are breaking the budget, people should demand that they stop paying for war.

August 2, 2011

War, Debt, and the President

President Barack Obama touted his debt ceiling deal Tuesday, saying, "We can't balance the budget on the backs of the very people who have borne the biggest brunt of this recession." Yet that is what he and his coterie of Wall Street advisers have done.

In the affairs of nations, Alexander Hamilton wrote in January 1790, "loans in times of public danger, especially from foreign war, are found an indispensable resource." It was his first report as secretary of the treasury to the new Congress of the United States. The country had borrowed to fight the Revolutionary War, and Hamilton proposed a system of public debt to pay those loans.

The history of the U.S. national debt is inexorably tied to its many wars. The resolution this week of the so-called debt ceiling crisis is no different. Not only did a compliant Congress agree to fund President George W. Bush's wars in Iraq and Afghanistan with emergency appropriations, it did so with borrowed money, raising the debt ceiling ten times since 2001 without quibbling.

So how did the Pentagon fare in the current budget battle? It looks like it did fine. Not to be confused with the soldiers and veterans who have fought these wars.

"This year is the 50th anniversary of [Dwight] Eisenhower's military-industrial complex speech," William Hartung of the Center for International Policy told me while the Senate assembled to vote on the debt ceiling bill. Speaking of the late general turned Republican U.S. president, Hartung said: "He talked about the need for a balanced economy, for a healthy population. Essentially, he's to the left of Barack Obama on these issues."

Michael Hudson, president of the Institute for the Study of Long-Term Economic Trends, explained the history of the debt ceiling's connection to war:

> It was put in in 1917 during World War I, and the idea was to prevent President Wilson from committing even more American troops and money to war. In every country of Europe—England, France—the parliamentary control over the budget was introduced to stop ambitious kings or rulers from waging wars. So the whole purpose was to limit a government's ability to run into debt for war, because that was the only reason that governments ran into debt.

The Budget Control Act of 2011 assures drastic cuts to the U.S. social safety net. Congress will appoint a committee of twelve, dubbed the "Super Congress," evenly split between Republicans and Democrats, to identify $1.2 trillion in cuts by Thanksgiving. If the committee fails to meet that goal, sweeping, mandatory, across-the-board cuts are mandated. Social services would get cut, but so would the Pentagon.

Or would it? The Congressional Black Caucus and the Congressional Progressive Caucus opposed the bill. Congressional Black Caucus Chair Emanuel Cleaver called it "a sugarcoated Satan sandwich." For fiscal years 2012 and 2013, the discretionary funding approved is split between "security" and "nonsecurity" categories. "Nonsecurity" categories like food programs, housing, Medicare and Medicaid (the basis of any genuine national security) will most likely be cut. But the "security" budget will get hit equally hard, which Democrats suggest would be an incentive for Republicans to cooperate with the process.

The security category includes "Department of Defense, the Department of Homeland Security, the Department of Veterans Affairs, the National Nuclear Security Administration, the intelligence community [and] international affairs." This sets up a dynamic where hawks will be trying to cut as much as possible from the State Department's diplomatic corps, and foreign aid, in order to favor their patrons at the Pentagon and in the weapons industry.

Hartung explained that the contractors, in addition to having the support of Speaker of the House John Boehner, "had Buck McKeon, the head of the House Armed Services Committee, whose biggest contributor is Lockheed Martin, who's got big military facilities in his district, [and] Randy Forbes, whose district is near the Newport News Shipbuilding complex, which builds attack submarines and aircraft carriers. They used their influence to get people on the inside, their allies in the House, to push their agenda."

President Obama's debt ceiling deal is widely considered a historic defeat for progressives, a successful attack on the New Deal and Great Society achievements of the past century. Congresswoman Donna Edwards, D-Md., summed up the disappointment, in which half the Democrats in the House voted against their president, tweeting: "Nada from million/billionaires; corp tax loopholes aplenty; only sacrifice from the poor/middle class? Shared sacrifice, balance? Really?"

The Project on Government Oversight says of the "Super Congress" that "the creation of the committee doesn't come with many requirements for transparency." Who will be the watchdog? With the 2012 election coming up, promising to be the most expensive ever, expect the committee's deficit-reduction proposal, due by Thanksgiving and subject to an up-or-down vote, to have very little to give thanks for.

MONEY IN POLITICS

June 27, 2012

Big Money Clouds the Big Skies of Montana

"I never bought a man who wasn't for sale," William A. Clark reportedly said. He was one of Montana's "Copper Kings," a man who used his vast wealth to manipulate the state government and literally buy votes to make himself a U.S. senator. That was more than 100 years ago, and the blatant corruption of Clark and the other Copper Kings created a furor that led to the passage, by citizen initiative, of Montana's Corrupt Practices Act in 1912. The century of transparent campaign-finance restrictions that followed, preventing corporate money from influencing elections, came to an end this week, as the U.S. Supreme Court summarily reversed the Montana law. Five justices of the U.S. Supreme Court reiterated: Their controversial Citizens United ruling remains the law of the land. Clark's corruption contributed to the passage of the Seventeenth Amendment to the U.S. Constitution. Now, close to 100 years later, it may take a popular movement to amend the Constitution again, this time to overturn Citizens United and confirm, finally and legally, that corporations are not people.

Citizens United v. Federal Election Commission is the case in which the U.S. Supreme Court ruled that corporations can contribute unlimited amounts of funds toward what are deemed "independent expenditures" in our elections. Thus, corporations, or shadowy "super PACs" that they choose to fund, can spend as much as they care to on negative campaign ads, just as long as they don't coordinate with a candidate's campaign committee. That 2010 ruling, approved by a narrow 5–4 majority of the court, has profoundly altered the electoral landscape—not only for the presidential election, but also for thousands of races around the country. According to a summary of the ruling's impact, prepared by the National Conference of State Legislatures, "While the ruling does not directly affect state laws, there are 24 states that currently prohibit or restrict corporate and/or union spending on candidate elections."

Montana, with its long history of banning corporate contributions, was alone among the states to defy those five U.S. Supreme Court justices. Twenty-two states and the District of Columbia filed a brief in support of Montana, noting that state elections are different. Their supporting brief read, "States— particularly resource-rich States with small populations, like Montana—face the risk that nonresident corporations with discrete and well-defined interests will dominate campaign spending in state and local election contests."

Montana is not known for bipartisanship these days. Democratic Gov. Brian Schweitzer says his veto pen has run out of ink from the number of "crazy" Republican bills that he has had to veto since taking office. Lacking ink, he now takes bills from the Republican-controlled legislature onto the capitol steps and emblazons them with a red-hot branding iron that says "Veto." So it was significant that, after the Supreme Court decision this week, Schweitzer and his lieutenant governor, John Bohlinger, a Republican, stood together before the capitol.

Bohlinger said, "Now, Republicans and Democrats don't always agree on policy matters, but there's one thing we do agree on, and that is, corporate money should not influence the outcome of an election." To which Schweitzer added: "Here in Montana, we have a proud, 100-year history of keeping corporate money out of our elections. Corporations aren't people, and they should not control our government. Montana stood up for democracy, here at home and on behalf of America, by fighting to keep our ban on corporate campaign spending. The United States Supreme Court blocked our state law, because they said corporations are people. I'll believe that when Texas executes one."

John Bonifaz is co-founder and director of Free Speech for People, one of a coalition of groups organizing for a constitutional amendment that specifies that "People, person, or persons as used in this Constitution does not include corporations, limited liability companies or other corporate entities." He told me:

> We've seen a growing mobilization across the country of people calling for an amendment to reclaim our democracy. Four states are now on record— Hawaii, Rhode Island, Vermont, New Mexico—calling for an amendment. Other states are likely to join that fight soon. Montana [has a] statewide ballot in November for an amendment. Hundreds of municipalities across the country have called for an amendment. Over a thousand business leaders have joined that call. And now there are some dozen amendment bills pending in the United States Congress calling for an amendment, with hearings to be held before the U.S. Senate Judiciary Committee this July.

Perhaps the only silver lining in the Supreme Court's decision to send Montana back to the age of the Copper Kings is that a mass movement is building to assert the rights of people over the power of money in politics.

June 6, 2012

It's One Person, One Vote, Not One Percent, One Vote

The failed effort to recall Wisconsin Gov. Scott Walker is widely seen as a crisis for the labor movement, and a pivotal moment in the 2012 U.S. presidential-election season. Walker launched a controversial effort to roll back the power of Wisconsin's public employee unions, and the unions pushed back, aided by strong, grassroots solidarity from many sectors. This week, the unions lost. Central to Walker's win was a massive infusion of campaign cash, saturating the Badger State with months of political advertising. His win signals less a loss for the unions than a loss for our democracy in this post–Citizens United era, when elections can be bought with the help of a few billionaires.

In February 2011, the newly elected Walker, a former Milwaukee county executive, rolled out a plan to strip public employees of their collective-bargaining rights, a platform he had not run on. The backlash was historic. Tens of thousands marched on the Wisconsin capitol, eventually occupying it. Walker threatened to call out the National Guard. The numbers grew. Despite Walker's strategy to "divide and conquer" the unions (a phrase he was overheard saying in a recorded conversation with a billionaire donor), the police and firefighters unions, whose bargaining rights he had strategically left intact, came out in support of the occupation. Across the world, the occupation of Tahrir Square in Egypt was in full swing, with signs in English and Arabic expressing solidarity with the workers of Wisconsin.

The demands for workers' rights were powerful and sustained. The momentum surged toward a demand to recall Walker, along with a slew of his Republican allies in the Wisconsin Senate. Then laws tempered the movement's power. The Wisconsin recall statute required that an elected official be in office for one year before a recall. Likewise, a loophole in the law allowed the target of the recall to raise unlimited individual donations, starting when the recall petitions are filed. Thus, Walker's campaign started raising funds in November 2011. His opponent, Tom Barrett, the mayor of Milwaukee, was limited to individual donations of up to $10,000, and had less than one month to campaign after winning the Democratic Party primary May 8.

Coupled with the impact of the U.S. Supreme Court's Citizens United decision, the Wisconsin loophole set the stage for grossly lopsided fundraising between Walker and Barrett, and an election battle that was the most expensive in Wisconsin's history. According to the most recent state campaign-finance filings, Walker's campaign raised over $30.5 million, more than seven times Barrett's reported $3.9 million. After adding in super PAC spending, estimates put the recall-election spending at more than $63.5 million.

According to *Forbes* magazine, fourteen billionaires made contributions to Walker, only one of whom lives in Wisconsin. Among the thirteen out-of-state billionaires was Christy Walton, the widow of John T. Walton, son of Walmart founder Sam Walton.

Nobel Prize–winning economist Joe Stiglitz writes about the Walton family in his new book, *The Price of Inequality: How Today's Divided Society Endangers Our Future*. He notes, "The six heirs to the Walmart empire command wealth of $69.7 billion, which is equivalent to the wealth of the entire bottom 30 percent of U.S. society." That is almost 95 million people. Stiglitz told me: "We've moved from a democracy, which is supposed to be based on one person, one vote, to something much more akin to one dollar, one vote. When you have that kind of democracy, it's not going to address the real needs of the 99 percent."

The voters of Wisconsin did return control of the state senate to the Democratic Party. The new majority will have the power to block the type of controversial legislation that made Walker famous. Meanwhile, three states over in Montana, the Democratic state attorney general, Steve Bullock, won his party's nomination for governor to run for the seat held by term-limited Democrat Brian Schweitzer. Bullock, as attorney general, has taken on Citizens United by defending the state's 100-year-old Corrupt Practices Act, which prohibits the type of campaign donations allowed under Citizens United. The case is now before the U.S. Supreme Court.

Wisconsin's recall is over, but the fight for democracy starts with one person, one vote, not one percent, one vote.

May 2, 2012

The Real Mad Men:
Following the Money Behind TV Political Ads

May Day, Murdoch, and the murder of Milly Dowler. What do they have to do with the 2012 U.S. general election? This year's election will undoubtedly be the most expensive in U.S. history, with some projections topping $5 billion. Not only has the amount of spending increased, but its nature has as well, following the 2010 U.S. Supreme Court's Citizens United ruling, which allows unlimited spending by corporations, unions, and so-called super PACs, all under the banner of "free speech." This campaign season will unfold amidst a resurgent Occupy Wall Street movement launched globally on May 1, the same day the British Parliament released a report on Rupert Murdoch's media empire charging that he is "not a fit person to exercise the stewardship of a major international company." Now more than ever, people should heed the advice of the famous Watergate source, Deep Throat: "Follow the money."

Most money in our elections goes to TV stations to run political advertisements. According to writers Robert McChesney and John Nichols in the *Monthly Review*, the amount of political ad spending is skyrocketing, such that "factoring for inflation, the 1972 election spent less than 3 percent of what will be spent on TV political ads in the 2012 election cycle."

For just one relatively small race, a recent Pennsylvania congressional primary between Democrats, journalist Ken Knelly provided a comprehensive analysis of the local TV news coverage compared with the amount of political ads that ran on the same TV stations. Knelly's headline says it all: "28 hours of political ads (and a few minutes of news)." More than 3,300 ad spots were run on the stations serving the predominantly Democratic district. Lost in the hours of ads, Knelly writes, was the "very occasional news report on the race," and he said the reports contained very little substance.

How Knelly was able to probe these details is crucial. The Federal Communications Commission requires that TV stations maintain a public inspection file, and any member of the public can view it. Within the disclosures are the details of the political advertising purchases made, the amounts paid, and what entity bought the airtime. Recent efforts have been made to compel these hugely profitable broadcast entities to publish these files online. The broadcasters have vigorously fought such efforts and, although they usually prevail in the industry-friendly halls of the FCC, have lost this battle. On Friday, April 27, the FCC voted 2–1 to require stations to transition from paper to online filing over a two-year period. ProPublica reporter Justin Elliot notes the files will not be provided in a standard format, and will likely not be searchable.

Most of the major U.S. broadcast networks lobbied against the new disclosure rules, including Fox Television, one of the crown jewels of Rupert Murdoch's News Corp. media empire. Murdoch received a stinging rebuke this week with the release of a British Parliament report on the phone-hacking scandal that has racked his newspapers in Britain. The scandal exploded in 2011, when the *Guardian* reported that *News of the World* reporters had hacked into the voice mail of thirteen-year-old murder victim Milly Dowler in 2002. While Dowler was still missing, reporters deleted some of her voice mails, which gave false hope to her family that she still might be alive.

Journalists, along with both a judicial inquiry and parliamentary hearings, have uncovered a culture of criminality behind much of the newsgathering facade at Murdoch's now-defunct *News of the World* newspaper in London. The parliamentary committee released its report this week, saying the Murdoch-controlled company "stonewalled, obfuscated and misled and [would] only come clean, reluctantly, when no other course of action was sensible."

The scandal also led to the discovery of bribery of British police officials, which, because News Corp. is a U.S. corporation, could fall under the U.S. federal Foreign Corrupt Practices Act, which prohibits bribery by U.S. companies overseas. In response, the nonpartisan group Citizens for Responsibility and Ethics in Washington petitioned the FCC to strip Murdoch of the twenty-seven television broadcast licenses he controls in the United States.

While it is a crime to bribe a police officer in London, it is perfectly legal to spend $5 billion to influence the course of U.S. elections, and for powerful broadcasters thereby to reap enormous profits. The FCC is to be applauded for its new transparency rules. Ultimately, political candidates should have free airtime to present their platform to the voters. Until then, it's up to journalists, activists, and regular citizens to follow the money.

January 4, 2012

Republicans Divided, Citizens United

The Republican caucuses in Iowa, with their cliffhanger ending, confirmed two key political points and left a third virtually ignored. First, the Republicans are not enthusiastic about any of their candidates. Second, we have entered a new era in political campaigning in the United States post–Citizens United, the U.S. Supreme Court decision that unleashed a torrent of unreported corporate money into our electoral process. And third, because President Barack Obama is running in this primary season unchallenged, scant attention has been paid to the growing discontent among the very people who put him in office in 2008. As a result, the 2012 presidential election promises to be long, contentious, extremely expensive, and perhaps more negative than any in history.

Mitt Romney technically prevailed in the Iowa caucuses, squeaking out an eight-vote margin over late-surging Rick Santorum. Libertarian Ron Paul garnered an impressive 21 percent of the vote in the crowded field. Note that the Republican Party does not allow a recount of the handwritten, hand-counted ballots, and that the final Romney edge was first reported on right-wing Fox News Channel by none other than its paid commentator Karl Rove, the architect of George W. Bush's two controversial presidential election wins.

So, the prevailing wisdom is that while Willard Mitt Romney retains the veneer of "electability," he cannot persuade more than 25 percent of Republicans to vote for him. Santorum's surge was a late-breaking coalescence of the anti-Romney vote, boosted by massive voter flight from Newt Gingrich that was inspired by a withering campaign of anti-Gingrich attack ads attributed to Romney.

While Romney's Iowa operation maintained a positive campaign strategy, a super PAC that supported him went on the offensive. Restore Our Future, according to NBC's Michael Isikoff, spent $2.8 million in ads in Iowa, more than twice the amount spent by the Romney campaign itself, all attacking Gingrich. The super PAC is not limited in how much corporate or individual money it can take in, and does not have to disclose the identity of its donors. While super PACs are prevented by law from coordinating with campaigns, three of the founders of the pro-Romney Restore Our Future were campaign staffers on Romney's failed 2008 presidential bid: Carl Forti, Charlie Spies, and Larry McCarthy.

The Iowa caucuses can be seen as the first instance in a presidential electoral race waged after the January 2010 U.S. Supreme Court's landmark *Citizens United v. Federal Election Commission* ruling. As summarized by the SCOTUSblog, the split court decided that "political spending is a form of protected speech under the First Amendment, and the government may not keep corporations or unions from spending money to support or denounce individual candidates in elections."

Election seasons are usually a boon for local TV stations, which sell airtime over the public airwaves. Iowa broadcasters were reporting a less-than-projected windfall, however, due to the record number of candidate debates, in which the candidates got to present themselves to the public, in essence, "for free." The last-minute onslaught of negative ads brought station revenues back up. Dale Woods, general manager of WHO TV in Des Moines, told *Broadcasting & Cable* magazine: "It's normally never negative here, but that's one dynamic I've seen change with the PAC money involved. The candidate buys are positive, but the PAC money is negative. I think that's a dynamic you'll see all over the country."

The advertising industry is watching campaign spending closely, predicting up to $4 billion in spending across all the campaigns, including those for president, Senate, House, and governorships.

But there's hope. People are fighting back against this flood of secret money infecting U.S. elections. State legislators in California are calling for a constitutional amendment overturning Citizens United. The New York City Council is voting on a similar measure, following Los Angeles; Oakland, California; Albany, New York; and Boulder, Colorado. Last week, Montana's Supreme Court restored a 100-year-old ban on corporate spending directed at political campaigns or candidates.

Harvard law professor Lawrence Lessig is calling for a constitutional convention. As defined in the U.S. Constitution, thirty-four state legislatures would need to call for a convention, which could allow an amendment banning corporate money from elections. Lessig, a favorite of progressives, is recruiting the right-wing Tea Party to help. He told me, "People can call for a convention for any purpose . . . the only option we have for intervening to fix this corrupted system is the only option the framers gave us, which is outsiders organizing to fix the problem in Washington."

CLIMATE CHANGE

September 2, 2009

New Light on Copenhagen Climate Talks

On September 1, the European Union stopped manufacturing and importing incandescent light bulbs. Europeans will now turn to the much more efficient compact fluorescent, halogen and LED (light-emitting diode) bulbs. Incandescents, critics argue, waste up to 95 percent of energy as heat, using only 5 percent for light. The EU hopes to save the equivalent of 11 million households' energy usage through the year 2020, worth $7.33 billion per year to the European economy.

The ban precedes the December 2009 Copenhagen climate conference, held by the United Nations to update the 1997 Kyoto Protocol. Greenhouse-gas emissions now occur faster than ever. Copenhagen will be critical to the success or failure of establishing a practical, binding global plan of action before human-caused climate change reaches the point of no return, creating a cascade of catastrophes.

Eventually, global warming will become irreversible if action is not taken. Greenhouse-gas concentrations in the atmosphere are measured in "parts per million" (ppm). Environmentalist Bill McKibben says that a sustainable level of carbon dioxide in the atmosphere is 350 ppm. He has named his organization 350.org to reinforce the point. We are currently at 387 ppm and climbing. McKibben and 350.org are calling for a global day of action, on October 24, to pressure governments before the Copenhagen summit.

A new generation of environmental activists is already in motion. This week, two young people were arrested in West Virginia for halting a Massey Energy Co. mountaintop coal-mining operation with a weeklong "tree sit," and six people in London were arrested at the Royal Bank of Scotland headquarters for protesting the bank's investment in fossil fuels. They glued themselves together and to the floor of the bank to hamper their removal, leading Reuters to headline its story "Protesters stick together in UK bank demonstration."

The road to Copenhagen also is paved with gold: money being spent by the wealthy oil, gas, and coal industries to derail or weaken any outcome. The American Petroleum Institute (API) has launched an "AstroTurf" (not to be confused with grassroots) campaign in the U.S., paying for and organizing rallies, largely attended by oil, gas, and coal company employees, under the banner of "Energy Citizens." Employees are bused in to the staged rallies with signs proclaiming "I'll pass on $4 gas" and "Congress, don't take away my job!" Similarities to the organized mobs at health care reform town-hall-style meetings are not merely coincidental; former Republican House Majority Leader Dick Armey's group FreedomWorks, funded by, among others, oil and pharmaceutical corporations, is listed as a consultant to each industry campaign.

The API is attempting to undermine the U.S. Senate's consideration of climate-change legislation, and it just might succeed. The House bill, referred to as the American Clean Energy and Security Act or the Waxman-Markey climate bill, is up for consideration by the Senate in September. Fast action would be required in order to grant President Barack Obama the room to negotiate at the G-20 meeting in Pittsburgh in late September, a key step in the lead-up to Copenhagen. But Sens. Barbara Boxer and John Kerry said this week that the bill will be delayed, citing the health care debate and the death of Sen. Edward Kennedy. How ironic. Every week that the health care and energy bills are delayed is a victory for the opponents of change, which is especially sad since these were two of the most important issues to Kennedy.

Genuine citizen action, in the U.S. and beyond, will be critical to counter industry influence over the Copenhagen talks. There is a light at the end of the climate tunnel—it just isn't incandescent.

• •

October 21, 2009

Trick or Treat for Climate Change

Halloween is around the corner, and children will soon be dressing up and chanting "trick or treat," their demand for candy backed up by the threat of a prank. Climate-change activists, from pranksters to presidents, are doing the same. This past Monday, the activist-artist group The Yes Men staged another of its hoaxes, with one member posing as an official from the U.S. Chamber of

Commerce, leading what appeared to be a legitimate press conference and stating the chamber's complete reversal on its historically adamant opposition to climate-change legislation.

Meanwhile, in the Indian Ocean, the president of the Maldives held the world's first underwater cabinet meeting, demonstrating that rising sea levels could very soon overwhelm his archipelago nation. With the Copenhagen climate conference less than fifty days away, people are stepping up the pressure.

The Yes Men stage elaborate hoaxes on global-trade organizations, multinational corporations, and politicians. They satirically skewer corporate, free-trade, pro-business positions by acting as genuine, sincere spokespeople for these institutions, often offering apologies for past corporate crimes or promoting absurd products with remarkably straight faces at industry conferences.

In December 2004, on the twentieth anniversary of the Bhopal, India, disaster in which a Union Carbide plant gas leak killed thousands of people, Andrew Bichlbaum of The Yes Men appeared on BBC News posing as a representative of Dow Chemical (which bought Union Carbide), claiming Dow would finally take full responsibility for the accident.

In 2007, Yes Men Bichlbaum and Mike Bonanno addressed Canada's largest oil conference, posing as executives of ExxonMobil and the National Petroleum Council. They announced a plan to convert the corpses of the expected millions of victims of climate change into a fuel they called "Vivoleum." They were ejected, after which Bonanno told the press: "While ExxonMobil continues to post record profits, they use their money to persuade governments to do nothing about climate change. This is a crime against humanity."

At this week's faux press conference in Washington, D.C., Bichlbaum read from a statement: "We at the Chamber have tried to keep climate science from interfering with business. But without a stable climate, there will be no business."

Fox Business News and other global news outlets carried the story of the chamber's surprise support for climate-change legislation. During the press conference, an actual U.S. Chamber of Commerce employee entered, loudly declaring the event a fraud, but exposing himself to probing questions about the chamber's position on climate change.

Several major corporations have quit the chamber because of its opposition to genuine climate-change legislation, including Apple, Exelon, PG&E, and Levi Strauss & Co.

The U.S. chamber's resistance to science-based climate policy is nothing new. Career public relations executive James Hoggan is the author of *Climate Cover-Up: The Crusade to Deny Global Warming*. Hoggan told me, "The PR stunt wasn't pulled off by The Yes Men; the PR stunt is basically being pulled off by the U.S. Chamber of Commerce, and it's been going on for decades."

Hoggan's book describes what he calls "a two-decade-long campaign by the energy industry in Canada and the United States, basically designed to confuse the public about climate change, and to give people the sense that there is a debate about the science of climate change."

October 24 is the global day of action organized by the group 350.org, which includes environmentalist Bill McKibben. Named after what scientists have identified as a sustainable target for carbon dioxide concentration in the atmosphere, 350 parts per million (we are currently at 387 ppm), 350.org lists close to 4,000 events around the world on October 24.

The goal is to pressure government representatives before their departure for the major United Nations climate summit that will be held in Copenhagen in December.

President Mohamed Nasheed of the Republic of Maldives is already taking action. Last week, he held an underwater cabinet meeting, donning scuba gear and literally meeting in twenty feet of water in the world's lowest-lying country. They signed an "SOS from the frontline" declaration, reading, in part, "If we can't save the Maldives today, you can't save the rest of the world tomorrow." He will carry the declaration to Copenhagen.

U.S. government leadership will be critical to clinching a substantive deal in Copenhagen, but the Senate has not finalized any climate legislation, which essentially ties the hands of U.S. negotiators. Oil, gas, and coal interests are spending $300,000 a day lobbying the government. The moment of climate-change truth is upon us, and the professional deniers are up to their old tricks.

December 9, 2009

Take Me to Your Climate Leader

COPENHAGEN—"Politicians talk, leaders act" read the sign outside the Bella Center in Copenhagen on the opening day of the United Nations climate summit. Inside the convention center, the official delegations from 192 countries, hundreds of NGOs (nongovernmental organizations)—an estimated 15,000 people in all—are engaging in two weeks of meetings aiming for a global agreement to stave off catastrophic global climate change. Five thousand journalists are covering the event.

Outside, Copenhagen has been transformed into a vibrant, global hub of climate-change activism, forums, and protest planning. In one square, an ice sculpture of a polar bear melts day by day, and an open-air exhibit of towering photos displays "100 places to remember that will disappear."

While the U.S. Environmental Protection Agency this week designated carbon dioxide as a threat to health, President Barack Obama has said that there will not be a binding agreement from this summit. Many see the U.S. as a key obstacle to it and are seizing the opportunity to assert a leadership role in what environmental writer and activist Bill McKibben has described as "the most important diplomatic gathering in the world's history." At stake are not only the rules that will govern entire economies, driven for well more than a century by fossil fuels, but the very existence of some nations and cultures, from the tropics to the Arctic.

The Republic of Maldives, an island nation in the Indian Ocean, sent fifteen-year-old Mohamed Axam Maumoon as a climate ambassador. After attending the Children's Climate Forum, he told me, "We are living at the very edge ... because our country is so fragile, only protected by the natural barriers, such as the coral reefs and the white sandy beaches."

Most of the 200 inhabited islands of the Maldives are at most three feet above sea level, and projected sea-level rises would inundate his country. Even at his age, Axam comprehends the enormousness of the threat he and his country face, and starkly frames the question he poses to people in the industrialized world: "Would you commit murder, even while we are begging for mercy and begging for you to stop what you're doing, change your ways and let our children see the future that we want to build for them?"

Farther north, in Arctic Village, Alaska, indigenous people are fighting to survive. Sarah James is an elder and a chair member of the Gwich'in Steering Committee. I met her this week at Copenhagen's Klimaforum09, dubbed "The People's Summit," where she told me: "Climate change, global warming is real in the Arctic. There's a lot of erosion, because permafrost is melting.... And last summer, there was a fire all summer long, no visibility. Last spring, twenty villages got flooded along the Yukon. Sixty villages within the Yukon area never got their fish."

Emerging economies like China and India are growing rapidly and are becoming top-tier carbon emitters, yet none approaches the per capita emission levels of the United States. With just four percent of the world's population, the U.S. produces about a quarter of the world's greenhouse gases. The model for the past century has been clear: If you want to escape poverty, grow your economy by industrializing with fossil fuels as your main source of energy. Yet the wealthy nations have not been willing to pay for the environmental damage they have caused, or significantly change the way they operate.

Author Ross Gelbspan says poverty is at the root of the problem: Take care of poverty, and humanity can solve the climate crisis. He says retooling the planet for a green economy can be the largest jobs program in history, can create more equality among nations, and is necessary, immediately, to avoid catastrophe.

Tuesday, between sessions at the Bella Center, in the cafe area packed with thousands, a group of activists dressed as space aliens, in white spacesuits and with green skin and goggles, walked in. "Take us to your climate leaders!" they demanded. "Show us your binding treaty!" In the rarified diplomatic atmosphere of the summit, such antics stand out. But the calls from the developing world, both inside and outside the summit, to cut emissions and to compensate countries, from Africa to Asia and Latin America, for the devastating effects of global warming they did not cause are no laughing matter.

Protesters are planning confrontations as more than 100 world leaders descend on Copenhagen next week. The battle cry at the Klimaforum09 is "Mobilize, Resist, Transform." The people are leading, while the politicians talk.

December 16, 2009

Copenhagen Climate Summit: The Empire's New Clothes

Denmark is the home of renowned children's author Hans Christian Andersen. Copenhagen is dotted with historical spots where Andersen lived and wrote. "The Little Mermaid" was one of his most famous tales, published in 1837, along with "The Emperor's New Clothes."

As the United Nations climate summit, called "COP 15," enters its final week, with more than 100 world leaders arriving amid growing protests, the notion that a binding agreement will come from this conference looks more and more like a fairy tale.

The reality is harsher. Negotiations have repeatedly broken down, with divisions between the global North, or industrialized countries, and the global South. Leading the North is the United States, the world's greatest polluter, historically, and a leader in per capita carbon emissions. Among the Southern nations are several groupings, including the least-developed countries, or LDCs; African nations; and nations from AOSIS, the Alliance of Small Island States. These are places where millions live on the edge, directly impacted by climate change, dealing with the effects, from cyclones and droughts to erosion and floods. Tuvalu, near Fiji, and other island nations, for example, are concerned that rising sea levels will wipe their countries off the map.

New conceptions of the crisis are emerging at COP 15. People are speaking of climate justice, climate debt, and climate refugees. Indian scientist and activist Vandana Shiva was among those who addressed a climate justice rally of 100,000 Saturday in Copenhagen. Afterward, I asked her to respond to U.S. climate negotiator Jonathan Pershing, who said the Obama administration is willing to pay its fair share, but added that donors "don't have unlimited largesse to disburse." Shiva responded, "I think it's time for the U.S. to stop seeing itself as a donor and recognize itself as a polluter, a polluter who must pay. . . . This is not about charity. This is about justice."

Shiva went on: "A climate refugee is someone who has been uprooted from their home, from their livelihoods, because of climate instability. It could be people who've had to leave their agriculture because of extended drought. It could be communities in the Himalayas who are having to leave their villages, either because flash floods are washing out their villages or because streams are disappearing."

Both inside and outside the summit there is a diverse cross section of nongovernmental organizations, or NGOs, from indigenous-peoples delegations to environmental and youth groups. Their separate but connected efforts have been coalescing into a new movement, a movement for climate justice. Broad consensus exists among the NGOs and the global South that any agreement coming out of the U.N. process must be fair, ambitious, and binding, or as they put it, "FAB."

The Bella Center itself, where the summit is being held, is said by the U.N. to be at capacity. Thousands of people line up daily in the cold, vainly hoping to get in to the Bella of the Beast. Thousands more, from the NGOs, are having their access stripped, ostensibly to make room for visiting heads of state, their entourages, and security.

Outside, Copenhagen is seeing an unprecedented police crackdown, with the largest and most expensive security operation in Denmark's history. More than 1,200 people were detained over the weekend, and as this column goes to press, targeted arrests of protest organizers and police raids of public protest convergence spaces are being reported. Heavy-handed police tactics give another meaning to "COP 15."

After South African Archbishop Desmond Tutu spoke at a candlelight vigil for children, I asked whether he thought President Barack Obama was following through on climate change. He responded: "We hope he will, yes. He has given the world a great deal of hope. I have said he's now a Nobel laureate—become what you are."

Last week, as a polar bear ice statue melted downtown, revealing the dinosaur skeleton hidden within, a small ice replica of Copenhagen's famous Little Mermaid statue sat outside the Bella Center, melting. She is now gone. Obama is making his second attempt to win a prize in Copenhagen, after the Chicago Olympics embarrassment. Unless he uses the U.S. Environmental Protection Agency's new determination that carbon dioxide is a public health hazard and nails down a fair, ambitious, and binding agreement, we may see Andersen's "The Emperor's New Clothes" played out on the global stage.

December 23, 2009

Climate Discord:
From Hopenhagen to Nopenhagen

Barack Obama said, minutes before racing out of the U.N. climate summit, "We will not be legally bound by anything that took place here today." These were among his remarks made to his own small White House press corps, excluding the 3,500 credentialed journalists covering the talks. It was late on December 18, the last day of the summit, and reports were that the negotiations had failed. Copenhagen, which had been co-branded for the talks on billboards with Coke and Siemens as "Hopenhagen," was looking more like "Nopenhagen."

As I entered the Bella Center, the summit venue, that morning, I saw several dozen people sitting on the cold stone plaza outside the police line. Throughout the summit, people had filled this area, hoping to pick up credentials. Thousands from nongovernmental organizations and the press waited hours in the cold, only to be denied. On the final days of the summit, the area was cold and empty.

Most groups had been stripped of their credentials so the summit could meet the security and space needs for traveling heads of state, the U.N. claimed. These people sitting in the cold were engaged in a somber protest: They were shaving their heads. One woman told me, "I am shaving my head to show how really deeply touched I feel about what is happening in there.... There are 6 billion people out there, and inside they don't seem to be talking about them." She held a white sign, with just a pair of quotation marks, but no words. "What does the sign say?" I asked her. She had tears in her eyes, "It says nothing because I don't know what to say anymore."

Obama reportedly heard Friday of a meeting taking place between the heads of state of China, India, Brazil, and South Africa, and burst into the room, leading the group to consensus on the "Copenhagen Accord." One hundred ninety-three countries were represented at the summit, most of them by their head of state. Obama and his small group defied U.N. procedure, resulting in the non-binding, take-it-or-leave-it document.

The accord at least acknowledges that countries "agree that deep cuts in global emissions are required according to science . . . so as to hold the increase in global temperature below 2 degrees Celsius." For some, after eight years with

President George W. Bush, just having a U.S. president who accepts science as a basis for policy might be considered a huge victory. The accord pledges "a goal of mobilizing jointly 100 billion dollars a year by 2020" for developing countries. This is less than many say is needed to solve the problem of adapting to climate change and building green economies in developing countries, and is only a nonbinding goal. Secretary of State Hillary Clinton refused to specify the U.S. share, only saying if countries didn't come to an agreement it would not be on the table anymore.

Respected climate scientist James Hansen told me, "The wealthy countries are trying to basically buy off these countries that will, in effect, disappear," adding, "based on our contribution to the carbon in the atmosphere, [the U.S. share] would be 27 percent, $27 billion per year."

I asked Bolivian President Evo Morales for his solution. He recommends "all war spending be directed towards climate change, instead of spending it on troops in Iraq, in Afghanistan or the military bases in Latin America." According to the Stockholm International Peace Research Institute, in 2008 the fifteen countries with the highest military budgets spent close to $1.2 trillion on armed forces.

Erich Pica, president of Friends of the Earth, one of the major NGOs stripped of credentials, criticized the outcome of the Copenhagen talks, writing: "The United States slammed through a flimsy agreement that was negotiated behind closed doors. The so-called 'Copenhagen Accord' is full of empty pledges." But he also applauded "concerned citizens who marched, held vigils and sent messages to their leaders, [who] helped to create unstoppable momentum in the global movement for climate justice."

Many feel that Obama's disruption of the process in Copenhagen may have fatally derailed twenty years of climate talks. But Pica has it right. The Copenhagen climate summit failed to reach a fair, ambitious, and binding agreement, but it inspired a new generation of activists to join what has emerged as a mature, sophisticated global movement for climate justice.

April 21, 2010

Cochabamba, the Water Wars, and Climate Change

COCHABAMBA, Bolivia—Here in this small Andean nation of 10 million people, the glaciers are melting, threatening the water supply of the largest urban area in the country, El Alto and La Paz, with 3.5 million people living at altitudes over 10,000 feet. I flew from El Alto International, the world's highest commercial airport, to the city of Cochabamba.

Bolivian President Evo Morales calls Cochabamba the heart of Bolivia. It was here, ten years ago this month, that, as one observer put it, "the first rebellion of the 21st century" took place. In what was dubbed the Water Wars, people from around Bolivia converged on Cochabamba to overturn the privatization of the public water system. As Jim Shultz, founder of the Cochabamba-based Democracy Center, told me, "People like a good David-and-Goliath story, and the water revolt is David not just beating one Goliath, but three. We call them the three Bs: Bechtel, Banzer and the Bank." The World Bank, Shultz explained, coerced the Bolivian government, under President Hugo Banzer, who had ruled as a dictator in the 1970s, to privatize Cochabamba's water system. The multinational corporation Bechtel, the sole bidder, took control of the public water system.

On Sunday, I walked around the Plaza Principal, in central Cochabamba, with Marcela Olivera, who was out on the streets ten years ago. I asked her about the movement's original banner, hanging for the anniversary, that reads, in Spanish, *"El agua es nuestra, carajo!"*—"The water is ours, damn it!" Bechtel was jacking up water rates. The first to notice were the farmers, dependent on irrigation. They appealed for support from the urban factory workers. Oscar Olivera, Marcela's brother, was their leader. He proclaimed, at one of their rallies, "If the government doesn't want the water company to leave the country, the people will throw them out."

Marcela recounted: "On the 4th of February, we called the people to a mobilization here. We call it '*la toma de la plaza*,' the takeover of the plaza. It was going to be the meeting of the people from the fields, meeting the people from the city, all getting together here at one time. . . . The government said that that wasn't going to be allowed to happen. Several days before this was going to happen, they sent policemen in cars and on motorcycles that were surrounding the city, trying to scare the people. And the actual day of the mobilization, they didn't let the people walk even 10 meters, and they started to shoot them with gases." The city was shut down by the coalition of farmers, factory workers, and coca growers, known as *cocaleros*. Unrest and strikes spread to other cities. During a military crackdown and state of emergency declared by then President Banzer, seventeen-year-old Victor Hugo Daza was shot in the face and killed. Amid public furor, Bechtel fled the city, and its contract with the Bolivian government was canceled.

The *cocaleros* played a crucial role in the victory. Their leader was Evo Morales. The Cochabamba Water Wars would eventually launch him into the presidency of Bolivia. At the United Nations climate summit in Copenhagen, he called for the most rigorous action on climate change.

After the summit, Bolivia refused to support the U.S.-brokered, nonbinding Copenhagen Accord. Bolivia's ambassador to the U.N., Pablo Solón, told me that, as a result, "we were notified, by the media, that the United States was cutting around $3 million to $3.5 million for projects that have to do with climate change." Instead of taking U.S. aid money for climate change, Bolivia is taking a leadership role in helping organize civil society and governments, globally, with one goal—to alter the course of the next major U.N. climate summit, set for Cancún, Mexico, in December.

Which is why more than 15,000 people from more than 120 countries have gathered here this week of Earth Day, at the People's World Conference on Climate Change and the Rights of Mother Earth. Morales called for the gathering to give the poor and the Global South an opportunity to respond to the failed climate talks in Copenhagen.

Ambassador Solón explained the reasoning behind this people's summit: "People are asking me how this is coming from a small country like Bolivia. I am the ambassador to the U.N. I know this institution. If there is no pressure from civilian society, change will not come from the U.N. The other pressure on governments comes from transnational corporations. In order to counteract that, we need to develop a voice from the grass roots."

August 11, 2010

News at 11: How Climate Change Affects You

Our daily weather reports, cheerfully presented with flashy graphics and state-of-the-art animation, appear to relay more and more information.

And yet, no matter how glitzy the presentation, a key fact is invariably omitted. Imagine if, after flashing the words "extreme weather" to grab our attention, the reports flashed "global warming." Then we would know not only to wear lighter clothes or carry an umbrella, but that we have to do something about climate change.

I put the question to Jeff Masters, co-founder and director of meteorology at Weather Underground, an Internet weather information service. Masters writes a popular blog on weather, and doesn't shy away from linking extreme weather to climate change:

"Heat, heat, heat is the name of the game on planet Earth this year," he told me, as the world is beset with extreme weather events that have caused the death of thousands and the displacement of millions.

Wildfires in Russia have blanketed the country with smoke, exacerbating the hottest summer there in 1,000 years. Torrential rains in Asia have caused massive flooding and deadly landslides in Pakistan, Kashmir, Afghanistan, and China. An ice shelf in Greenland has broken off, sending an ice island four times the size of Manhattan into the ocean. Droughts threaten Niger and the Sahel.

Masters relates stark statistics:

2010 has seen the most national extreme heat records for a single year: 17.
The past decade was the hottest decade in the historical record.
The first half of 2010 was the warmest such six-month period in the planet's history.
The five warmest months in history for the tropical Atlantic have all occurred this year (likely leading to more frequent and severe Atlantic hurricanes).

"We will start seeing more and more years like this year when you get these amazing events that caused tremendous death and destruction," Masters said. "As this extreme weather continues to increase in the coming decades and the population increases, the ability of the international community to respond and provide aid to victims will be stretched to the limit."

And yet the U.N. talks aimed at climate change seem poised for collapse.

When the Copenhagen climate talks last December were derailed, with select industrialized nations, led by the United States, offering a "take it or leave it" accord, many developing nations decided to leave it. The so-called Copenhagen Accord is seen as a tepid, nonbinding document that was forced on the poorer countries as a ploy to allow countries like the U.S., Canada, and China to escape the legally binding greenhouse-gas emissions targets of the Kyoto Protocol, which is up for renewal.

Bolivia, for example, is pursuing a more aggressive global agreement on emissions. It's calling for strict, legally binding limits on emissions, rather than the voluntary goals set forth in the Copenhagen Accord. When Bolivia refused to sign on to the accord, the U.S. denied it millions in promised aid money. Bolivia's United Nations ambassador, Pablo Solón, told me: "We said: 'You can keep your money. We're not fighting for a couple of coins. We are fighting for life.'"

While Bolivia did succeed in passing a U.N. resolution last month affirming the right to water and sanitation as a human right, a first for the world body, that doesn't change the fact that as Bolivia's glaciers melt as a result of climate change, its water supply is threatened.

Pacific Island nations like Tuvalu may disappear from the planet entirely if sea levels continue to rise, which is another consequence of global warming.

The U.N. climate conference will convene in Cancún, Mexico, in December, where prospects for global consensus with binding commitments seem increasingly unlikely. Ultimately, policy in the United States, the greatest polluter in human history, must be changed. That will come only from people in the United States making the vital connection between our local weather and global climate change. What better way than through the daily drumbeat of the weather forecasts? Meteorologist Jeff Masters defined for me the crux of the problem:

> A lot of TV meteorologists are very skeptical that human-caused global climate change is real. They've been seduced by the view pushed by the fossil-fuel industry that humans really aren't responsible . . . we're fighting a battle against an enemy that's very well-funded, that's intent on providing disinformation about what the real science says.

It just may take a weatherperson to tell which way the wind blows.

September 15, 2010

A Little Missed Sunshine

BONN, Germany—When first lady Michelle Obama started an organic garden at the White House, she sparked a national discussion on food, obesity, health, and sustainability. But the green action on the White House lawn hasn't made it to the White House roof, unfortunately.

Back in 1979, President Jimmy Carter installed solar panels on the roof of the West Wing as part of a new solar strategy. "In the year 2000," Carter said, "the solar water heater behind me, which is being dedicated today, will still be here, supplying cheap, efficient energy. A generation from now, this solar heater can either be a curiosity, a museum piece, an example of a road not taken, or it can be just a small part of one of the greatest and most exciting adventures ever undertaken by the American people."

Sadly, after President Ronald Reagan came into office, he had the panels removed, and some of them did end up in museums. Environmental activist Bill McKibben, founder of the group 350.org, told me, "You know where one of these other panels is? It's in the private museum of the Chinese entrepreneur who's built the world's largest solar thermal company on earth, Himin Solar. They've installed 60 million arrays like this across China."

In 1990, the White House panels were retrieved from government storage and put back into use by Unity College in Maine. To make the case for solar, McKibben joined with a group of Unity College students and drove one of the panels from their campus to the White House, asking that it be put back on the roof. The White House declined the offer.

President Barack Obama campaigned on the pledge that he would create millions of new green jobs. He hired Van Jones as his White House green jobs czar—only to fire him shortly after Jones became the target of what he called a "vicious smear campaign," which was promulgated by Fox News Channel. Now Obama faces a massive unemployment problem, jeopardizing not only the livelihoods of tens of millions, but the political prospects for the Democrats.

Here in Bonn, the answer couldn't be clearer: Use stimulus money and policy to jump-start a green job sector, to help create, for example, solar panel manufacturing, installation, and servicing.

Germany, one of the most advanced economies in the world, did just that.

Now, as reported in the *Financial Times*, German photovoltaic cell installations last year amount to more than one-half of those in the world.

I'm here covering the thirtieth anniversary of the Right Livelihood Awards, an amazing gathering of scores of activists and thinkers from around the world. Among them is Hermann Scheer, a member of the German Parliament.

When he received his Right Livelihood Award, he said: "Solar energy is the energy of the people. To use this energy does not require big investments of only a few big corporations. It requires billions of investments by billions of people. They have the opportunity to switch from being a part of the problem to becoming a part of the global solution."

And Germany is making this happen. Small-scale residential and commercial solar power installations are not only providing jobs, increased efficiency, and cost savings—they actually are allowing the owners of the systems to sell excess power back to the power grid, running their meters in reverse, when conditions allow.

Here, too, are representatives of the Bangladeshi organization Grameen Shakti, which makes loans and offers technical assistance to allow poor, rural people to install solar power in their homes, often granting access to electricity for the first time in their family's history. They have helped install more than 110,000 systems, often with a woman hired to maintain the system—creating jobs, empowering women, and raising the standard of living.

Also in Bonn is the headquarters of the United Nations Framework Convention on Climate Change, the sponsor of the failed Copenhagen climate talks last year. U.N. member countries and other stakeholders will meet again in December in Cancún, Mexico, with expectations for substantial progress declining almost daily.

The Obamas' organic garden shows that when the most powerful, public couple takes a stand, people pay attention. Instead of just saying no, President Obama could make an important statement in restoring the White House solar panels to the roof: After the BP Gulf oil disaster, after the reckless invasion and profoundly costly occupation of Iraq (which many believe was based on our need for oil), after the massive, ongoing loss of jobs, we are changing. We will power a vital movement away from fossil fuels, to sustainable energy, to green jobs.

December 8, 2010

Cancún, Climate Change, and WikiLeaks

CANCÚN, Mexico—Critical negotiations are under way here in Cancún, under the auspices of the United Nations, to reverse human-induced global warming. This is the first major meeting since the failed Copenhagen summit last year, and it is happening at the end of the hottest decade on record. While the stakes are high, expectations are low, and, as we have just learned with the release of classified diplomatic cables from WikiLeaks, the United States, the largest polluter in the history of the planet, is engaged in what one journalist here called "a very, very dirty business."

Dirty business, indeed. In Copenhagen last year, President Barack Obama swept into town and sequestered a select, invite-only group of nations to hammer out what became known as the "Copenhagen Accord." It outlined a plan for nations to make a public "pledge" to reduce carbon emissions, and to submit to some kind of verification process. In addition, wealthy, developed nations would, under the accord, pay billions of dollars to help poor, developing nations adapt to climate change and to pursue green-energy economies as they develop. That might sound nice, but the accord was designed, in effect, to supplant the Kyoto Protocol, a legally binding global treaty that more than 190 countries have signed. The United States, notably, has never signed Kyoto.

The WikiLeaks cables help explain what happened. One of the most outspoken critics of developed countries in the lead-up to Copenhagen, President Mohamed Nasheed of the Republic of Maldives, a nation of small islands in the Indian Ocean, ultimately signed on to the Copenhagen Accord. A secret U.S. State Department memo leaked via WikiLeaks, dated February 10, 2010, summarized the consultations of the newly appointed Maldives ambassador to the U.S., Abdul Ghafoor Mohamed. The memo reports that the ambassador said, when meeting with U.S. deputy special envoy for climate change Jonathan Pershing, "Maldives would like to see that small countries, like Maldives, that are at the forefront of the climate debate, receive tangible assistance from the larger economies. Other nations would then come to realize that there are advantages to be gained by compliance." He asked for $50 million, for projects to protect the Maldives from rising sea levels.

Pershing appears in a related memo, dated a week after the Maldives memo, regarding a meeting he had with Connie Hedegaard, the European commissioner for climate action, who played a key role in Copenhagen, as she does in Cancún. According to the memo, "Hedegaard suggested the AOSIS (Alliance of Small Island States) countries 'could be our best allies' given their need for financing." Another memo from February 17, 2010, reported, "Hedegaard responded that we will need to work around unhelpful countries such as Venezuela or Bolivia." That was from a meeting with deputy national security adviser for international economic affairs Michael Froman. The memo went on, "Froman agreed that we will need to neutralize, co-opt or marginalize these and others such as Nicaragua, Cuba, Ecuador."

The message is clear: Play along with the U.S., and the aid will flow. Oppose, and be punished.

Here in Cancún, I asked Pershing and the lead U.S. negotiator, special envoy for climate change Todd Stern, about the memos, and whether the U.S. role amounted to bribery or democracy. Stern wouldn't comment on the WikiLeaks cables, and said nations "can't . . . ask for . . . climate assistance and then . . . turn around and accuse us of bribery." I followed up by asking about countries that had U.S. aid money for climate stripped, like Ecuador and Bolivia, for opposing the Copenhagen Accord. He and Pershing ignored the question.

Pablo Solón, Bolivia's ambassador to the United Nations, did have an answer. He said the facts speak for themselves: "One thing that I can say for sure is they cut aid to Bolivia and to Ecuador. That is a fact. And they said it very clearly: 'We're going to cut it, because you don't support the Copenhagen Accord.' And that is blackmail." Solón is not optimistic about what can come from the Cancún negotiations. He told me: "The current pledges on the table will raise up the temperature by four degrees Celsius [7.2 degrees Fahrenheit]. That is catastrophic for human life and for Mother Earth."

April 20, 2011

Renewed Energy for Renewable Energy

More than 10,000 people converged in Washington, D.C., this past week to discuss, organize, mobilize, and protest around the issue of climate change. While tax day Tea Party gatherings of a few hundred scattered around the country made the news, this massive gathering, Power Shift 2011, was largely ignored by the media.

They met the week before Earth Day, around the first anniversary of the BP oil rig explosion and the twenty-fifth anniversary of the Chernobyl disaster, while the Fukushima nuclear plant still spews radioactivity into the environment. Against such a calamitous backdrop, this renewed movement's power and passion ensure that it won't be ignored for long.

Rallying those attending to the work ahead, environmentalist, author, and founder of 350.org Bill McKibben said:

> This city is as polluted as Beijing. But instead of coal smoke, it's polluted by money. Money warps our political life, it obscures our vision [...] We know now what we need to do, and the first thing we need to do is build a movement. We will never have as much money as the oil companies, so we need a different currency to work in, we need bodies, we need creativity, we need spirit.

The organizers of Power Shift describe it as an intensive boot camp, training a new generation of activists to go back to their communities and build the movement that McKibben called for. Three areas are targeted by the organizers: Catalyzing the Clean Energy Economy, Campus Climate Challenge 2.0, and Beyond Dirty Energy. The campaigns cross major sectors of U.S. society. The move for a clean energy economy has been embraced by the AFL-CIO, seeing the potential for employment in construction of wind turbines, installation of solar panels and, one of the potentially greenest and oft-ignored sectors, retrofitting of existing buildings with energy efficiencies like better insulation and weatherproofing.

On Monday, April 18, tax day in the United States, thousands held a "Make Big Polluters Pay" rally, targeting the fossil fuel and non-renewable energy industries. The demonstrators gathered in Lafayette Park, a traditional protest square wedged between the White House and the U.S. Chamber of Commerce.

As Bill McKibben said, the Chamber "spends more money lobbying than the next five lobbies combined...."

It spent more money on politics last year than the Republican National Committee and the Democratic National Committee combined, and 94 percent of that went to climate deniers.

The protests also targeted BP's offices, just after the BP shareholders' meeting was held last week in London. There, security officers blocked the entrance of a delegation of four fishermen and women from the Louisiana and Texas Gulf Coast areas heavily damaged by last year's oil spill. Diane Wilson, a fourth-generation fisherwoman, was arrested for disturbing the peace. She said "That was pretty outrageous. They had disrupted our lives down there. But just appearing at the door of a BP general assembly, and we're disrupting the peace."

Many of those gathered at Power Shift 2011 were not yet born when the Three Mile Island and Chernobyl nuclear disasters happened. These young people, seeking sustainable, renewable futures, are now learning about what President Barack Obama calls the "nuclear renaissance." The Fukushima nuclear crisis has escalated in severity to the top rating of seven, on par with Chernobyl. Best estimates are that the radiation leaks will persist for months, with ongoing impacts on health and the environment impossible to forecast.

Will Obama proceed to deliver $80 billion in loan guarantees to build more nuclear power plants in the United States? He claims he's against tax cuts for the rich, but what about public subsidies for oil, gas, coal, and nuclear, among the richest industries on earth?

We recently built new studios from which to broadcast the *Democracy Now!* news hour on public television and radio around the United States. Ours is the greenest TV/radio/Internet broadcast facility in the nation, receiving the top rating, LEED Platinum (Leadership in Energy and Environmental Design), from the U.S. Green Building Council. The medium is the message. We all need to do our part in pursuit of sustainability.

June 8, 2011

Weiner's No Longfellow

"The troubled sky reveals / The grief it feels."

These two lines were written by Henry Wadsworth Longfellow in his poem "Snow-Flakes," published in a volume in 1863 alongside his epic and better-known "The Midnight Ride of Paul Revere." Much of the news chatter this week has been about Sarah Palin's flubbing of the history of Revere's famous ride in April 1775. Revere was on a late-night, clandestine mission to alert American revolutionaries of an impending British attack. Palin's incorrect version had Revere loudly ringing a bell and shooting a gun on horseback as a warning to the British to back off.

Pathetically, as well, the media has been awash with New York Congressmember Anthony Weiner's string of electronic sexual peccadilloes. Punctuating the sensationalism, and between the TV commercials from the oil, gas, coal, and nuclear industries, are story after story of extreme weather events. Herein lies the real scandal: Why aren't the TV meteorologists, with each story, following the words "extreme weather" with another two, "climate change"? We need modern-day eco-Paul (or Paula) Revere to rouse the populace to this imminent threat.

If anyone fits that role, it's Bill McKibben. He's been speaking, writing, and organizing globally to stop climate change for more than two decades. I recently asked him about the extreme weather / climate change connection:

> We're making the Earth a more dynamic and violent place. . . . We're trapping more of the sun's energy in this narrow envelope of atmosphere, and that's now expressing itself in many ways. We don't know for sure that any particular tornado comes from climate change. There have always been tornadoes. We do know that we're seeing epic levels of thunderstorm activity, of flooding, of drought, of all the things that climatologists have been warning us about.

McKibben, founder of the grassroots climate-action organization 350.org, critiques media coverage of the disasters: "You didn't see . . . pictures from Sri Lanka, from Vietnam, from the Philippines, from Brazil northeast of Rio, where they've had similar kinds of megafloods, now Colombia."

When McKibben speaks of a "more dynamic and violent place," he's talking about the climate. But climate change, increasingly, can cause actual political violence. This week in Oslo, people gathered for the Nansen Conference on Climate Change and Displacement, to work on the growing problem of climate refugees. The United Nations High Commissioner for Refugees, Antonio Guterres, warned of two threats: slow onset disasters like drought and desertification that lead to "a tipping point at which people's lives and livelihoods come under such serious threat that they have no choice but to leave their homes," and "natural disasters [that] uproot large numbers of people in a matter of hours."

A principal concern is that these millions, even billions, who are or will be displaced will be denied safe haven. As Naomi Klein, a true Paula Revere, warned recently, "This crisis will be exploited to militarize our societies, to create fortress continents."

UNHCR's Guterres notes that most of the climate refugees will be internally displaced within their home country. And you needn't look as far away as Pakistan to see evidence of that. Just this week in the United States, people have been forced to flee tornadoes in western Massachusetts, flooding in Iowa and Colorado, and wildfires in Arizona. Record-breaking heat levels in Washington, D.C., and Texas are threatening lives, with the hottest summer months yet to come.

Not far from Oslo, in Bonn, Germany, more than 3,000 participants from some 180 countries are gathered to plan for this December's U.N. climate talks in Durban, South Africa. Addressing the meeting, Tove Ryding of Greenpeace said, "What we are talking about here is actually millions of green jobs, to transform our societies to energy systems that are safe, that are stable and that are based on renewable energy and energy efficiency."

That move, away from fossil fuels and nuclear toward renewable energy, is being embraced now by more and more countries, especially after the Fukushima disaster. Japan just revealed that there were three full nuclear meltdowns at Fukushima.

Switzerland and Germany have announced they will be phasing out nuclear power. China, Germany, and Japan, three of the world's top five economies, are charging ahead on renewable-energy research and deployment.

The Obama administration's paltry funding for renewable-energy research pales in comparison with the tens of billions in subsidies for the oil, coal, and nuclear industries.

The global climate is changing, and humans are the principal cause. Will we in the U.S., the world's historically largest polluter, heed the warnings of our environmental Reveres, or will the troubled sky, as Longfellow wrote, increasingly reveal the grief it feels?

• •

November 30, 2011

Cry, the Beloved Climate

The United Nations annual climate summit descended on Durban, South Africa, this week, but not in time to prevent the tragic death of Qodeni Ximba. The seventeen-year-old was one of ten people killed in Durban on Sunday, the night before the U.N. conference opened. Torrential rains pummeled the seaside city of 3.5 million. Seven hundred homes were destroyed by the floods.

Ximba was sleeping when the concrete wall next to her collapsed. One woman tried to save a flailing one-year-old baby whose parents had been crushed by their home. She failed, and the baby died along with both parents. All this, as more than 20,000 politicians, bureaucrats, journalists, scientists, and activists made their way to what may be the last chance for the Kyoto Protocol.

How might the conference have prevented the deaths? A better question is, how might the massive deluge, which fell on the heels of other deadly storms this month, be linked to human-induced climate change, and what is the gathering in Durban doing about it? Durban has received twice the normal amount of rain for November. The trends suggest that extreme weather is going to get worse.

The Intergovernmental Panel on Climate Change is a group with thousands of scientists who volunteer their time "to provide the world with a clear scientific view on the current state of knowledge in climate change." The group won the Nobel Peace Prize in 2007. Last week, the IPCC released a summary of its findings, clearly linking changing climate to extreme weather events such as drought, flash floods, hurricanes, heat waves, and rising sea levels. The World Meteorological Organization released a summary of its latest findings, noting, to date, that 2011 is the tenth-warmest year on record, that the Arctic sea ice is at its all-time low volume this year, and that thirteen of the warmest years on record have occurred in the past fifteen years.

Which brings us to Durban. This is the 17th Conference of the Parties to the United Nations Framework Convention on Climate Change, or, simply, COP 17. One of the signal achievements of the U.N. process to date is the Kyoto Protocol, an international treaty with enforceable provisions designed to limit greenhouse-gas emissions. In 1997, when Kyoto was adopted, China was considered a poor, developing country, and, as such, had far fewer obligations under Kyoto. Now, the U.S. and others say that China must join the wealthy, developed nations and comply with that set of rules. China refuses. That is one of the major, but by no means the only, stumbling blocks to renewing the Kyoto Protocol (another major problem is that the world's historically largest polluter, the United States, signed Kyoto but did not ratify it in Congress).

In Copenhagen in late 2009 (at COP 15), President Barack Obama swept in; organized back-door, invite-only meetings; and crafted a voluntary—i.e., unenforceable—alternative to Kyoto, angering many. COP 16 in Cancún, Mexico, in 2010 heightened the distance from the Kyoto Protocol. The prevailing wisdom in Durban is that this is make-or-break time for the U.N. climate process.

Exacerbating Obama's failures is the Republican majority in the House of Representatives that largely holds human-made climate change as being either a hoax or simply nonexistent, as do eight of nine Republican presidential candidates. Oil and gas corporations spend tens of millions of dollars annually to promote junk science and climate-change deniers. Their investment has paid off, with an increasing percentage of Americans believing that climate change is not a problem.

Coincident with the disappointing U.N. proceedings has been a growing movement for climate justice in the streets. Protests against fossil-fuel dependence, which accelerates global warming, range from the nonviolent direct action against mountaintop-removal coal mining in West Virginia to the arrest of more than 1,200 people at the White House opposing the Keystone XL tar sands oil pipeline.

Which is why Durban, South Africa, is such a fitting place for civil society to challenge the United Nations process. The continent of Africa is projected to experience the impact of climate change more severely than many other locales, and most populations here are less well-equipped to deal with climate disasters, without proper infrastructure or a reserve of wealth to deploy. Yet these are the people who threw off the oppressive yoke of apartheid.

South African novelist Alan Paton wrote of apartheid in 1948, the system's first year, anticipating a long fight to overturn it, "Cry, the beloved country, these things are not yet at an end." The same determination is growing in the streets of Durban, providing the leadership so lacking in the guarded, air-conditioned enclave of COP 17.

• •

December 7, 2011

Listen to the People, Not the Polluters

It was no simple task. Despite the morning sun and blue sky, the wind was ferocious, and the group hanging the banner wasn't exactly welcome. They were with Greenpeace, hanging off the roof of the Protea Hotel Edward.

Inside, executives gathered at the World Business Council for Sustainable Development (WBCSD), an organization that touts itself as "a CEO-led organization of forward-thinking companies that galvanizes the global business community to create a sustainable future for business, society and the environment." Down at street level, as the police gathered and scores held signs and banners and sang in solidarity with the climbers, Kumi Naidoo lambasted the WBCSD, labeling it one of Greenpeace's "Dirty Dozen."

Naidoo is no stranger to action on the streets of Durban. While he is now the executive director of Greenpeace International, one of the largest and most visible global environmental organizations, in 1980, at the age of fifteen, he was one of millions of South Africans fighting against the racist apartheid regime. He was thrown out of high school and eventually had to go underground. He emerged in England, living in exile, and went on to become a Rhodes scholar. Naidoo has long struggled for human rights, against poverty, and for action to combat climate change.

A colleague and I scrambled up to the roof to film as the seven banner-hanging activists were arrested. South African climber Michael Baillie, one of them, told me: "Our goal here today was to highlight how governments are being unduly influenced by a handful of corporations who are trying to adversely influence the climate negotiations that are happening here in Durban. They are holding the climate hostage."

Later, at the U.N. conference inside the Alfred Luthuli International Conference Center, named after an early president-general of the African National Congress and the first African to win the Nobel Peace Prize, Naidoo told me about that morning's action: "We are not opposed to the idea of dialogue with corporations, but clearly corporations are not actually moving as fast as we need them to move and, in fact, are actually holding us back. Therefore, we think that calling them out, naming and shaming them, is critically necessary so that people know why these climate talks here are not actually going as fast as we need them to go."

The Dirty Dozen in Durban include Royal Dutch Shell, ExxonMobil, Koch Industries, and BASF, along with industry trade groups such as the U.S. Chamber of Commerce, the WBCSD, and the American Petroleum Institute. Greenpeace highlighted these corporations and corporate umbrella groups for their presence in Durban, and for their actions throughout the global-climate-change negotiating process, in undermining meaningful progress. The full report, titled "Who's holding us back? How carbon-intensive industry is preventing effective climate legislation," details how these corporations not only derail national legislation on climate change across the globe, but are also gaining privileged access to the global negotiations like these crucial United Nations talks in Durban.

Former South African Archbishop Desmond Tutu addressed a rally before the summit, describing climate change as a "huge enemy. . . . We are saying this is the last chance, please for goodness' sake take the right decision, this is the only world we have, the only home we have, if it is destroyed, we all sink." Former Irish President Mary Robinson added, "People are suffering because of the impact of climate change, those who are suffering most are not responsible, so the rich world has to take its responsibility, we have to have a continuation of Kyoto, a track that leads to a fair, ambitious and binding agreement, and we have to do it here in Durban."

There is a growing consensus here in Durban that the United States is the main impediment to progress at these crucial talks. A consortium of sixteen of the major environmental groups in the U.S. wrote a letter to Secretary of State Hillary Clinton, who directly oversees the U.S. climate negotiations. They pointed out that, while President Barack Obama originally campaigned on a promise to lead in global climate negotiations, "three years later, America risks being viewed not as a global leader on climate change, but as a major obstacle to progress."

The fossil-fuel industry exerts enormous influence over the U.S. government, and over the U.S. public, with tens of millions of dollars on lobbying and PR campaigns to shape public opinion. Kumi Naidoo, who has been jailed many times for his activism, compared the struggle against apartheid to the fight against climate change: "If people around the world can actually unite—trade unions, social movements, religious leaders, environmental groups and so on, which we saw in the march on Saturday—I pray and hope that we will have a similar kind of miracle to get these climate negotiations to deliver a fair, ambitious and legally binding outcome."

• •

December 14, 2011

Climate Apartheid

"You've been negotiating all my life," Anjali Appadurai told the plenary session of the U.N.'s seventeenth "Conference of Parties," or COP 17, the official title of the United Nations Climate Change Conference in Durban, South Africa. Appadurai, a student at the ecologically focused College of the Atlantic in Bar Harbor, Maine, addressed the plenary as part of the youth delegation. She continued: "In that time, you've failed to meet pledges, you've missed targets, and you've broken promises. But you've heard this all before."

After she finished her address, she moved to the side of the podium, off microphone, and in a manner familiar to anyone who has attended an Occupy protest, shouted into the vast hall of staid diplomats, "Mic check!" A crowd of young people stood up, and the call-and-response began:

Appadurai: "Equity now!"
Crowd: "Equity now!"
Appadurai: "You've run out of excuses!"
Crowd: "You've run out of excuses!"
Appadurai: "We're running out of time!"
Crowd: "We're running out of time!"
Appadurai: "Get it done!"
Crowd: "Get it done!"

That was Friday, at the official closing plenary session of COP 17. The negotiations were extended, virtually nonstop, through Sunday, in hopes of avoiding complete failure. At issue were arguments over words and phrases—for instance, the replacement of "legal agreement" with "an agreed outcome with legal force," which is said to have won over India to the Durban Platform.

The countries in attendance agreed to a schedule that would lead to an agreement by 2015, which would commit all countries to reduce emissions starting no sooner than 2020, eight years into the future.

"Eight years from now is a death sentence on Africa," Nigerian environmentalist Nnimmo Bassey, chairperson of Friends of the Earth International, told me. "For every one-degree Celsius change in temperature, Africa is impacted at a heightened level." He lays out the extent of the immediate threats in his new book about Africa, *To Cook a Continent.*

Bassey is one among many concerned with the profound lack of ambition embodied in the Durban Platform, which delays actual, legally binding reductions in emissions until 2020 at the earliest, whereas scientists globally are in overwhelming agreement: The stated goal of limiting average global temperature rise to 2 degrees Celsius (3.6 degrees Fahrenheit) will soon be impossible to achieve. The International Energy Agency, in its annual World Energy Outlook released in November, predicted "cumulative CO2 [carbon dioxide] emissions over the next 25 years amount to three-quarters of the total from the past 110 years, leading to a long-term average temperature rise of 3.5 [degrees] C."

Despite optimistic pronouncements to the contrary, many believe the Kyoto Protocol died in Durban. Pablo Solón, the former Bolivian ambassador to the United Nations and former chief climate negotiator for that poor country, now calls Kyoto a "zombie agreement," staggering forward for another five or seven years, but without force or impact. On the day after the talks concluded, Canadian Environment Minister Peter Kent announced that Canada was formally withdrawing from the Kyoto Protocol. Expected to follow are Russia and Japan, the very nation where the 1997 meeting was held that gives the Kyoto Protocol its name.

The largest polluter in world history, the United States, never ratified the Kyoto Protocol and remains defiant. Both Bassey and Solón refer to the outcome of Durban as a form of "climate apartheid."

Despite the pledges by President Barack Obama to restore the United States to a position of leadership on the issue of climate change, the trajectory from Copenhagen in 2009, to Cancún in 2010, and, now, to Durban reinforces the statement made by then President George H. W. Bush prior to the Rio Earth Summit in 1992, the forerunner to the Kyoto Protocol, when he said, "The American way of life is not up for negotiation."

The "American way of life" can be measured in per capita emissions of carbon. In the U.S., on average, about twenty metric tons of CO_2 is released into the atmosphere annually, one of the top ten on the planet. Hence, a popular sticker in Durban read "Stop CO2lonialism."

By comparison, China, the country that is the largest emitter currently, has per capita emissions closer to five metric tons, ranking it about eightieth. India's population emits a meager 1.5 tons per capita, a fraction of the U.S. level.

So it seems U.S. intransigence, its unwillingness to get off its fossil-fuel addiction, effectively killed Kyoto in Durban, a key city in South Africa's fight against apartheid. That is why Anjali Appadurai's closing words were imbued with a sense of hope brought by this new generation of climate activists:

"[Nelson] Mandela said, 'It always seems impossible, until it's done.' So, distinguished delegates and governments around the world, governments of the developed world, deep cuts now. Get it done."

April 12, 2012

The Long, Hot March of Climate Change

The Pentagon knows it. The world's largest insurers know it. Now, governments may be overthrown because of it. It is climate change, and it is real. According to the U.S. National Oceanic and Atmospheric Administration, last month was the hottest March on record for the United States since 1895, when records were first kept, with average temperatures of 8.6 degrees F above average. More than 15,000 March high-temperature records were broken nationally. Drought, wildfires, tornadoes, and other extreme weather events are already plaguing the country.

Across the world in the Maldives, rising sea levels continue to threaten this Indian Ocean archipelago. It is the world's lowest-lying nation, on average only 1.3 meters above sea level. The plight of the Maldives gained global prominence when its young president, the first-ever democratically elected there, Mohamed Nasheed, became one of the world's leading voices against climate change, especially in the lead-up to the 2009 U.N. climate-change summit in Copenhagen. Nasheed held a ministerial meeting underwater, with his cabinet in scuba gear, to illustrate the potential disaster.

In February, Nasheed was ousted from his presidency at gunpoint. The Obama administration, through State Department spokesperson Victoria Nuland, said of the coup d'etat, "This was handled constitutionally." When I spoke to Nasheed last month, he told me: "It was really shocking and deeply disturbing that the United States government so instantly recognized the former dictatorship coming back again.... The European governments have not recognized the new regime in the Maldives." There is a parallel between national positions on climate change and support or opposition to the Maldives coup.

Nasheed is the subject of a new documentary, *The Island President,* in which his remarkable trajectory is traced. He was a student activist under the dictatorship of Maumoon Abdul Gayoom and was arrested and tortured, along with many others. By 2008, when elections were finally held, Gayoom lost, and Nasheed was elected. As he told me, though: "It's easy to beat a dictator, but it's not so easy to get rid of a dictatorship. The networks, the intricacies, the institutions and everything that the dictatorship has established remains, even after the elections." On the morning of February 7, 2012, under threat of death to him and his supporters from rebelling army generals, Nasheed resigned.

While no direct link has been found yet between Nasheed's climate activism and the coup, it was clear in Copenhagen in 2009 that he was a thorn in the Obama administration's side. Nasheed and other representatives from AOSIS, the Alliance of Small Island States, were taking a stand to defend their nations' very existence, and building alliances with grassroots groups like 350.org, which challenge corporate-dominated climate policy.

Back in the U.S., March delivered this year's first weather disaster that caused more than $1 billion in damage, with tornadoes ravaging four central states and killing forty-one. Dr. Jeff Masters of the weather website Weather Underground blogged about March that "records not merely smashed, but obliterated." On March 23, conservative Texas Gov. Rick Perry renewed the state of emergency declared there last year as a result of massive droughts.

Texas lists 1,000 of the state's 4,710 community water systems under restrictions. Spicewood, Texas, population 1,100, has run dry, and is now getting water trucked in. Residents have severe restrictions on water use. But for Perry, restricting corporations whose greenhouse-gas emissions lead to climate change is heresy.

Mitt Romney is on track to be the Republican candidate for president, with the support of former challengers like Perry. They are already attacking President Obama on climate change. The American Legislative Exchange Council, or ALEC, has been promoting legislation in statehouses to oppose any climate legislation, and rallying members of Congress to block federal action, especially by hampering the work of the Environmental Protection Agency. As the Center for Media and Democracy has detailed in its "ALEC Exposed" reporting, ALEC is funded by the country's major polluters, including ExxonMobil, BP America, Chevron, Peabody Energy, and Koch Industries. The Koch brothers have also funded Tea Party groups like FreedomWorks, to create the appearance of grassroots activism.

This election season will likely be marked by more extreme weather events, more massive loss of life, and billions of dollars in damages.

President Nasheed is working to run again for his lost presidency, as President Obama tries to hold on to his. The climate may hang in the balance.

July 4, 2012

Climate Change: "This Is Just the Beginning"

Evidence supporting the existence of climate change is pummeling the United States this summer, from the mountain wildfires of Colorado to the recent "derecho" storm that left at least twenty-three dead and 1.4 million people without power from Illinois to Virginia. The phrase "extreme weather" flashes across television screens from coast to coast, but its connection to climate change is consistently ignored, if not outright mocked. If our news media, including—or especially—the meteorologists, continue to ignore the essential link between extreme weather and climate change, then we as a nation, the greatest per capita polluters on the planet, may not act in time to avert even greater catastrophe.

More than 2,000 heat records were broken last week around the United States. The National Oceanic and Atmospheric Administration (NOAA), the government agency that tracks the data, reported that the spring of 2012 "marked the largest temperature departure from average of any season on record for the contiguous United States." These record temperatures in May, NOAA says, "have been so dramatically different that they establish a new 'neighborhood' apart from the historical year-to-date temperatures."

In Colorado, at least seven major wildfires are burning at the time of this writing. The Waldo Canyon fire in Colorado Springs destroyed 347 homes and killed at least two people. The High Park fire farther north burned 259 homes and killed one. While officially "contained" now, that fire won't go out, according to Colorado's Office of Emergency Management, until an "act of nature such as prolonged rain or snowfall." The derecho storm system is another example. "Derecho" is Spanish for "straight ahead," and that is what the storm did, forming near Chicago and blasting east, leaving a trail of death, destruction, and downed power lines.

Add drought to fire and violent thunderstorms. According to Dr. Jeff Masters, one of the few meteorologists who frequently makes the connection between extreme weather and climate change, "across the entire continental U.S., 72 percent of the land area was classified as being in dry or drought conditions" last week. "We're going to be seeing a lot more weather like this, a lot more impacts like we're seeing from this series of heat waves, fires and storms. . . . This is just the beginning."

Fortunately, we might be seeing a lot more of Jeff Masters, too. He was a co-founder of the popular weather website Weather Underground in 1995. Just this week he announced that the site had been purchased by the Weather Channel, perhaps the largest single purveyor of extreme weather reports. Masters promises the same focus on his blog, which he hopes will reach the much larger Weather Channel audience. He and others are needed to counter the drumbeat denial of the significance of human-induced climate change, of the sort delivered by CNN's charismatic weatherman Rob Marciano. In 2007, a British judge was considering banning Al Gore's movie *An Inconvenient Truth* from schools in England. After the report, Marciano said on CNN, "Finally. Finally . . . you know, the Oscars, they give out awards for fictional films, as well. . . . Global warming does not conclusively cause stronger hurricanes like we've seen." Masters responded to that characteristic clip by telling me, "Our TV meteorologists are missing a big opportunity here to educate and tell the population what is likely to happen."

Beyond the borders of wealthy countries like the United States, in developing countries where most people in the world live, the impacts of climate change are much more deadly, from the growing desertification of Africa to the threats of rising sea levels and the submersion of small island nations.

The U.S. news media have a critical role to play in educating the public about climate change. Imagine if just half the times that they flash "Extreme Weather" across our TV screens, they alternated with "Global Warming." This Independence Day holiday week might just be the beginning of people demanding the push to wean ourselves off fossil fuels and to pursue a sane course toward sustainable energy independence.

DIRTY ENERGY

February 17, 2010

Obama's Nuclear Option

President Barack Obama is going nuclear. He announced the initial $8 billion in loan guarantees for construction of the first new nuclear power plants in the United States in close to three decades. Obama is making good on a campaign pledge, like his promises to escalate the war in Afghanistan and to unilaterally attack in Pakistan. And like his "Af-Pak" war strategy, Obama's publicly financed resuscitation of the nuclear power industry in the U.S. is bound to fail, another taxpayer bailout waiting to happen.

Opponents of the plan, which includes a tripling of existing nuclear plant construction-loan guarantees to $54.5 billion, span the ideological spectrum. On its most basic level, the economics of nuclear power generation simply doesn't make sense. The cost to construct these behemoths is so huge, and the risks are so great, that no sensible investor, no banks, no hedge funds will invest in their construction.

No one will loan a power company the money to build a power plant, and the power companies refuse to spend their own money. Obama himself professes a passion for the free market, telling *Bloomberg BusinessWeek*, "We are fierce advocates for a thriving, dynamic free market." Well, the free market long ago abandoned nuclear power. The right-wing think tank Heritage Foundation remarked, "Expansive loan guarantee programs... are wrought with problems. At a minimum, they create taxpayer liabilities, give recipients preferential treatment, and distort capital markets."

Amory Lovins of the Rocky Mountain Institute, a longtime critic of the nuclear power industry, told me, "If you buy more nuclear plants, you're going to get about two to 10 times less climate solution per dollar, and you'll get it about 20 to 40 times slower, than if you buy instead the cheaper, faster stuff that is walloping nuclear and coal and gas."

In his 2008 report "The Nuclear Illusion," Lovins writes, "Nuclear power is continuing its decades-long collapse in the global marketplace because it's grossly uncompetitive, unneeded, and obsolete—so hopelessly uneconomic that one needn't debate whether it's clean and safe; it weakens electric reliability and national security; and it worsens climate change compared with devoting the same money and time to more effective options."

The White House Office of Management and Budget, in the same statement announcing the $54.5 billion for nuclear power, also listed a "credit subsidy funding of $500 million to support $3 [billion] to $5 billion of loan guarantees for energy efficiency and renewable energy projects." Thus, just one-tenth the amount for nuclear is being dedicated to energy efficiency and renewable energy technologies. At the same time, the Obama administration plans to cancel funding for the hugely unpopular Yucca Mountain nuclear waste storage facility. Edwin Lyman of the Union of Concerned Scientists told the *Christian Science Monitor* the Obama administration "doesn't have a plan for [storing] radioactive waste from a new generation of nuclear power plants. That is irresponsible."

The waste from nuclear power plants is not only an ecological nightmare, but also increases the threats of nuclear proliferation. Obama said in his recent State of the Union address, "We're also confronting perhaps the greatest danger to the American people—the threat of nuclear weapons." Despite this, plans that accompany what Obama has proposed, his "new generation of safe, clean nuclear power plants," include increased commercial "nuclear fuel reprocessing," which the Union of Concerned Scientists calls "dangerous, dirty and expensive," and which it says would increase the global risks of both nuclear proliferation and nuclear terrorism.

Both Lovins and the Union of Concerned Scientists debunk the myth that nuclear energy is essential to combat global warming. Lovins writes, "Every dollar invested in nuclear expansion will worsen climate change by buying less solution per dollar." Obama said that this first tranche of public funding, which will benefit the energy giant Southern Co., "will create thousands of construction jobs in the next few years, and some 800 permanent jobs." Yet investment in solar, wind, and cogeneration technologies could do the same thing, quickly creating industries here in the U.S. that are thriving in Europe. What's more, the risks of failure of a windmill or a solar panel are minute when compared with nuclear power plant disasters like Three Mile Island and Chernobyl.

From economics to the environment to the prevention of nuclear threats, Obama's nuclear loan guarantees fail on all counts.

February 24, 2010

Cracking Down on Fracking

Mike Markham of Colorado has an explosive problem: His tap water catches fire. Markham demonstrates this in a new documentary, *Gasland*, which just won the Sundance Film Festival Special Jury Prize. Director Josh Fox films Markham as he runs his kitchen faucet, holding a cigarette lighter up to the running water. After a few seconds, a ball of fire erupts out of the sink, almost enveloping Markham's head.

The source of the flammable water, and the subject of *Gasland*, is the mining process called hydraulic fracturing, or "fracking."

Fracking is used to access natural gas and oil reserves buried thousands of feet below the ground. Companies like Halliburton drill down vertically, then send the shaft horizontally, crossing many small, trapped veins of gas and oil. Explosive charges are then set off at various points in the drill shaft, causing what Fox calls "mini-earthquakes." These fractures spread underground, allowing the gas to flow back into the shaft to be extracted. To force open the fractures, millions of gallons of liquid are forced into the shaft at very high pressure.

The high-pressure liquids are a combination of water, sand, and a secret mix of chemicals. Each well requires between 1 million and 7 million gallons of the fluid every time gas is extracted. Drillers do not have to reveal the chemical cocktail, thanks to a slew of exemptions given to the industry, most notably in the 2005 Energy Policy Act, which actually granted the fracking industry a specific exemption from the Safe Drinking Water Act. California Congressman Henry Waxman, chair of the House Energy and Commerce Committee, has just announced an investigation into the composition of the proprietary chemicals used in fracking. In a February 18 letter, Waxman commented on the Safe Drinking Water Act exemption: "Many dubbed this provision the 'Halliburton loophole' because of Halliburton's ties to then Vice President Cheney and its role as one of the largest providers of hydraulic fracturing services." Before he was vice president, Dick Cheney was the CEO of Halliburton.

In an earlier investigation, Waxman learned that Halliburton had violated a 2003 nonbinding agreement with the government in which the company promised not to use diesel fuel in the mix when extracting from certain wells.

Halliburton pumped hundreds of thousands of gallons of toxic, diesel-containing liquids into the ground, potentially contaminating drinking water.

According to the Department of Energy, there were more than 418,000 gas wells in the U.S. as of 2006. Since the Environmental Protection Agency lacks authority to investigate and regulate fracking, the extent of the pollution is unknown. Yet, as Josh Fox traveled the country, becoming increasingly engrossed in the vastness of the domestic drilling industry and the problems it creates, he documented how people living near gas wells are suffering water contamination, air pollution, and numerous health problems that crop up after fracking. It's personal for Fox: He lives in Pennsylvania, on a stream that feeds into the Delaware River, atop the "Marcellus Shale," a subterranean region from New York to Tennessee with extensive natural gas reserves. Fracking in the Marcellus Shale could potentially contaminate the water supplies of both New York City and Philadelphia. Fox was offered almost $100,000 for the gas rights to his nineteen acres, which led him to investigate the industry, and ultimately to produce his award-winning documentary.

There is virtually no federal oversight of fracking, leaving the budget-strapped states to do the job with a patchwork of disparate regulations. They are no match for the major, multinational drilling and energy companies that are exploiting the political goal of "energy independence." The nonprofit news website ProPublica.org found that, out of thirty-one states examined, twenty-one have no regulations specific to hydraulic fracturing, and none requires the companies to report the amount of the toxic fluid remaining underground.

Reports indicate that almost 600 different chemicals are used in fracking, including diesel fuel and the "BTEX" chemicals: benzene, toluene, ethylbenzene and xylenes, which include known carcinogens.

Dr. Theo Colborn, zoologist and expert on chemical pollution from fracking, appears in *Gasland*, saying, "Every environmental law we wrote to protect public health is ignored.... We can't monitor until we know what they're using."

Fox ends *Gasland* with an excerpt of a congressional hearing. Rep. Diana DeGette, D-Colo., and Rep. Maurice Hinchey, D-N.Y., aggressively question gas industry executives about water contamination. The two have submitted a bill, the proposed FRAC Act, which would remove the "Halliburton loophole," forcing drillers to reveal the chemical components used in fracking. It's time to close the door on the Cheney energy policy and take immediate steps to protect clean water.

April 14, 2010

Massey Disaster Not Just Tragic, but Criminal

Massey Energy runs the Upper Big Branch (UBB) mine in Montcoal, West Virginia, where twenty-nine miners were killed last week. The loss of life is tragic, but the UBB explosion is more than tragic; it is criminal. When corporations are guilty of crimes, however, they don't go to prison, they don't forfeit their freedom—they just get fined, which often amounts to a slap on the wrist, the cost of doing business. No one makes this clearer than the CEO of Massey Energy, Don Blankenship. He has been the bane of climate-change activists and mine safety advocates for years. This latest mine disaster, if nothing else, will surely bring needed attention to this poster boy for malevolent big business trampling on communities, the environment, and workers' rights.

Days after the Massey explosion, Blankenship admitted in a radio interview: "Violations are, you know, unfortunately, a normal part of the mining process . . . there are violations at every coal mine in America. And UBB was a mine that had violations." The *Charleston Gazette* of West Virginia has consistently reported critically on Massey Energy and Blankenship, prompting him to attack its editors in a November 2008 speech, saying: "It is as great a pleasure to me to be criticized by the communists and the atheists of the *Gazette* . . . would we be upset if Osama bin Laden were to be critical of us? I don't think so."

Initial speculation on the cause of the explosion is methane in the mine. The Massey UBB mine has received thousands of citations for violations, including many for failing to remove the methane with ventilation. Another cause may be the mine's proximity to Massey mountaintop removal operations. Mountaintop removal involves the massive blasting away of mountaintops, providing access to seams of coal, but causing widespread destruction of the environment. The *Wall Street Journal* reported Monday that a West Virginia state investigation into the explosion will include possible impact of nearby mountaintop mining operations. Environmental Protection Agency Administrator Lisa Jackson issued new rules restricting mountaintop removal on April 1, just days before the Massey explosion. Massey is the principal target of a growing grassroots campaign against mountaintop removal. Among those arrested at protests have been renowned climate scientist James Hansen, director of the NASA Goddard Institute for Space Studies, and actress Daryl Hannah.

Sixteen miners died in Massey mines between the years 2000 and 2007. Elvis Hatfield, forty-six, and Don Bragg, thirty-three, were killed in January 2006 in the Aracoma mine fire. Their widows sued Massey Energy and Blankenship. At the trial, their lawyers presented a memo written by Blankenship months before the fatal fire, instructing his deep-mine superintendents to focus on extracting coal over safety projects: "If any of you have been asked by your group presidents, your supervisors, engineers or anyone else to do anything other than run coal (i.e. build overcasts, do construction jobs, or whatever), you need to ignore them and run coal. This memo is necessary only because we seem not to understand that the coal pays the bills."

Coal pays the bills. And pays Blankenship's salary, which, estimated by the Associated Press at $19.7 million, is the highest in the coal industry. Blankenship, who is a board member of the U.S. Chamber of Commerce, is a fierce opponent of organized labor, a relentless denier of climate change, and a staunch opponent of regulation. He said of government regulators, last Labor Day at an anti-union rally, "The very idea that they care more about coal-miner safety than we do is as silly as global warming."

Blankenship poured $3 million into the election campaign of a candidate for the West Virginia Supreme Court, in order to replace a sitting judge whom he feared would rule against Massey in an appeal against a $50 million judgment. The candidate he backed, Brent Benjamin, won the seat and voted to overturn the judgment. (The U.S. Supreme Court overturned that decision, citing Blankenship's funding of the election, and the case served as the basis of John Grisham's 2008 legal thriller, *The Appeal*.)

Pension funds and other large institutional investors are demanding that Massey fire Blankenship. The last of the twenty-nine bodies of the miners killed in the Massey mine have been recovered. Their deaths should not be counted by Don Blankenship as the cost of doing business, but, rather, should top his criminal indictment.

May 5, 2010

BP: Billionaire Polluter

Less than a week after British Petroleum's Deepwater Horizon drilling platform exploded in the Gulf of Mexico, killing eleven workers and unleashing what could be the worst industrial environmental disaster in U.S. history, the company announced more than $6 billion in profits for the first quarter of 2010, more than doubling profits from the same period the year before. Oil industry analyst Antonia Juhasz notes: "BP is one of the most powerful corporations operating in the United States. Its 2009 revenues of $327 billion are enough to rank BP as the third-largest corporation in the country. It spends aggressively to influence U.S. policy and regulatory oversight." The power and wealth that BP and other oil giants wield are almost without parallel in the world, and pose a threat to the lives of workers, to the environment, and to our prospects for democracy.

Sixty years ago, BP was called the Anglo-Iranian Oil Co. (AIOC). A popular, progressive, elected Iranian government had asked the AIOC, a largely British-owned monopoly, to share more of its profits from Iranian oil with the people of Iran. The AIOC refused, so Iran nationalized its oil industry. That didn't sit well with the U.S., so the CIA organized a coup d'état against Prime Minister Mohammed Mossadegh. After he was deposed, the AIOC, renamed British Petroleum, got a large part of its monopoly back, and the Iranians got the brutal Shah of Iran imposed upon them, planting the seeds of the 1979 Iranian revolution, the subsequent hostage crisis, and the political turmoil that besets Iran to this day.

In 2000, British Petroleum rebranded itself as BP, adopting a flowery green-and-yellow logo, and began besieging the U.S. public with an advertising campaign claiming it was moving "beyond petroleum." BP's aggressive growth, outrageous profit, and track record of petroleum-related disasters paint a much different picture, however. In 2005, BP's Texas City refinery exploded, killing fifteen people and injuring 170. In 2006, a BP pipeline in Alaska leaked 200,000 gallons of crude oil, causing what the Environmental Protection Agency calls "the largest spill that ever occurred on the [Alaskan] North Slope." BP was fined $60 million for the two disasters. Then, in 2009, the Occupational Safety and Health Administration (OSHA) fined BP an additional $87 million for the refinery blast. Secretary of Labor Hilda Solis said: "BP has allowed hundreds of potential hazards to continue unabated.... Workplace safety is more than a slogan. It's the law." BP responded by formally contesting all of OSHA's charges.

President Barack Obama said of the Gulf of Mexico oil spill, "Let me be clear: BP is responsible for this leak; BP will be paying the bill." Riki Ott is not so sure. She is a marine toxicologist and former "fisherma'am" from Alaska, and was one of the first people to respond to the 1989 *Exxon Valdez* oil disaster. Exxon deployed an army of lawyers to delay and defeat the legal claims of the people who were physically and/or financially harmed by the *Valdez* spill. "What we know is that the industry does everything it can to limit its liability," she told me.

The *Press-Register* of Mobile, Alabama, reported that Alabama Attorney General Troy King told BP to "stop circulating settlement agreements among coastal Alabamians." Apparently, BP was requiring owners of fishing boats seeking work mitigating the spill to waive any and all rights to sue BP in the future. Despite a BP spokesperson's pledge that the waivers would not be enforced, the news report stated, "King said late Sunday that he was still concerned that people would lose their right to sue by accepting settlements from BP of up to $5,000."

Even if BP doesn't trick victims into signing away the right to sue, the 1990 Oil Pollution Act, while requiring polluters to pay the actual hard costs of the cleanup, caps the additional financial liability of a spill at just $75 million. Given that millions of people will be impacted by the spill, by the loss of fisheries and tourism, and by the cascade of impacts on related industries, $75 million is small change.

That is why Sen. Robert Menendez, D-N.J., introduced a bill to raise the economic-damages liability cap to $10 billion, calling the bill the Big Oil Bailout Prevention Act. Riki Ott is touring New Orleans and the Gulf Coast, educating people about the toxic effects of the spill, and helping them prepare for the long fight ahead to hold BP accountable.

BP will surely continue its dirty practices, fighting accountability in the courts, in the press, and on the oil-drenched beaches. BP: be prepared.

June 2, 2010

In Memory of All That Is Lost

NEW ORLEANS—The anger is palpable across the Mississippi Delta. As the Deepwater Horizon oil geyser, almost a mile underwater, continues unabated, the brunt of this, the largest environmental catastrophe in United States history, is rolling onto the coast, impacting the ecology, the economy, and entire ways of life.

I traveled across the bayous and towns of coastal Louisiana for four days, meeting the people on the front lines of the onrush of BP's oil slick. They are angry and out of work and read the papers about people getting sick.

One person, whose job remains intact—at least so far—is BP's CEO, Tony Hayward. Hayward, who was paid more than $4.5 million in 2009, lamented Sunday: "There's no one who wants this thing over more than I do. You know, I'd like my life back." Hayward becomes more vilified with almost each of his utterances, which are clearly aimed at minimizing the perceived impact of the BP disaster. He will probably be increasingly guarded in his remarks, as U.S. Attorney General Eric Holder just toured the area and, in a public statement, said: "We must also ensure that anyone found responsible for this spill is held accountable. That means enforcing the appropriate civil—and if warranted, criminal—authorities to the full extent of the law."

On Grand Isle, we met Dean Blanchard, who owns the largest shrimp business in the area. He took us out on his boat, where he expressed his strong feelings about President Barack Obama: "I thought he was a man of the people, that he would've come out and met the businesses that are suffering, and look at us, and tell us, give us a little assurance that he would help us, but he just hid by the Coast Guard station like all the other presidents." Blanchard's parents and grandparents were shrimpers. With his strong Cajun accent, he explained the effect of the tides on the oil:

> I made my living off of watching tides. We hunt shrimp. You can't see a shrimp. You know how we know where the shrimp's at? Because of the tides. When the tide goes out, the more water goes out, the more water comes back, and when it comes back, it brings everything with it. It usually brings the shrimp, but this time it's going to be bringing the oil.

Blanchard says fishermen are like farmers: "We lose money in January, February, March, and April, preparing to harvest our crop in May, June, and July. So we spend a lot of money preparing to get to May." When the Deepwater Horizon exploded April 20, thousands of fisherfolk, their families, and the businesses and communities that depend on them saw their annual income disappear, with bleak prospects.

Many shrimp-boat owners have now been hired by BP to work on the cleanup. One local fisherman, John Wunstell Jr., was rushed to the hospital with respiratory problems that he attributed to the noxious environment.

He and others claim BP has prohibited the use of masks, and he has filed a request for an injunction to force BP to provide masks and other protective gear to cleanup workers. The response of BP's Hayward? "I'm sure they were genuinely ill, but whether it was anything to do with dispersants and oil, whether it was food poisoning or some other reason for them being ill. . . . It's one of the big issues of keeping the army operating. You know, armies march on their stomachs."

Blanchard was enraged. Why, he asked, did BP confiscate the clothing of their workers once they donned hospital gowns? He said: "I don't think you need people's clothes to test for food poisoning. You'd only need people's clothes to test for chemical poisoning."

Blanchard took us out into the Gulf to see the skimming operations. None of the boat owners would talk to us. Blanchard explained, "They're scared to talk, and they're scared to be seen, because BP has threatened them that if they talk to the media, they're going to be fired."

One fisherman, Glenn Swift, whom we met in Buras, Louisiana, confirmed that he signed a contract with a clause stating that speaking to the media was grounds for termination. When I asked him why, then, he was talking to me, he said: "I don't feel it's the right thing to shut somebody up. We're supposed to live in the United States, and we're supposed to have freedom of speech."

Down the road from Blanchard, a family has erected 101 crosses in their front yard, each one commemorating something they love, like "brown pelicans," "beach sunsets," and "sand between the toes." The sign next to the cemetery of dreams reads, "In memory of all that is lost, courtesy of BP and our federal government."

July 7, 2010

If Only Information Flowed as Freely as Oil

"Deep Spill 2" sounds like a sequel to a Hollywood thriller.

Unfortunately, it is more of a reality show. "Deep Spill 2" is the name of an ambitious series of proposed scientific experiments that should be happening right now. Scientists from around the globe are ready, literally, to dive in to understand what is happening with the oil and gas that are spewing into the Gulf of Mexico with the force of a volcano.

There is one problem, though: BP won't let them.

Ira Leifer is a scientist on the government-appointed Flow Rate Technical Group and a researcher in the Marine Science Institute at the University of California, Santa Barbara. He organized a team of scientists to develop intensive study of the Deepwater Horizon oil gusher, since so little is known about how oil and gas behave underwater, especially at the depths and temperatures one mile below the surface. The group of scientists presented the plan to BP, which ignored them, then to Rep. Ed Markey, D-Mass., of the House Energy and Commerce Committee. Markey wrote to BP on June 10:

"My understanding is that BP has not yet responded to Dr. Leifer's request to make direct flow measurement. . . . I request that you provide whatever budget and ROV [robotic vehicle] access is needed to allow these scientists to deploy their measurement activities."

A month later, Dr. Leifer told me: "We have heard nothing from BP. . . . Other scientists I know who are doing and trying to do research find themselves blocked at every turn from actually learning what we need to know so we can address this spill safely."

Ten years ago, scientists conducted "Deep Spill 1," a limited, 750-barrel controlled release off the coast of Norway, to study deep-sea oil spill phenomena. The lack of scientific knowledge of deep-water oil disasters allows BP officials like Tony Hayward to pronounce, as he did in late May, that "The oil is on the surface. . . . There aren't any plumes."

So, while BP scientists, executives, and public relations experts produce sound bites with their own fake "news teams," the world's leading experts are being shut out by BP itself.

Also shut out in the BP Gulf disaster are the media. The Coast Guard has announced new rules keeping the public, including photographers and reporters covering the spill, from coming within sixty-five feet of any response vessels or booms on the water or on beaches. Violators could face a fine of up to $40,000 and felony charges. In order to get within the sixty-five-foot limit, media must get direct permission from the Coast Guard captain of the Port of New Orleans.

The sixty-five-foot limit follows the rule requiring overhead flights with media to stay above 3,000 feet. Just like the Bush administration barring photographs of flag-draped coffins, the Obama administration seems to be colluding with BP to limit the images of the disaster. With current rules, and with photographers potentially facing felony charges, you can expect far fewer photos and videos of oil-soaked pelicans and dying sea turtles. You probably likely see fewer overhead close-ups showing how woefully inadequate the cleanup is, as 4 million gallons of oil jet into the Gulf every day.

Stories of denial of media access accumulate like tar balls on the beach (which have now made their way into Louisiana's Lake Pontchartrain and to beaches in Texas). *PBS NewsHour* reporters were repeatedly denied access to a Department of Health and Human Services "National Disaster Medical System" trailer, ringed with barbed wire. A *CBS Evening News* crew on a boat was accosted by another boat with five BP contractors and two U.S. Coast Guard members, and denied access to an oil-drenched beach.

Dr. Leifer sees reporting as an essential part of the overall process: "Reporters having access is part of the learning process as a society so that when there are accidents in the future, we actually can respond intelligently and not with a lot of unknown assumptions."

If only BP and the federal government allowed information to flow as freely as the oil, we might well be on the road to dealing with this catastrophe.

March 15, 2011

A Warning to the World

A reporter, describing the devastation of one city in Japan, wrote: "It looks as if a monster steamroller had passed over it and squashed it out of existence. I write these facts . . . as a warning to the world." The reporter was Wilfred Burchett, writing from Hiroshima, Japan, on September 5, 1945. Burchett was the first Western reporter to make it to Hiroshima after the atomic bomb was dropped there. He reported on the strange illness that continued to kill people, even a full month after that first, dreadful use of nuclear weapons against humans. His words could well describe the scenes of annihilation in northeastern Japan today. Given the worsening catastrophe at the Fukushima nuclear power plant, his grave warning to the world remains all too relevant.

The disaster deepens at the Fukushima complex in the aftermath of the largest recorded earthquake in Japanese history and the tsunami that followed, killing thousands. Explosions in Fukushima reactors No. 1 and No. 3 released radiation that was measured by a U.S. Navy vessel as far away as 100 miles, prompting the ship to move farther out to sea. A third explosion happened at reactor No. 2, leading many to speculate that the vital containment vessel, holding uranium undergoing fission, may have been breached. Then reactor No. 4 caught fire, even though it wasn't running when the earthquake hit. Each reactor also has spent nuclear fuel stored with it, and that fuel can cause massive fires, releasing more radiation into the air. The cooling systems and their backups all have failed, and a small crew of courageous workers remains on-site, despite the life-threatening radiation, trying to pump seawater into the damaged structures to cool the radioactive fuel.

President Barack Obama had hoped to usher in a "nuclear renaissance," and proposed $36 billion in new federal, taxpayer-subsidized loan guarantees to entice energy corporations to build new plants (adding to the $18.5 billion already approved during the George W. Bush administration). The first energy corporation in line to receive the public largesse was Southern Co., for two reactors slated for Georgia. The last time new construction on a nuclear power plant in the U.S. was ordered, and ultimately built, was back in 1973, when Obama was a seventh-grader at the Punahou School on Honolulu. The Three Mile Island disaster in 1979 and the Chernobyl disaster in 1986 effectively shut down new commercial nuclear projects in the U.S. Nevertheless, this country remains the largest producer of commercial nuclear power in the world. The 104 licensed commercial nuclear plants are old, close to the end of their originally projected life spans. Plant owners are petitioning the federal government to extend their operating licenses.

These licenses are controlled by the Nuclear Regulatory Commission (NRC). On March 10, the NRC issued a press release "regarding renewal of the operating license for the Vermont Yankee Nuclear Power Station near Brattleboro, Vt., for an additional 20 years. The NRC staff expects to issue the renewed license soon." Harvey Wasserman, of NukeFree.org, told me, "The first reactor at Fukushima is identical to the Vermont Yankee plant.... There are 23 reactors in the United States that are identical or close to identical to the first Fukushima reactor." A majority of Vermonters, including the state's governor, Peter Shumlin, support shutting down the Vermont Yankee reactor, designed and built by General Electric.

The Japanese nuclear crisis has sparked global repercussions. Protests erupted across Europe. Eva Joly, a French member of the European Parliament, said at one protest, "We know how to get out of the nuclear plants: We need renewable energy, we need windmills, we need geothermal, and we need solar energy." Switzerland has halted plans to relicense its reactors, and 10,000 protesters in Stuttgart prompted German Chancellor Angela Merkel to order an immediate shutdown of Germany's seven pre-1980 nuclear plants. In the U.S., Rep. Ed Markey, D-Mass., said, "What is happening in Japan right now shows that a severe accident at a nuclear power plant can happen here."

The nuclear age dawned not far from Fukushima, when the United States became the sole nation in human history to drop nuclear bombs on another country, destroying Hiroshima and Nagasaki, and killing hundreds of thousands of civilians. Journalist Wilfred Burchett described, for the first time, the "atomic plague," writing: "In these hospitals I found people who, when the bomb fell, suffered absolutely no injuries, but now are dying from the uncanny after-effects. For no apparent reason their health began to fail." More than sixty-five years after he sat in the rubble with his battered Hermes typewriter and typed his warning to the world, what have we learned?

June 22, 2011

Japan's Meltdowns Demand New No-Nukes Thinking

New details are emerging that indicate the Fukushima nuclear disaster in Japan is far worse than previously known, with three of the four affected reactors experiencing full meltdowns. Meanwhile, in the U.S., massive flooding along the Missouri River has put Nebraska's two nuclear plants, both near Omaha, on alert. The Cooper Nuclear Station declared a low-level emergency and will have to close down if the river rises another three inches. The Fort Calhoun nuclear power plant has been shut down since April 9, in part due to flooding. At Prairie Island, Minnesota, extreme heat caused the nuclear plant's two emergency diesel generators to fail. Emergency-generator failure was one of the key problems that led to the meltdowns at Fukushima.

In May, in reaction to the Fukushima disaster, Nikolaus Berlakovich, Austria's federal minister of agriculture, forestry, environment, and water management, convened a meeting of Europe's eleven nuclear-free countries. Those gathered resolved to push for a nuclear-free Europe, even as Germany announced it will phase out nuclear power in ten years and push ahead on renewable-energy research. Then, in last week's national elections in Italy, more than 90 percent of voters resoundingly rejected Prime Minister Silvio Berlusconi's plans to restart the country's nuclear power program.

Leaders of national nuclear-energy programs are gathering this week in Vienna for the International Atomic Energy Agency's Ministerial Conference on Nuclear Safety. The meeting was called in response to Fukushima. Ironically, the ministers, including U.S. Nuclear Regulatory Commission (NRC) Chairman Gregory Jaczko, held their meeting safely in a country with no nuclear power plants. Austria is at the forefront of Europe's new anti-nuclear alliance.

The IAEA meeting was preceded by the release of an Associated Press report stating that consistently, and for decades, U.S. nuclear regulators lowered the bar on safety regulations in order to allow operators to keep the nuclear plants running. Nuclear power plants were constructed in the U.S. in the decades leading up to the Three Mile Island disaster in 1979. These 104 plants are all getting on in years. The original licenses were granted for forty years.

The AP's Jeff Donn wrote, "When the first ones were being built in the 1960s and 1970s, it was expected that they would be replaced with improved models long before those licenses expired." Enormous upfront construction costs, safety concerns, and the problem of storing radioactive nuclear waste for thousands of years drove away private investors. Instead of developing and building new nuclear plants, the owners—typically for-profit companies like Exelon Corp., a major donor to the Obama campaigns through the years—simply try to run the old reactors longer, applying to the NRC for twenty-year extensions.

Europe, already ahead of the U.S. in development and deployment of renewable-energy technology, is now poised to accelerate in the field. In the U.S., the NRC has provided preliminary approval of the Southern Company's planned expansion of the Vogtle power plant in Georgia, which would allow the first construction of new nuclear power plants in the U.S. since Three Mile Island. The project got a boost from President Barack Obama, who pledged an $8.3 billion federal loan guarantee. Southern plans on using Westinghouse's new AP1000 reactor. But a coalition of environmental groups has filed to block the permit, noting that the new reactor design is inherently unsafe.

Obama established what he called his Blue Ribbon Commission on America's Nuclear Future. One of its fifteen members is John Rowe, the chairman and chief executive officer of Exelon Corp. (the same nuclear-energy company that has lavished campaign contributions on Obama). The commission made a fact-finding trip to Japan to see how that country was thriving with nuclear power—one month before the Fukushima disaster. In May, the commission reiterated its position, which is Obama's position, that nuclear ought to be part of the U.S. energy mix.

The U.S. energy mix, instead, should include a national jobs program to make existing buildings energy efficient, and to install solar and wind-power technology where appropriate. These jobs could not be outsourced and would immediately reduce our energy use and, thus, our reliance on foreign oil and domestic coal and nuclear. Such a program could favor U.S. manufacturers, to keep the money in the U.S. economy. That would be a simple, effective, and sane reaction to Fukushima.

August 10, 2011

From Hiroshima to Fukushima: Japan's Atomic Tragedies

In recent weeks, radiation levels have spiked at the Fukushima nuclear power reactors in Japan, with recorded levels of 10,000 millisieverts per hour (mSv/hr) at one spot. This is the number reported by the reactor's discredited owner, Tokyo Electric Power Co., although that number is simply as high as the Geiger counters go. In other words, the radiation levels are literally off the charts. Exposure to 10,000 millisieverts for even a brief time would be fatal, with death occurring within weeks. (For comparison, the total radiation from a dental X-ray is 0.005 mSv, and from a brain CT scan is less than 5 mSv.) The *New York Times* has reported that government officials in Japan suppressed official projections of where the nuclear fallout would most likely move with wind and weather after the disaster in order to avoid costly relocation of potentially hundreds of thousands of residents.

"Secrecy, once accepted, becomes an addiction." While those words could describe how the Japanese government has handled the nuclear catastrophe, they were said by atomic scientist Edward Teller, one of the key creators of the first two atomic bombs. The uranium bomb dubbed "Little Boy" was dropped on August 6, 1945, on the city of Hiroshima, Japan. Three days later, the second, a plutonium bomb called "Fat Man," was dropped over the city of Nagasaki, Japan. Close to a quarter-million people were killed by the massive blasts and the immediate aftereffects. No one knows the full extent of the death and disease that followed, from the painful burns that thousands of survivors suffered to the later effects of radiation sickness and cancer.

The history of the bombing of Hiroshima and Nagasaki is itself the history of U.S. military censorship and propaganda. In addition to the suppressed film footage, the military kept the blast zones off-limits to reporters. When Pulitzer Prize–winning journalist George Weller managed to get in to Nagasaki, his story was personally killed by Gen. Douglas MacArthur. Australian journalist Wilfred Burchett managed to sneak in to Hiroshima not long after the blast and reported what he called "a warning to the world," describing widespread illnesses as an "atomic plague." The military deployed one of its own. It turns out that William Laurence, the *New York Times* reporter, was also on the payroll of the War Department. He faithfully reported the U.S. government position, that "the Japanese described 'symptoms' that did not ring true." Sadly, he won the Pulitzer Prize for his propaganda.

Greg Mitchell has been writing about the history and aftermath of Hiroshima and Nagasaki for decades. On this anniversary of the Nagasaki bombing, I asked Mitchell about his latest book, *Atomic Cover-Up: Two U.S. Soldiers, Hiroshima and Nagasaki, and The Greatest Movie Never Made.*

"Anything that nuclear weapons or nuclear energy touches leads to suppression and leads to danger for the public," he told me. For years, Mitchell sought newsreel footage shot by the U.S. military in the months following the atomic blasts. Tracking down the aging filmmakers, and despite decades-old government classification, he was one of the journalists who publicized the incredible color film archives. As part of the U.S. Strategic Bombing Survey, the film crews documented not only the devastation of the cities, but also close-up, clinical documentation of the severe burns and disfiguring injuries suffered by the civilians, including children.

In one scene, a young man is shown with red, raw wounds all over his back, undergoing treatment. Despite the massive burns and being treated months late, the man survived.

Now eighty-two, Sumiteru Taniguchi is director of the Nagasaki Council of A-Bomb Sufferers. Mitchell found recent comments from Taniguchi in a Japanese newspaper linking the atomic bombing to the Fukushima disaster:

> Nuclear power and mankind cannot coexist. We survivors of the atomic bomb have said this all along. And yet, the use of nuclear power was camouflaged as "peaceful" and continued to progress. You never know when there's going to be a natural disaster. You can never say that there will never be a nuclear accident.

In a poignant fusion of the old and new disasters, we should listen to the surviving victims of both.

August 24, 2011

D.C. Protests That Make Big Oil Quake

The White House was rocked Tuesday, not only by a 5.8-magnitude earthquake, but by the protests mounting outside its gates. More than 2,100 people say they'll risk arrest there during the next two weeks. They oppose the Keystone XL pipeline project, designed to carry heavy crude oil from the tar sands of Alberta, Canada, to refineries on the U.S. Gulf Coast.

A "keystone" in architecture is the stone at the top of an arch that holds the arch together; without it, the structure collapses. By putting their bodies on the line—as more than 200 have already at the time of this writing—these practitioners of the proud tradition of civil disobedience hope to collapse not only the pipeline, but the fossil-fuel dependence that is accelerating disruptive global climate change.

Bill McKibben was among those already arrested. He is an environmentalist and author who founded the group 350.org, named after the estimated safe upper limit of carbon dioxide in the atmosphere of 350 ppm (parts per million—the planet is currently at 390 ppm). In a call to action to join the protest, McKibben, along with others including journalist Naomi Klein, actor Danny Glover, and NASA scientist James Hansen, wrote the Keystone pipeline is "a 1,500-mile fuse to the biggest carbon bomb on the continent, a way to make it easier and faster to trigger the final overheating of our planet."

The movement to oppose Keystone XL ranges from activists and scientists to indigenous peoples of the threatened Canadian plains and boreal forests, where the tar sands are located, to rural farmers and ranchers in the ecologically fragile Sand Hills region of Nebraska, to students and physicians.

Asked why the White House protests are taking place while President Obama is away on a family vacation on Martha's Vineyard, McKibben replied: "We'll be here when he gets back too. We're staying for two weeks, every day. This is the first real civil disobedience of this scale in the environmental movement in ages."

Just miles to the east of Martha's Vineyard, and almost exactly 170 years earlier, on Nantucket, Frederick Douglass, the escaped slave, abolitionist, journalist, and publisher, gave one of his first major addresses before the Massachusetts

Anti-Slavery Society. Douglass is famous for stating one of grassroots organizing's central truths: "Power concedes nothing without a demand. It never did and it never will."

Demanding change is one thing, while getting change in Washington, D.C., is another, especially with the Republican-controlled House of Representatives' hostility to any climate-change legislation. That is why the protests against Keystone XL are happening in front of the White House. Obama has the power to stop the pipeline. The Canadian corporation behind the project, TransCanada, has applied for a permit from the U.S. State Department to build the pipeline. If the State Department denies the permit, Keystone XL would be dead. The enormous environmental devastation caused by extracting petroleum from the tar sands might still move forward, but without easy access to the refineries and the U.S. market, it would certainly be slowed.

TransCanada executives are confident that the U.S. will grant the permit by the end of the year. Republican politicians and the petroleum industry tout the creation of well-paying construction jobs that would come from the project, and even enjoy some union support.

In response, two major unions, the Amalgamated Transit Union and the Transport Workers Union, representing more than 300,000 workers, called on the State Department to deny the permit. In a joint press release, they said: "We need jobs, but not ones based on increasing our reliance on Tar Sands oil. . . . Many jobs could also be created in energy conservation, upgrading the grid, maintaining and expanding public transportation—jobs that can help us reduce air pollution, greenhouse gas emissions and improve energy efficiency."

Two Canadian women, indigenous actress Tantoo Cardinal, who starred in *Dances with Wolves,* and Margot Kidder, who played Lois Lane in *Superman,* were arrested with about fifty others just before the earthquake hit Tuesday. Bill McKibben summed up: "It takes more than earthquakes and hurricanes to worry us—we'll be out here through September 3. Our hope is to send a Richter 8 tremor through the political system on the day Barack Obama says no to Big Oil and reminds us all why we were so happy when he got elected. The tar sands pipeline is his test."

November 9, 2011

Keystone XL: Ring Around the Rose Garden

More than 10,000 people gathered in Washington, D.C., last Sunday with a simple goal: Encircle the White House. They succeeded, just weeks after 1,253 people were arrested in a series of protests at the same spot. These thousands, as well as those arrested, were unified in their opposition to the planned Keystone XL pipeline, intended to run from the tar sands of Alberta, Canada, to the Gulf Coast of Texas. A broad, international coalition against the pipeline has formed since President Barack Obama took office, and now the deadline for its approval or rejection is at hand.

Bill McKibben, founder of the global movement against climate change 350.org, told me: "This has become not only the biggest environmental flash point in many, many years, but maybe the issue in recent times in the Obama administration when he's been most directly confronted by people in the street. In this case, people willing, hopeful, almost dying for him to be the Barack Obama of 2008."

The president, until recently, simply hid behind the legal argument that, as the pipeline was coming from Canada, the proper forum for the decision fell with the U.S. Department of State and Secretary of State Hillary Clinton. That was until a key Clinton insider was exposed as a lobbyist for the company trying to build Keystone XL, TransCanada. The environmental group Friends of the Earth has exposed a series of connections between the Clinton political machine and Keystone XL. Paul Elliott is TransCanada's top lobbyist in Washington on the pipeline. He was a high-level campaign staffer on Hillary Clinton's bid for the White House in 2008, and worked as well on Bill Clinton's campaign in 1996 and Hillary Clinton's Senate campaign in 2000.

Friends of the Earth (FOE) received emails following a Freedom of Information Act request, documenting exchanges in 2010 between Elliott and Marja Verloop, whom FOE describes as a "member of the senior diplomatic staff at the U.S. Embassy in Ottawa." Verloop in one email cheers Elliott for obtaining the buy-in on Keystone XL from conservative Democratic Sen. Max Baucus, writing: "Go Paul! Baucus support holds clout."

Another person arrested at the White House during the August-September protests was Canadian author Naomi Klein. Of the cozy email exchange, she said, "The response of the State Department was, 'Well, we meet with environmentalists, too.' But just imagine them writing an email to Bill McKibben: when he says, 'We got more than 1,200 people arrested,' and they would write back, 'Go Bill!'? The day that happens, I'll stop worrying." Klein went on to explain the environmental impact of the project: "Tar sands oil emits three times as much greenhouse gases as a regular barrel of Canadian crude, because, of course, it is in solid form. So, you have to use all of this energy to get it out and to liquefy it."

Adding to the controversy, the New York Times revealed that the State Department chose as an outside group to run the environmental impact study of Keystone XL, a company called Cardno Entrix. It turns out Cardno Entrix listed as one of its major clients none other than TransCanada. The environmental impacts are potentially extreme, with, first, the potential for a catastrophic leak of the toxic tar sands extract, and, secondly but no less significant, the potential long-term impacts on the global climate. The Obama campaign also drew fire for hiring Broderick Johnson, a lobbyist who formerly represented TransCanada.

Nebraska's Republican governor, Dave Heineman, called a special session of the state legislature, beginning November 1, to discuss the pipeline. After a week of deliberation, several bills are being reviewed, including LB1, the Major Oil Pipeline Siting Act, which would require stringent review of any pipeline passing through Nebraska, seriously slowing the Keystone XL approval process. The movement in Nebraska is broad-based, from environmentalists to ranchers to Native Americans.

The State Department inspector general is investigating whether all federal laws and regulations were followed in the permitting process, and President Obama now says he will make the final decision. He has powerful corporations pushing for the pipeline, but a ring of people he needs for re-election outside his window. As Bill McKibben said of the human chain at the White House: "Every banner that people carried yesterday had quotes from that wonderful rhetoric of that election: 'Time to end the tyranny of oil,' 'In my administration, the rise of the oceans will begin to slow.' We're looking for some kind of glimmer, some kind of echo, of that Barack Obama to re-emerge."

March 8, 2012

The Bipartisan Nuclear Bailout

Super Tuesday demonstrated the rancor rife in Republican ranks, as the four remaining major candidates slug it out to see how far to the right of President Barack Obama they can go. While attacking him daily for the high cost of gasoline, both sides are traveling down the same perilous road in their support of nuclear power. This is mind-boggling, on the first anniversary of the Fukushima nuclear disaster, with the chair of the U.S. Nuclear Regulatory Commission warning that lessons from Fukushima have not been implemented in this country. Nevertheless, Democrats and Republicans agree on one thing: They're going to force nuclear power on the public, despite the astronomically high risks, both financial and environmental.

One year ago, on March 11, 2011, the Tohoku earthquake and tsunami hit the northeast coast of Japan, causing more than 15,000 deaths, with 3,000 more missing and thousands of injuries. Japan is still reeling from the devastation—environmentally, economically, socially, and politically. Naoto Kan, Japan's prime minister at the time, said last July, "We will aim to bring about a society that can exist without nuclear power." He resigned in August after shutting down production at several power plants. He said that another catastrophe could force the mass evacuation of Tokyo, and even threaten "Japan's very existence." Only two of the fifty-four Japanese power plants that were online at the time of the Fukushima disaster are currently producing power. Kan's successor, Prime Minister Yoshihiko Noda, supports nuclear power, but faces growing public opposition to it.

This stands in stark contrast to the United States. Just about a year before Fukushima, President Obama announced $8 billion in loan guarantees to the Southern Company, the largest energy producer in the southeastern U.S., for the construction of two new nuclear power plants in Waynesboro, Georgia, at the Vogtle power plant, on the South Carolina border. Since the 1979 nuclear accident at Three Mile Island in Pennsylvania, and then the catastrophe at Chernobyl in 1986, there have been no new nuclear power plants built in the U.S. The 104 existing nuclear plants are all increasing in age, many nearing their originally slated life expectancy of forty years.

While campaigning for president in 2008, Barack Obama promised that nuclear power would remain part of the U.S.'s "energy mix." His chief adviser, David Axelrod, had consulted in the past for Illinois energy company ComEd, a subsidiary of Exelon, a major nuclear-energy producer. Obama's former chief of staff Rahm Emanuel played a key role in the formation of Exelon. In the past four years, Exelon employees have contributed more than $244,000 to the Obama campaign—and that is not counting any soft-money contributions to PACs, or direct, corporate contributions to the new super PACs. Lamented by many for breaking key campaign promises (like closing Guantánamo, or accepting super PAC money), President Obama is fulfilling his promise to push nuclear power.

That is why several groups sued the Nuclear Regulatory Commission last month. The NRC granted approval to the Southern Company to build the new reactors at the Vogtle plant despite a no vote from the NRC chair, Gregory Jaczko. He objected to the licenses over the absence of guarantees to implement recommendations made following the Japanese disaster. Jaczko said, "I cannot support issuing this license as if Fukushima never happened."

Stephen Smith, executive director of the Southern Alliance for Clean Energy, one of the plaintiffs in the suit against the NRC, explained how advocates for nuclear power "distort market forces," since private investors simply don't want to touch nuclear: "They've asked the federal government for loan guarantees to support the project, and they have not revealed the terms of that loan guarantee . . . it's socializing the risk and privatizing the profits."

The Nuclear Information and Resource Service, noting the ongoing Republican attack on President Obama's loan guarantee to the failed solar power company Solyndra, said, "The potential for taxpayer losses that would dwarf the Solyndra debacle is extraordinarily high . . . this loan would be 15 times larger than the Solyndra loan, and is probably 50 times riskier."

As long as our politicians dance to the tune of their donors, the threat of nuclear disaster will never be far off.

RACE, RACISM,
AND THE MYTH OF
POST-RACIAL AMERICA

July 22, 2009

Henry Louis Gates Jr., Troy Anthony Davis, and the Twenty-First-Century Color Line

W. E. B. Du Bois' classic 1903 work *The Souls of Black Folk* opens with "The problem of the Twentieth Century is the problem of the color line." Du Bois helped form the NAACP, the National Association for the Advancement of Colored People, which just celebrated its 100th anniversary.

Henry Louis Gates Jr., who directs Harvard University's W. E. B. Du Bois Institute for African and African American Research, knows much about the color line—not only from his life's work, but from life experience, including last week, when he was arrested in his own home.

Gates' lawyer, Harvard Law professor Charles Ogletree, said in a statement that the arrest occurred as Gates returned from the airport:

> Professor Gates attempted to enter his front door, but the door was damaged. Professor Gates then entered his rear door with his key, turned off his alarm, and again attempted to open the front door. With the help of his driver they were able to force the front door open, and then the driver carried Professor Gates' luggage into his home.

Both Gates and his driver are African-American. According to the Cambridge Police report, a white woman saw the two black men attempting to enter the home and called police.

Ogletree continued: "The officer ... asked Professor Gates whether he could prove that he lived there and taught at Harvard. Professor Gates said that he could, and ... handed both his Harvard University identification and his valid Massachusetts driver's license to the officer. Both include Professor Gates' photograph, and the license includes his address." Police officer James Crowley reported that Gates responded to his request for identification: "Why? Because I'm a black man in America?" Despite his positive identification, Gates was then arrested for disorderly conduct.

Meanwhile, in Philadelphia, more than sixty mostly African-American and Latino children attending the Creative Steps camp were disinvited from a suburban Valley Swim Club, which their camp had paid for pool access.

Suspicions of racism were exacerbated when Valley Swim Club president John Duesler said, "There was concern that a lot of kids would change the complexion . . . and the atmosphere of the club." The U.S. Department of Justice has opened an investigation.

The Senate Judiciary Committee hearings on Supreme Court nominee Sonia Sotomayor were permeated by the race question, especially with white, male senators questioning her comments on how a "wise Latina" might rule in court. If confirmed, one of the first cases she will hear will be that of Georgia death-row prisoner Troy Anthony Davis, an African-American.

As it moves into its second century, the NAACP is, unfortunately, as relevant as ever. It is confronting the death penalty head-on, demanding Davis' claims of innocence be heard and asking Attorney General Eric Holder to investigate the case of Pennsylvania death-row prisoner Mumia Abu-Jamal. Another new NAACP initiative asks people to record instances of bias, discrimination, and police brutality with their cell-phone cameras, and upload them to NAACP.org.

At the group's centennial, longtime board chair Julian Bond said, paraphrasing Jay Leno: "When I started, my hair was black and my president was white. Now my hair's white, and my president is black. I hold the NAACP responsible for both." Though the Cambridge Police Department has dropped the charges against Gates, his charges of racial discrimination remain. W. E. B. Du Bois' color line has shifted—but it hasn't been erased.

* *

September 9, 2009

Van Jones and the Boycott of Glenn Beck

Glenn Beck was mad. He's the right-wing talk radio host who has a television program on the Fox News Channel. Advertisers were fleeing his Fox program en masse after the civil rights group Color of Change mounted a campaign urging advertisers to boycott Beck, who labeled President Barack Obama a "racist." As the campaign progressed, Beck began his attacks against Van Jones. Jones was appointed by Obama in March to be special adviser for green jobs. He co-founded Color of Change four years ago. After weeks of attacks from Beck, Jones resigned his position at the White House last Sunday.

Beck said on *Fox & Friends*, the network's morning show, July 28: "This president I think has exposed himself as a guy over and over and over again who has a deep-seated hatred for white people.... This guy is, I believe, a racist." This inspired ColorOfChange.org to launch its campaign urging advertisers to drop their sponsorship of Beck's Fox program. The campaign had a powerful impact, with companies like Progressive Insurance, Geico, and Procter & Gamble immediately pulling their advertising. Since then, more than fifty companies have joined, including Best Buy, Capital One, CVS, Discover, GMAC Financial Services, HSBC, Mercedes-Benz, Travelocity, and Walmart.

Van Jones was named one of *Time* magazine's 100 most influential people in the world for 2009. His book, *The Green Collar Economy*, was a national best-seller. A Yale Law School graduate, Jones didn't go after the lucrative jobs that were available to him, but moved to San Francisco, where he founded Bay Area PoliceWatch, a hot line for victims of alleged police brutality. He then founded the Ella Baker Center for Human Rights, based in Oakland, California, "a strategy and action center working for justice, opportunity and peace in urban America." The center thrived, growing to a staff of more than twenty and building a solid record of fighting police violence and youth incarceration, along with spearheading green-job initiatives. The fusion of racial justice and economic and environmental sustainability is at the core of Jones' work.

Jones told me last October: "The clean energy revolution ... would put literally millions of people to work, putting up solar panels all across the United States, weatherizing buildings so they don't leak so much energy ... you could put Detroit back to work not making SUVs to destroy the world, but making wind turbines. We think that you can fight pollution and poverty at the same time."

Beck alleged Jones was a former black nationalist and communist, that he signed a petition calling for a congressional investigation into the events of 9/11, and that Jones referred to Republicans as "assholes" in a February 2009 talk. (Beck failed to note that Jones referred to himself in the talk with the same term.) Jones apologized for the remark, which is more than George W. Bush did when recorded referring to *New York Times* reporter Adam Clymer with the same term in 2000.

Jones said Beck's attacks were a "vicious smear campaign ... using lies and distortions to distract and divide." Ben Jealous, president and CEO of the National Association for the Advancement of Colored People, said, "The only thing more outrageous than Mr. Beck's attack on Van Jones is the fact that there are sponsors that continue to pay him to provide this type of offensive commentary." He recalled Beck's 2006 radio attack on a seven-year-old African-American girl, when Beck, responding to her poem about her heritage, said: "You want to go to Africa? I will personally purchase your airfare. I'll do it. It's one-way."

Glenn Beck may claim a notch in his belt, but he's also helped push Van Jones back into an arena where he can be much more effective, as a grassroots organizer working for progressive change from outside the administration. And with groups like the NAACP paying more attention to Beck, the advertiser boycott of his show is unlikely to just go away.

• •

January 13, 2010

Holding Corporations Accountable for Apartheid Crimes

A landmark class action case is under way in a New York federal court, with victims of apartheid in South Africa suing corporations that they say helped the pre-1994 regime. Among the multinational corporations are IBM, Fujitsu, Ford, GM, and banking giants UBS and Barclays. The lawsuit accuses the corporations of "knowing participation in and/or aiding and abetting of the crimes of apartheid; extrajudicial killing; torture; prolonged unlawful detention; and cruel, inhuman and degrading treatment." Attorneys are seeking up to $400 billion in damages.

The late anti-apartheid activist Dennis Brutus, who died just weeks ago, is a listed plaintiff. Back in 2008, he told me that "for [the corporations], apartheid was a very good system, and it was a very profitable system." As the U.S. observes the Rev. Martin Luther King Jr.'s birthday, marks the first anniversary in office of the first African-American president, and ponders the exposure of a racial gaffe spoken by Sen. Harry Reid, the issue of race is front and center, making this case timely and compelling.

The Alien Tort Statute dates from the U.S. Revolutionary War era and allows people from outside the United States to bring a civil suit against another party for alleged crimes committed outside the United States. Cases have been brought in recent years to address forced labor on an oil pipeline in Burma, the killing of labor organizers in Colombia, and the killing of activists in the Niger delta. This suit alleges that the apartheid regime could not have succeeded in its violent oppression of millions of people without the active support of the foreign corporations.

Ford and General Motors built manufacturing centers in Port Elizabeth, South Africa, where Dennis Brutus grew up. He told me, "They were using . . . very cheap black labor, because there was a law in South Africa which said blacks are not allowed to join trade unions, and they're not allowed to strike, so that they were forced to accept whatever wages they were given. They lived in ghettos . . . actually in the boxes in which the parts had been shipped from the U.S. to be assembled in South Africa. So you had a whole township called Kwaford, meaning 'the place of Ford.'"

Likewise with IBM and Fujitsu. The complaint states, "The South African security forces used computers supplied by . . . IBM and Fujitsu . . . to restrict Black people's movements within the country, to track non-whites and political dissidents, and to target individuals for the purpose of repressing the Black population and perpetuating the apartheid system." Black South Africans were issued passbooks, which the apartheid regime used to restrict movement and track millions of people, and to enable politically motivated arrests and disappearances over decades.

UBS and Barclays, the suit alleges, "directly financed the South African security forces that carried out the most brutal aspects of apartheid." The United Nations Special Committee Against Apartheid stated, in 1979, that "we learn today that more than $5.4 billion has been loaned in a six-year period to bolster a regime which is responsible for some of the most heinous crimes ever committed against humanity." Banks (including UBS) were punished for helping the Nazis during World War II, so precedent exists for reparations in the case of apartheid.

One of the plaintiffs' attorneys, Michael Hausfeld, told me: "Who is a corporation and what are its responsibilities? If companies can affect lives in ways that make those lives worse, so that people are suppressed or terrorized ... you are basically ascribing to eternity the fact that companies can act with both impunity and immunity."

South Africa went through a historic process after apartheid, the Truth and Reconciliation Commission (TRC), led by Nobel Peace laureate Archbishop Desmond Tutu. Thousands of people took responsibility for their actions, along with scores of South African corporations. Not one multinational company accepted the invitation to speak at the TRC. The case, says Marjorie Jobson, national director of the Khulumani Support Group, which is filing the lawsuit, "takes forward the unfinished business of the TRC."

The election of Barack Obama, the son of an African, was a historic moment in the fight against racism. But unless U.S. courts are open to addressing wrongs, past and present, corporations will still feel free to go abroad and profit from racist and repressive policies.

* *

April 29, 2010

Boycotting Arizona's Racism

Arizona was the only territory west of Texas to secede from the Union and join the Confederacy during the Civil War. A century later, it fought recognition of the Martin Luther King Jr. federal holiday. This week, an anti-immigrant bill was signed into law by Republican Gov. Jan Brewer. Arizona Senate Bill 1070 empowers state and local law enforcement to stop, question, and arrest whomever they suspect may not be in the state legally. The law is an open invitation to sweeping racial profiling and arbitrary detention.

The law ostensibly offers "cooperative enforcement of federal immigration laws throughout all of Arizona." It provides that a "law enforcement officer, without a warrant, may arrest a person if the officer has probable cause to believe that the person has committed any public offense that makes the person removable from the United States."

Thus, if a police officer suspects a Latino person of being an undocumented immigrant, he or she can lock that person up. Day laborers are targeted. The new law makes it illegal to offer or accept a job in some roadside settings, and even makes "communication by a gesture or a nod" in accepting a work offer an arrestable offense. S.B. 1070 goes further, facilitating anonymous reporting of businesses that anyone suspects has undocumented employees.

President Barack Obama denounced the bill, saying: "Our failure to act responsibly at the federal level will only open the door to irresponsibility by others, and that includes, for example, the recent efforts in Arizona, which threaten to undermine basic notions of fairness that we cherish as Americans, as well as the trust between police and their communities that is so crucial to keeping us safe. In fact, I've instructed members of my administration to closely monitor the situation and examine the civil-rights and other implications of this legislation."

There is a serious backlash against the bill in Arizona and around the country. Rep. Raul Grijalva, a Democrat from Tucson and co-chair of the Congressional Progressive Caucus, is front and center in opposing the controversial law. He told me: "It's a license to racially profile. It creates a second-class status for primarily Latinos and people of color in the state of Arizona.... Arizona's been the petri dish for these kinds of harsh, racist initiatives."

Legal groups are mounting challenges to the law. Sunita Patel is a staff attorney with the Center for Constitutional Rights. According to Patel, "It allows the local law-enforcement agencies to check not only the FBI databases, which they've traditionally always done, it also allows them to sync up with immigration databases, which are notoriously unreliable because of errors with the data entry because they just have incorrect information on citizenship status . . . so you have this very broad net being cast."

Grijalva is calling on the federal government to refuse to cooperate with Arizona. "Immigration is a federal law, and if we're asking the president for him not to cooperate in the implementation of this law through Homeland Security, through Border Patrol, through detention and a noncooperative stance by the United States government and the federal agencies, [it] would render much of this legislation moot and ineffective," he said.

He also is calling for people to boycott his own state: "I support some very targeted economic sanctions on the state of Arizona. We will be asking national organizations, civic, religious, political organizations not to have conferences and conventions in the state of Arizona. That there has to be an economic consequence to this action and to this legislation. And good organizations across this country, decent organizations that agree with us that this bill is patently racist, that it is unconstitutional and it's harsh, it's unjust, that they should refrain from bringing their business to the state."

Already, the American Immigration Lawyers Association has decided to move its fall 2010 annual conference from Arizona to another state. San Francisco Board of Supervisors member David Campos, saying that Arizona "with a stroke of a pen set the clock back on a generation of civil-rights gains," is confident that his resolution calling for the city to boycott Arizona will pass. Similar city boycotts are being considered in Oakland, California, and El Paso, Texas. Sportswriter Dave Zirin is supporting a boycott of the Diamondbacks, Arizona's Major League Baseball team.

Close to 30 percent of the Arizona population identifies itself as Hispanic. It was a boycott that eventually forced the state to recognize Martin Luther King Jr. Day. It is a shame that similar tactics are needed again.

• •

May 26, 2010

Alleged Chicago Torturer's Overdue Day in Court

Abu Ghraib has nothing over Chicago. Forty years ago, Jon Burge returned from Vietnam, joined the Chicago Police Department, and allegedly began torturing people. He rose in the ranks to become a commander in Chicago's South Side, called Area 2. Electric shocks to the genitals, mock executions, suffocation with bags over the head, beatings, and painful stress positions are among the torture techniques that Burge and police officers under his command are accused of using to extract confessions in Chicago, mostly from African-American men. More than 110 men are known to have been victims of Burge and his associates. Victims often went to prison, some to death row. Facing mounting evidence and increasing community outcry, Burge was fired from the Chicago Police Department in 1993. He now lives in Florida, collecting his pension.

This week, in a federal criminal trial beginning in Chicago, Burge faces charges, not for torture, but for lying about torture under oath in an earlier civil suit brought by one of his victims (since the statute of limitations on torture, remarkably, has expired). He faces up to forty-five years in prison. Burge's co-conspirators remain uncharged. Also untouched in the trial is the role played by the current mayor of Chicago, Richard M. Daley, who as state's attorney for Cook County from 1980 to 1989, and as mayor since then, has consistently fought investigations or prosecutions of the alleged torturers.

Darrell Cannon is one of the men alleging torture against Burge and his associates. He says police tortured him in 1983 and forced him to confess to a murder he didn't commit. He spent more than twenty years in prison, but after a hearing on his tortured confession, prosecutors dismissed his case in 2004. It took him three more years to gain release from prison.

At 6 a.m. on November 2, 1983, Chicago cops under Burge's command arrested Cannon and drove him to an isolated industrial area on the Chicago waterfront. He related his ordeal to me:

> They did a mock hanging, where I'm cuffed behind my back and one of the detectives would get on the bumper of the detective car, the other two detectives would lift me up to him, and he would grab my handcuffs from behind. They would let me go. That will cause my arms to go up backwards, almost wrenching the inside of my shoulders.... Then they switched to a second torture treatment, where they got their shotgun. . . . One of them said, "Go ahead, blow that ni—r's head off." And that's when [Detective] Peter Dignan forced the shotgun in my mouth.... They did a mock execution three times.

Cannon refused to confess. He went on: "They then put me in the backseat of a detective car.... They pulled my pants and my shorts down ... took an electric cattle prod, turned it on and proceeded to shock me on my testicles."

Cannon finally made a false and coerced statement, implicating himself as an accomplice to murder, to make the torture stop.

His attorney, Flint Taylor, is with the People's Law Office, which has been representing scores of Burge's alleged torture victims. Taylor pointed out the controversial role of Mayor Daley. "Darrell Cannon here, my client, was tortured in

1983. If Daley had moved in 1982 with the evidence he had to remove Burge from the police force and prosecute him for torture, we would not have Darrell Cannon spending 20, 25 years behind bars and not having him tortured by electric shock. So, the real crime here started many years ago with the cover-up, a cover-up that was engineered by the mayor himself."

In January 2003, before leaving office, Illinois Gov. George Ryan, a Republican, commuted the death sentences of all 156 people on Illinois' death row, after the innocence of thirteen other death row inmates had been proved. Ryan pardoned four on death row who were known to be victims of Burge's torture.

Where did it all begin? One thing is clear: In 1968–69, Burge was an MP at the U.S. Army's Dong Tam camp in Vietnam's Mekong Delta, where captured suspected Viet Cong soldiers were allegedly interrogated with electric, hand-cranked field telephones supplying shocks. Torture techniques similar to this were rampant under Burge's command in Chicago.

Given ongoing reports of torture in Iraq and Afghanistan, we have to wonder how many Jon Burges are being bred in President Barack Obama's two wars.

• •

August 18, 2010

Mosque-Issippi Burning

Salman Hamdani died on September 11, 2001. The twenty-three-year-old research assistant at Rockefeller University had a degree in biochemistry. He was also a trained emergency medical technician and a cadet with the New York Police Department. But he never made it to work that day. Hamdani, a Muslim-American, was among that day's first responders. He raced to Ground Zero to save others. His selfless act cost him his life.

Hamdani was later praised by President George W. Bush as a hero and mentioned by name in the USA Patriot Act. But that was not how he was portrayed in the immediate aftermath of 9/11. In October, his parents went to Mecca to pray for their son. While they were away, the *New York Post* and other media outlets portrayed Hamdani as a possible terrorist on the run. "MISSING—OR HIDING? MYSTERY OF THE NYPD CADET FROM PAKISTAN" screamed the *Post* headline. The sensational article noted that someone fitting Hamdani's description had been seen near the Midtown Tunnel a full month after 9/11. His family was interrogated. Hamdani's Internet use and politics were investigated.

His parents, Talat and Saleem Hamdani, had been frantically searching the hospitals, the lists of the dead and the injured. "There were patients who had lost their memory," his mother, Talat, said. "We hoped he would be one of them, we would be able to identify him."

The ominous reports on Hamdani were typical of the increasing, overt bigotry against Arab-Americans, Muslim-Americans, and people of South Asian heritage. Talat, who worked as a teacher, told me how children in her extended family had to Anglicize their names to avoid discrimination: "They were in second grade ... Armeen became Amy, and one became Mickey and the other one became Mikey and the fourth one became Adam. And we asked them, 'Why did you change your names?' And they said 'because we don't want to be called terrorists in the school.'"

On March 20, 2002, the Hamdanis received word that Salman's DNA had been found at Ground Zero, and thus he was officially a victim of the attacks. At his funeral, held at the Islamic Community Center at East 96th Street in Manhattan, Mayor Michael Bloomberg, Police Commissioner Ray Kelly, and Rep. Gary Ackerman all spoke.

Which brings us to the controversy around the proposed Islamic community center, slated to be built at 51 Park Place in lower Manhattan. The facility is not, for the record, a mosque. And it is not at Ground Zero (it's two blocks away). The Cordoba Initiative, the nonprofit group spearheading the project, describes it as a "community center, much like the YMCA or the Jewish Community Center ... where people from any faith are allowed to use the facilities. Beyond having a gym, the Cordoba House will house a pool, restaurant, 500-person auditorium, 9/11 memorial, multifaith chapel, office and conference space, and prayer space."

Opposition to the center started among fringe, right-wing blogs, and has since been swept into the mainstream. While the hole at Ground Zero has yet to be filled, as billionaire developers bicker over the plans, the news hole that August brings has been readily filled with the "Ground Zero Mosque" controversy. There is another hole that needs to be filled, namely, the absence of people in the U.S. in leadership positions in every walk of life, of every political stripe, speaking out for freedom of religion and against racism. As the Rev. Martin Luther King Jr. once said, "In the end, we will remember not the words of our enemies, but the silence of our friends."

Does anyone seriously say that there shouldn't be a Christian church near the site of the Oklahoma City bombing, just because Timothy McVeigh was a Christian?

People who are against hate are not a fringe minority, not even a silent majority, but are a silenced majority. They are silenced by the chattering classes, who are driving this debate throughout the media.

Hate breeds violence. Marginalizing an entire population, an entire religion, is not good for our country. It endangers Muslims within America, and provokes animosity toward America around the world.

When I asked Daisy Khan, executive director of the American Society for Muslim Advancement, which is a partner in the proposed community center, if she feared for herself, for her children or for Muslims in New York, she replied, "I'm afraid for my country."

• •

March 17, 2010

NYC's Jihad Against Debbie Almontaser

Debbie Almontaser has won a victory in her battle against discrimination. She was the founding principal of the first Arabic-language public school in the United States, until a campaign of hate forced her out. She is well known for her success in bridging cultural divides, bringing together Muslims, Christians, and Jews, yet as the new school neared its opening date in the summer of 2007, she became the target of anti-Muslim and anti-Arab attacks. Last week, the federal Equal Employment Opportunity Commission (EEOC) ruled that the New York City Department of Education (DOE) discriminated against her "on account of her race, religion and national origin."

The school is called the Khalil Gibran International Academy. Gibran was a Lebanese-born writer and philosopher. His best-known book, *The Prophet,* published in 1923, has sold more than 100 million copies in forty languages. A line from *The Prophet,* prominent on the academy's website, reads, "The teacher who is indeed wise does not bid you to enter the house of his wisdom but rather leads you to the threshold of your mind."

But open-mindedness was hardly the response of a fringe group called Stop the Madrassa. The group used the Arabic word for *school* because of its negative connotations with religious schools in Afghanistan and Pakistan. The academy was developed as a secular, dual-language public school for sixth through twelfth grades and had no religious curriculum. As the small but vocal group of opponents continued to take issue with the planned school, the DOE compelled Almontaser to submit to an interview with Rupert Murdoch's *New York Post.* The article's headline read: "City Principal Is 'Revolting.'"

· In the interview, Almontaser was asked to explain the use of the word *intifada,* because the word appeared on a T-shirt of a women's organization that sometimes used the offices of a community group where she was a board member. The T-shirt had nothing to do with the Khalil Gibran International Academy. Almontaser told me: "He asked me one or two questions about the school and then asked me for the root word of the word *intifada.* As an educator, I simply responded and said to him that it comes from the root word of the word *infad* in Arabic, which is 'shake off'; however, this word has developed a negative connotation based on the Palestinian-Israeli conflict, where thousands of people have died. Within the interview, I stated that I . . . condemn all violence, any shape, way or form."

Her lawyer, Alan Levine, told me: "Debbie was the victim of a smear campaign. . . . The bigots in the community had no power to fire; the Department of Education did. They succumbed to the bigots." The EEOC report concluded, "DOE succumbed to the very bias that the creation of the school was intended to dispel, and a small segment of the public succeeded in imposing its prejudices on DOE as an employer." Almontaser is seeking reinstatement as principal of the KGIA, along with back pay, damages, and legal fees. The New York City Law Department has vowed to fight her. Levine hopes for a settlement, but is prepared to file a lawsuit, saying: "The EEOC, which has no ax to grind [and] is the country's premier agency with regard to employment discrimination claims, says that they did discriminate. I'll go with the EEOC. I'm confident that a judge or jury will." Days after the EEOC letter was delivered, the non-Arab-American principal of the KGIA stepped down, without explanation, and was replaced by an Arab-American educator.

Three years ago, in the midst of the firestorm, a group of prominent Jewish leaders, including fifteen rabbis, wrote an open letter to the Jewish community in support of Almontaser, saying, "We seek your support and respect for a colleague and friend who has suffered and continues to suffer from a disturbing and growing prejudice in our midst . . . her return to her children [at the KGIA] will only bring greater peace and understanding between people of all faiths in our educational system and in our city as a whole." This case, as a metaphor, has broader implications, as protests continue in the streets of Jerusalem following the Israeli announcement of thousands of new housing units in occupied East Jerusalem, blindsiding Vice President Joe Biden as he began a peacemaking visit there. Almontaser told me, "It's my life's dream . . . to lead a school, to establish an institution that would set precedents in helping building bridges of understanding and certainly creating young people who will be global thinkers, competing in the twenty-first-century work force." Hers is a vision the New York City Department of Education should embrace, with her prompt reinstatement.

• •

October 6, 2010

From Tuskegee to Guatemala via Nuremberg

News broke last week that the U.S. government purposely exposed hundreds of men in Guatemala to syphilis in ghoulish medical experiments conducted during the late 1940s. As soon as the story got out, President Barack Obama phoned President Álvaro Colom of Guatemala to apologize. Colom called the experiments "an incredible violation of human rights." Colom also says his government is studying whether it can bring the case to an international court.

The revelations came about through research conducted by Wellesley College medical historian Susan Reverby on the notorious Tuskegee syphilis study. The two former, equally noxious U.S. government research projects, in Tuskegee, Alabama, and Guatemala, are mirror images of each other. Both point to the extremes to which ethics can be disregarded in the pursuit of medical knowledge, and serve as essential reminders that medical research needs constant supervision and regulation.

Reverby is the author of the recently published book *Examining Tuskegee*, a comprehensive history of the Tuskegee syphilis study.

Tuskegee, Alabama, is in the heart of the Deep South. From 1932 until it was exposed by the press in 1972, the U.S. government conducted a long-term study on the effects of syphilis when left untreated. Four hundred men with syphilis were told that they would be given a "special treatment" for their "bad blood." Unbeknownst to them, the men were given useless placebos, not the promised cure, and their debilitation caused by the untreated syphilis was tracked over decades. In its advanced stages, syphilis can disfigure and can cause dementia, blindness and extreme, chronic pain. It is a horrible way to die. Ten years into the Tuskegee Study, penicillin was found to cure syphilis. Yet the men were not told about the potential cure and were actively denied treatment when some of them sought it.

In Tuskegee, infected men were left untreated. In Guatemala, the opposite happened.

There, U.S. government researchers actively infected men in prison with syphilis, then treated them with penicillin to measure the antibiotic's effect immediately after exposure. Syphilis is a sexually transmitted disease, and that is how the lead doctor, Dr. John Cutler of the U.S. Public Health Service, attempted to infect the prisoners. First, they hired prostitutes with syphilis to have sex with the prisoners. When transmission rates were not sufficiently high, the researchers lacerated the men's penises and applied syphilis-infected cotton to the wounds, or directly injected a fresh "syphilitic mixture" into their spines.

Similar procedures were used on mental patients and soldiers.

Ironically, the Guatemala study began in 1946, the same year as the Nuremberg tribunals, the first of which tried Nazi doctors accused of conducting heinous experiments on concentration-camp prisoners. Half of those accused were put to death. The tribunals produced the Nuremberg Code, which set ethical standards for human medical experimentation and informed consent. Yet Nuremberg didn't seem to bother the U.S. researchers.

Dr. Cutler, the head of the Guatemala project, later joined the Tuskegee Study. He said in a 1993 PBS *NOVA* documentary, "It was important that they were supposedly untreated, and it would be undesirable to go ahead and use large amounts of penicillin to treat the disease, because you'd interfere with the study."

The U.S. government has frequently conducted experiments without the informed consent of the subjects. Women in Puerto Rico were given estrogen, at dangerous levels, when testing birth control pills.

Researchers injected unwitting hospital patients with plutonium to study its effects on the human body. Dow Chemical, Johnson & Johnson, and Pennsylvania prison authorities exposed inmates to chemicals, including dioxin, to test their effects. Subjects of a number of these experiments and others have died or had their lives indelibly harmed, all in the name of progress or profit.

Researchers are quick to point out that such practices are a thing of the past and have led to strict guidelines ensuring informed consent of subjects. Yet efforts are being made to loosen restrictions on medical experimentation in prisons. We need to ask what "informed consent" means inside a prison, or in a poor community when money is used as an incentive to "volunteer" for research. Medical research should only happen with humane standards, informed consent, and independent oversight, if the lessons of Nuremberg, Tuskegee and, now, Guatemala are to have meaning.

● ●

January 12, 2011

A Tale of Two Sheriffs

The Tucson massacre that left six dead and fourteen injured, including Rep. Gabrielle Giffords, brought into sharp public focus the local sheriff, Clarence Dupnik. He's been the sheriff of Pima County, which includes Tucson, Arizona's second-largest city, for thirty years. For the twenty years before that, he was a police officer. Dupnik has gained attention this week for linking the shooting to the vitriolic political climate in the U.S., and in particular, Arizona.

Speaking at a press conference shortly after the shooting, Sheriff Dupnik said: "The anger, the hatred, the bigotry that goes on in this country is getting to be outrageous. And unfortunately, Arizona, I think, has become the capital. We have become the mecca for prejudice and bigotry."

Arizona is one of three states in the country that allow people to carry concealed weapons without a permit. When asked about the law, the sheriff was emphatic: "We are the Tombstone of the United States of America. . . . I have never been a proponent of letting everybody in this state carry weapons under any circumstances that they want. And that's almost where we are." He also decried a proposed Arizona bill that would allow students and professors to carry guns on campus.

The suspected shooter, twenty-two-year-old Jared Loughner, by most accounts suffers from some form of mental illness. Yet he was able to buy a semi-automatic pistol, along with extended-capacity magazines to hold more bullets. He bought the bullets the same morning as the attack.

When I interviewed Dupnik, he called Arizona's gun laws "insane," and reaffirmed the link he made between political rhetoric and the shooting: "I think that there are a lot of people in the radio industry, especially, and some in the TV industry, who make millions of dollars off of inflaming the public, purveying hate against the government, and distrust. In my judgment, people who are mentally unstable are very susceptible to the kind of rhetoric that's going on in our country."

One of those whose rhetoric has attracted attention is Sarah Palin. She published a map of the United States on her political action committee's website that listed twenty congressional seats held by Democrats whom she was "targeting" in the 2010 elections, including Gabrielle Giffords. The map marked each district with the cross hairs of a gun. More controversially, she linked to the cross hairs map through a tweet that read, "Don't Retreat, Instead—RELOAD!"

Giffords spoke directly to Palin's use of the cross hairs when they first appeared, noting that "When people do that . . . there are consequences to that action." Giffords' opponent in the midterm elections, the Tea Party–backed Iraq veteran Jesse Kelly, held an event advertised with the words: "Get on Target for Victory in November. Help remove Gabrielle Giffords from office. Shoot a fully automatic M16 with Jesse Kelly."

As Giffords' father rushed to her hospital bedside, he was asked if she had any enemies. "Yeah," he said. "The whole Tea Party."

As direct and offensive as Palin's campaign was, it was a small part of the political vitriol that has consumed Arizona in recent years. Republican Gov. Jan Brewer gained national notoriety when she signed into law the controversial immigration bill S.B. 1070, which Dupnik fiercely opposed:

> Every Hispanic in this country, especially in Arizona, must have awakened the next day to feel like they've been kicked in the teeth, like they are now second-class citizens, they have a target on their back, because when they leave the house, they're going to have to take papers with them and prepare to be stopped and questioned.

Contrast Dupnik with the sheriff of nearby Maricopa County, Joe Arpaio. He is notorious for the harsh conditions in which he jails people, using canvas tents in the searing summer heat. He has pledged to expand his tent city to accommodate the expected influx of detained immigrants. He is the subject of a U.S. Justice Department federal civil-rights lawsuit focusing on his treatment of prisoners and immigrants, and on abuse of power.

The *Arizona Republic* reports that Jared Loughner, charged in federal court for the murders and attacks, normally would have been remanded to the Maricopa County Jail, but "given the high profile of the case and Maricopa County Sheriff Joe Arpaio's penchant for publicity, they moved Loughner instead to [a] federal facility."

As the country unites against the terror in Tucson, let's take the targets off the backs of all innocent civilians, and hope the humanity of Sheriff Dupnik prevails over the cruel vitriol of Arpaio and his ilk.

January 19, 2011

Tucson, Juarez, and an Assault Weapons Ban

The Glock 19 semiautomatic pistol that Jared Loughner is accused of using in his rampage in Tucson, Arizona, is, according to Glock's website, "ideal for versatile use through reduced dimensions" and is "suitable for concealed carry." The site continues, "Compact and subcompact Glock pistol model magazines can be loaded with a convincing number of rounds," from the standard fifteen up to thirty-three. The shooter was able to kill and wound to the extent that he did, with six dead and thirteen injured, because he had a semiautomatic, concealed weapon, along with the "extended magazine." He was attempting to reload the weapon with another extended magazine when a brave, unarmed woman knocked his next clip from his hand.

Jared Loughner confirmed Glock's claim that thirty-three is a "convincing" number of rounds. Rep. Carolyn McCarthy, D-N.Y., doesn't need convincing, though. Her husband, Dennis McCarthy, was gunned down on the Long Island Rail Road on December 7, 1993, when Colin Ferguson pulled a semiautomatic pistol out of his bag and methodically made his way along the afternoon commuter train, randomly shooting passengers. He, too, killed six people and wounded nineteen, including McCarthy's son, Kevin. Ferguson was tackled, as was Loughner, while reloading his weapon. In both cases, the act of reloading the gun created a pause in the shooting that allowed unarmed citizens to take action.

Carolyn McCarthy mourned the loss of her husband and nursed her critically injured son back to health. He had been shot in the head. Carolyn McCarthy then decided to go further, to try to heal the nation. She lobbied her Long Island member of Congress, Republican Daniel Frisa, to support the 1994 Federal Assault Weapons Ban. He refused. McCarthy had been a nurse for thirty years, and a lifelong Republican. Turning her anger into action, she switched to the Democratic Party, ran for Congress against Frisa and defeated him in 1996. She has been in Congress ever since, and is one of the staunchest supporters there of common sense gun laws.

The 1994 law prohibited a number of weapons outright, as well as extended-capacity magazines like Loughner used. The law expired in 2004 under President George W. Bush. In response to the Tucson shooting, McCarthy is introducing the Large Capacity Ammunition Feeding Devices Act. In a letter to other members of Congress seeking co-sponsors, she says the bill "will prohibit the transfer, importation, or possession of high-capacity magazines manufactured after the bill is enacted," and, thus, "the increased difficulty in obtaining these devices will reduce their use and ultimately save lives."

The ban on these bullet clips is a start. But ultimately, the guns themselves—semiautomatic weapons—are the personal weapons of mass destruction that are designed not to hunt animals, but to kill people. These guns need to be controlled. By controlling them, we will reduce violence not only in the United States, but across the border in Mexico as well.

In Ciudad Juarez, just 300 miles from Tucson, directly across the border from El Paso, Texas, Mexican officials say more than 3,100 people were killed in drug violence last year, the bloodiest year to date. In May 2010, President Felipe Calderon spoke before a joint session of the U.S. Congress and called for a reinstatement of the assault weapons ban. According to law enforcement officials, 90 percent of the guns picked up in Mexico from criminal activity are purchased in the United States.

Susana Chavez was a poet and activist in Ciudad Juarez. She popularized the phrase "Not one more dead." She was buried last week in Mexico, just as the bodies of Tucson's youngest victim, nine-year-old Christina Greene, and federal Judge John Roll were being prepared for burial in Arizona. A month earlier, anti-violence campaigner Marisela Escobedo Ortiz was shot in the head while maintaining a vigil to demand that the government take action in pursuit of the killers of her seventeen-year-old daughter, Rubi Frayre Escobedo.

The U.S. group Mayors Against Illegal Guns has just released the results of a bipartisan survey, which found that 86 percent of Americans and 81 percent of gun owners support background checks on all gun sales. The group maintains a website, CloseTheLoophole.org. Gun shows, the ready access to semiautomatic weapons, and the additional availability of extended-capacity magazines are a recipe for the massacres that occur every few years in the U.S., and every few weeks in Mexico.

In the wake of the Tucson shooting, amidst calls for bipartisanship and civility, now is the time for Democrats and Republicans to join together to pass a permanent ban on assault weapons, and make us all safer.

December 28, 2011

If You Can't Beat Them, Enjoin Them (From Voting)

All eyes are on Iowa this week, as the hodgepodge field of Republican contenders gallivants across that farm state seeking a win, or at least "momentum," in the campaign for the party's presidential nomination. But behind the scenes, a battle is being waged by Republicans—not against each other, but against American voters. Across the country, state legislatures and governors are pushing laws that seek to restrict access to the voting booth, laws that will disproportionately harm people of color, low-income people, and young and elderly voters.

The National Association for the Advancement of Colored People and the NAACP Legal Defense and Educational Fund have just released a comprehensive report on the crisis, "Defending Democracy: Confronting Modern Barriers to Voting Rights in America." In it, they write: "The heart of the modern block the vote campaign is a wave of restrictive government-issued photo identification requirements. In a coordinated effort, legislators in thirty-four states introduced bills imposing such requirements. Many of these bills were modeled on legislation drafted by the American Legislative Exchange Council (ALEC)—a conservative advocacy group whose founder explained: 'Our leverage in the elections quite candidly goes up as the voting populace goes down.'"

It is interesting that the right wing, long an opponent of any type of national identification card, is very keen to impose photo-identification requirements at the state level. Why? Ben Jealous, president of the NAACP, calls the voter ID laws "a solution without a problem. . . . It's not going to make the vote more secure. What it is going to do is put the first financial barrier between people and their ballot box since we got rid of the poll tax."

You don't have to look far for people impacted by this new wave of voter-purging laws. Darwin Spinks, an eighty-six-year-old World War II veteran from Murfreesboro, Tennessee, went to the Department of Motor Vehicles to get a photo ID for voting purposes, since drivers over sixty there are issued driver's licenses without photos. After waiting in two lines, he was told he had to pay $8. Requiring a voter to pay a fee to vote has been unconstitutional since the poll tax was outlawed in 1964. Over in Nashville, ninety-three-year-old Thelma Mitchell had a state-issued ID—the one she used as a cleaner at the state capitol building for more than thirty years. The ID had granted her access to the governor's office for decades, but now, she was told, it wasn't good enough to get her into the voting booth. She and her family are considering a lawsuit, an unfortunate turn of events for a woman who is older than the right of women to vote in this country.

It is not just the elderly being given the disenfranchisement runaround. The Brennan Center for Justice at the New York University School of Law points to "bills making voter registration drives extremely difficult and risky for volunteer groups, bills requiring voters to provide specific photo ID or citizenship documents . . . bills cutting back on early and absentee voting, bills making it hard for students and active-duty members of the military to register to vote locally, and more."

U.S. Attorney General Eric Holder recently spoke on this alarming trend. He said: "Our efforts honor the generations of Americans who have taken extraordinary risks, and willingly confronted hatred, bias, and ignorance—as well as billy clubs and fire hoses, bullets and bombs—to ensure that their children, and all American citizens, would have the chance to participate in the work of their government. The right to vote is not only the cornerstone of our system of government—it is the lifeblood of our democracy."

Just this week, the Justice Department blocked South Carolina's new law requiring voters to show photo IDs at the polls, saying data submitted by South Carolina showed that minority voters were about 20 percent more likely to lack acceptable photo ID required at polling places.

By some estimates, the overall population that may be disenfranchised by this wave of legislation is upward of 5 million voters, most of whom would be expected to vote with the Democratic Party. The efforts to quash voter participation are not genuine, grassroots movements. Rather, they rely on funding from people like the Koch brothers, David and Charles. That is why thousands of people, led by the NAACP, marched on the New York headquarters of Koch Industries two weeks ago en route to a rally for voting rights at the United Nations.

Despite the media attention showered on the Iowa caucuses, the real election outcomes in 2012 will likely hinge more on the contest between billionaire political funders like the Kochs and the thousands of people in the streets, demanding one person, one vote.

March 21, 2012

Walking While Black: The Killing of Trayvon Martin

On the rainy night of Sunday, February 26, seventeen-year-old Trayvon Martin walked to a convenience store in Sanford, Florida. On his way home, with his Skittles and iced tea, the African-American teenager was shot and killed. The gunman, George Zimmerman, didn't run. He claimed that he killed the young man in self-defense. The Sanford police agreed and let him go. Since then, witnesses have come forward, 911 emergency calls have been released, and outrage over the killing has gone global.

Trayvon Martin lived in Miami. He was visiting his father in Sanford, near Orlando, staying in the gated community known as The Retreat at Twin Lakes, where Zimmerman volunteered with the Neighborhood Watch program. The *Miami Herald* reported that Zimmerman was a "habitual caller" to the police, making forty-six calls since January 2011. He was out on his rounds as a self-appointed watchman, packing his concealed 9 mm pistol, when he called 911: "We've had some break-ins in my neighborhood, and there's a real suspicious guy . . . this guy looks like he's up to no good, or he's on drugs or something."

Later in the call, Zimmerman exclaims, "OK. These a—holes always get away. . . . [Expletive], he's running."

Sounds of Zimmerman moving follow, along with a controversial utterance from Zimmerman, under his breath, considered by many to be "[Expletive] coons." The sound of his running prompted the 911 operator to ask, "Are you following him?" Zimmerman replied, "Yeah," to which the dispatcher said, "OK, we don't need you to do that."

One of the attorneys representing the Martin family, Jasmine Rand, told me: "The term 'coon' on the audiotape . . . is a very obvious racial slur against African-Americans. We also heard the neighbors come forward and say, 'Yeah, in this particular neighborhood, we look for young black males to be committing criminal activity.' And that's exactly what George Zimmerman did that night. He found a young black male that he did not recognize, assumed that he did not belong there, and he targeted him."

Another 911 call that has been released is from a woman who hears someone crying for help, then a gunshot.

Eyewitnesses Mary Cutcher and Selma Mora Lamilla both heard the cries, which police say could have been from Zimmerman, thus supporting his claim, even though he had a gun and outweighed Trayvon Martin by eighty pounds. Cutcher said at a press conference: "I feel it was not self-defense, because I heard the crying. And if it was Zimmerman that was crying, Zimmerman would have continued crying after the shot went off. The only thing I saw that night—I heard the crying. We were in the kitchen. I heard the crying. It was a little boy. As soon as the gun went off, the crying stopped. Therefore, it tells me it was not Zimmerman crying."

Sanford Police Chief Bill Lee has defended his department's decision not to arrest Zimmerman. They bagged Martin's body and took it away, labeling him a "John Doe," even though they had his cell phone, which anyone, let alone law enforcement with a shooting victim, could have used to easily identify a person. They tested Martin's corpse for drugs and alcohol. Zimmerman was not tested. Neighbors say that Zimmerman loaded things into a U-Haul truck and left the area.

So, while the police and State Attorney Norm Wolfinger have defended their inaction, a democratic demand for justice has ricocheted around the country, prompting a U.S. Justice Department investigation and leading Wolfinger to promise to convene a grand jury. The Rev. Glenn Dames, pastor of St. James AME Church in nearby Titusville, has called Martin's death "a modern-day lynching." His demand for the immediate arrest of Zimmerman was echoed by the organizers of the "Million Hoodie March" in New York City, named after the often racially stereotyped sweatshirt Martin was wearing in the rain when he was shot.

The National Association for the Advancement of Colored People has called for the removal of Sanford Police Chief Lee. NAACP President Ben Jealous, recounting a mass meeting in a Sanford-area church Tuesday night, quoted a local resident who stood up and said, "'If you kill a dog in this town, you'd be in jail the next day.' Trayvon Martin was killed four weeks ago, and his killer is still walking the streets."

With his gun.

April 4, 2012

Black in White Plains:
The Police Killing of Kenneth Chamberlain

"My name is Kenneth Chamberlain. This is my sworn testimony. White Plains police are going to come in here and kill me."

And that's just what they did.

In the early hours of Saturday, November 19, 2011, U.S. Marine veteran Kenneth Chamberlain Sr. accidentally hit his LifeAid medical-alert pendant, presumably while sleeping. The sixty-eight-year-old retired corrections officer had a heart condition, but wasn't in need of help that dawn. Within two hours, the White Plains, New York, police department broke down his apartment door and shot him dead. Chamberlain was African-American. As with Trayvon Martin, the black teen recently killed in Florida, there are recordings of the events, recordings that include a racial slur directed at the victim.

The opening quote, above, was related to us by Kenneth Chamberlain Jr., when he appeared on the *Democracy Now!* news hour talking about the police killing of his father. Ken Jr. was holding on to the LifeAid pendant that his father wore around his neck in case of a medical emergency. Perhaps unbeknownst to the White Plains police who arrived at Ken Sr.'s door that morning, the LifeAid system includes a box in the home that, when activated, transmits audio to the LifeAid company, where it is recorded. Ken Jr. and his lawyers heard the recording in a meeting at the office of the Westchester County district attorney, Janet DiFiore.

Ken Jr. repeated what he heard his father say on the tape: "He says, 'I'm a sixty-eight-year-old man with a heart condition. Why are you doing this to me?' ... You also hear him pleading with the officers again, over and over. And at one point, that's when the expletive is used by one of the police officers."

One of Chamberlain's attorneys, Mayo Bartlett, told me about the racial slur. Bartlett is a former Westchester County prosecutor, so he knows the ropes. He was very explicit in recounting what he heard on the recording.

"Kenneth Chamberlain Sr. said to the police, 'I'm a sick old man.' One of the police officers replied, 'We don't give a f—k, n——!'" (that last word rhymes with "trigger," which they would soon pull). The recording also includes a taunt from the police, as related by Bartlett, "Open the door, Kenny, you're a grown-ass man!" It was when Ken Jr. related how the police mocked his father's military service that he broke down. "He said, 'Semper fi.' So they said, 'Oh, you're a Marine. Hoo-rah. Hoo-rah.' And this is somebody that served this country. Why would you even say that to him?" Ken Jr. wept as he held his father's Marine ring and Veterans Administration card.

The LifeAid operator that November morning, hearing the exchange live, called the White Plains police in a desperate attempt to cancel the call for emergency medical aid. Chamberlain's niece, who lives in the building, ran down, trying to intervene. Chamberlain's sister was on her cell phone, offering to talk to her brother. The police denied any attempt at help. One was heard on the recording saying, "We don't need any mediator."

The heavily armed police used a special device to take Chamberlain's door completely off the hinges and, as chillingly captured in the Taser-mounted camera, burst into the apartment. Mayo Bartlett recounted seeing Chamberlain shirtless in the video, hands at his sides, without the knife or hatchet that police claim he wielded, standing in his boxer shorts. "The minute they got into the house, they didn't even give him one command. They never mentioned, 'Put your hands up.' They never told him to lie down on the bed. They never did any of that. The first thing they did, as soon as that door was finally broken off the hinges, you could see the Taser light up, and it was charged, and you could see it going directly toward him."

The last thing Bartlett hears on the Taser tape is "shut it off," meaning, turn off the video recording, which the police did. Within minutes, they would shoot Chamberlain twice. Four months later, no one has been charged with the killing. *Democracy Now!* co-host Juan Gonzalez revealed the name of the shooter, through his reporting in the New York *Daily News*, as White Plains Officer Anthony Carelli. Carelli is to be tried in coming months for alleged police brutality against two brothers, the sons of Jordanian immigrants, who say Carelli beat one of them, Jereis Hatter, while handcuffed, and called him a "raghead."

Trayvon Martin was killed February 26. A Florida grand jury is expected to begin the investigation into his killing on April 10. The next day, April 11, a New York grand jury is scheduled to begin hearing evidence in the case of Kenneth Chamberlain Sr. He was killed last November. In both cases, an African-American male was gunned down. In both cases, the shooter is known to the police. In Chamberlain's case, it is the police. And in both cases, no one has been arrested.

CAPITAL PUNISHMENT:
THE MACHINERY OF DEATH

August 19, 2009

Troy Davis and the Meaning of "Actual Innocence"

Sitting on death row in Georgia, Troy Davis has won a key victory against his own execution. On August 17, the U.S. Supreme Court instructed a federal court in Georgia to consider, for the first time in a formal court proceeding, significant evidence of Davis' innocence that surfaced after his conviction. This is the first such order from the U.S. Supreme Court in almost fifty years. Remarkably, the Supreme Court has never ruled on whether it is unconstitutional to execute an innocent person.

The order read, in part, "The District Court should receive testimony and make findings of fact as to whether evidence that could not have been obtained at the time of trial clearly establishes petitioner's innocence." Behind the order lay a stunning array of recantations from those who originally testified as eyewitnesses to the murder of off-duty Savannah police officer Mark Allen MacPhail on August 19, 1989. Seven of the nine nonpolice witnesses who originally identified Davis as the murderer of MacPhail have since recanted, some alleging police coercion and intimidation in obtaining their testimony. Of the remaining two witnesses, one, Sylvester "Redd" Coles, is accused by others as the shooter and identified Davis as the perpetrator probably to save himself from arrest.

On the night of the murder, MacPhail was off duty, working as a security guard at a Burger King. A homeless man was being beaten in the parking lot. The altercation drew Davis and others to the scene, along with MacPhail. MacPhail intervened, and was shot fatally with a .38-caliber gun. Later, Coles arrived at the police station, accompanied by a lawyer, and identified Davis as the shooter. The police engaged in a high-profile manhunt, with Davis' picture splayed across the newspapers and television stations. Davis turned himself in. With no physical evidence linking him to the crime, Davis was convicted and sentenced to death.

Jeffrey Sapp is typical of those in the case who recanted their eyewitness testimony. He said in an affidavit: "The police ... put a lot of pressure on me to say 'Troy said this' or 'Troy said that.' They wanted me to tell them that Troy confessed to me about killing that officer ... they made it clear that the only way they would leave me alone is if I told them what they wanted to hear."

Despite the seven recantations, Georgia's parole commission has refused to commute Davis' sentence. Courts have refused to hear the evidence, mostly on procedural grounds. Conservatives like former Georgia Congressman and prosecutor Bob Barr and former FBI Director William Sessions have called for justice in his case, along with Pope Benedict XVI, President Jimmy Carter, the NAACP, and Amnesty International.

Supreme Court Justice John Paul Stevens wrote for the majority, "The substantial risk of putting an innocent man to death clearly provides an adequate justification for holding an evidentiary hearing." Yet conservative Justice Antonin Scalia dissented (with Justice Clarence Thomas), writing that Davis' case "is a sure loser," and "[t]his Court has never held that the Constitution forbids the execution of a convicted defendant who has had a full and fair trial but is later able to convince a habeas court that he is 'actually' innocent."

Davis has had three execution dates, and in one instance was within two hours of lethal injection. Now he will finally have his day in court. With the courageous support of his sister, Martina Correia (who has been fighting for his life as well as her own—she has stage 4 breast cancer), and his nephew, Antone De'Jaun Correia, who at fifteen is a budding human rights activist, Davis may yet defy death. That could lead to a long-overdue precedent in U.S. law: It is unconstitutional to execute an innocent person.

• •

March 30, 2011

Georgia and the U.S. Supreme Court: Tinkering with the Machinery of Death

On March 28, the Supreme Court refused to hear the death penalty case of Troy Anthony Davis. It was his last appeal. Davis has been on Georgia's death row for close to twenty years after being convicted of shooting to death off-duty police officer Mark MacPhail in Savannah. Since his conviction, seven of the nine nonpolice witnesses have recanted their testimony, alleging police coercion and intimidation in obtaining the testimony. Despite the doubt surrounding his case, Troy Anthony Davis could be put to death within weeks.

Davis is now at the mercy of the Georgia State Board of Pardons and Parole, which could commute his sentence to life without parole. It will be a tough fight, despite widespread national and international support for clemency from figures such as Pope Benedict XVI, Archbishop Desmond Tutu, and former President Jimmy Carter.

Davis' sister, Martina Correia, has tirelessly campaigned for justice for her brother. In response to the Supreme Court decision, she told me: "We were really shocked and appalled yesterday when we received the news . . . no one wants to look at the actual innocence, and no one wants to look at the witness recantation as a real strong and viable part of this case, even though new witnesses have come forward. There needs to be a global mobilization about Troy's case, and the fact that in the United States it's not unconstitutional to execute an innocent person needs to be addressed once and for all by the U.S. Supreme Court."

Correia brings up a significant but little-known fact about death penalty law in the U.S., namely, that current court precedent allows the execution of innocent people. Remarkably, the Supreme Court, in a 1993 opinion, suggested that "actual innocence" is not a sufficient cause to be let free. The court only cares if the legal rules are followed, while acknowledging that innocent people could still be convicted and put to death. In such cases, a prisoner could appeal for executive clemency. It seems the court has not yet learned what many states have, that the death penalty system is broken beyond repair.

Illinois recently became the sixteenth state in the U.S. to outlaw the death penalty. Gov. Pat Quinn, after signing the bill into law, said, "I have concluded that our system of imposing the death penalty is inherently flawed . . . it is impossible to devise a system that is consistent, that is free of discrimination on the basis of race, geography or economic circumstance, and that always gets it right." He follows an earlier Illinois governor, Republican George Ryan, who commuted the death sentences of 120 death row prisoners in that state.

Both Illinois governors bring to mind former Supreme Court Justice Harry A. Blackmun, who wrote, in a dissenting opinion in 1994 after the court denied yet another death row inmate's last appeal, "From this day forward, I no longer shall tinker with the machinery of death."

Tinkering with the machinery of death is just what some states seem to be doing. Thiopental is one of the three drugs used in the lethal "cocktail" administered in most executions in this country. Hospira, the last U.S.-based company to make sodium thiopental, quit making the controlled drug, creating a national shortage. States began scrambling to keep their death chambers well-stocked. When California borrowed a similar drug from Arizona, California Undersecretary of Corrections and Rehabilitation Scott Kernan wrote in an email, "You guys in AZ are life savers...."

Georgia, it turns out, seems to have illegally imported its supply from a dubious, London-based company called Dream Pharma Ltd., run by a husband and wife out of a rented space in the back of a driving school. Georgia is not currently licensed by the Drug Enforcement Administration to import controlled substances, so the DEA recently confiscated the state's thiopental supply. Pending an investigation, Georgia will not have this key ingredient and will not be able to execute Davis or any other death row inmate.

On the same day that the Supreme Court denied Davis' appeal, Amnesty International issued its annual report on the death penalty. The United States remains among the world's leading executioners, along with China, Iran, Saudi Arabia, Yemen, and North Korea.

In addition to leading the fight for her brother, Martina Correia has been fighting for her own life. The day of the court decision was the tenth anniversary of her ongoing battle against breast cancer. Her face adorns the mobile mammography van that helps save the lives of poor women in Savannah. The National Breast Cancer Coalition named her and former House Speaker Nancy Pelosi "Women Who Get It Right." Correia, with customary humility, feels she won't have earned the title until her brother's life is saved as well.

April 27, 2011

Capital Punishment:
One of America's Worst Crimes

The death penalty case of Mumia Abu-Jamal took a surprising turn this week, as a federal appeals court declared, for the second time, that Abu-Jamal's death sentence was unconstitutional. The third U.S. circuit court of appeals, in Philadelphia, found that the sentencing instructions the jury received, and the verdict form they had to use in the sentencing, were unclear. While the disputes surrounding Abu-Jamal's guilt or innocence were not addressed, the case highlights inherent problems with the death penalty and the criminal justice system, especially the role played by race.

Early on December 9, 1981, Philadelphia Police Officer Daniel Faulkner pulled over a car driven by William Cook, Abu-Jamal's brother. What happened next is in dispute. Shots were fired, and both Officer Faulkner and Abu-Jamal were shot. Faulkner died, and Abu-Jamal was found guilty of his murder in a court case presided over by Judge Albert Sabo, who was widely considered to be a racist. In just one of too many painful examples, a court stenographer said in an affidavit that she heard Sabo say, in the courtroom antechamber, "I'm going to help them fry the ni—r."

This latest decision by the Court of Appeals relates directly to Sabo's conduct of the sentencing phase of Abu-Jamal's court case. The Pennsylvania Supreme Court is considering separate arguments surrounding whether or not Abu-Jamal received a fair trial at all. What the Court of Appeals unanimously found this week is that he did not receive a fair sentencing. Philadelphia District Attorney Seth Williams has decided to appeal the decision to the U.S. Supreme Court, saying, "The right thing for us to do is to ask the U.S. Supreme Court to hear this and to make a ruling on it."

As a result of this ruling, Abu-Jamal could get a new, full sentencing hearing, in court, before a jury. In such a hearing, the jury would be given clear instructions on how to decide between applying a sentence of life in prison versus the death penalty, something the court found he did not receive back in 1982. At best, Abu-Jamal would be removed from the cruel confines of solitary confinement on Pennsylvania's death row at SCI Greene.

John Payton, director-counsel of the NAACP Legal Defense Fund, which is representing Abu-Jamal in court, said: "This decision marks an important step forward in the struggle to correct the mistakes of an unfortunate chapter in Pennsylvania history . . . and helps to relegate the kind of unfairness on which this death sentence rested to the distant past."

His other attorney, Judith Ritter, a professor at Widener University School of Law, told me: "This is extremely significant. It's a life or death decision." I asked her if she had spoken to Abu-Jamal yet, and she told me that the prison failed to approve her request for an emergency legal phone call. I was not surprised, given my many years of covering his case.

Abu-Jamal has faced multiple obstacles as he has tried to have his voice heard. On August 12, 1999, as I was hosting *Democracy Now!*, Abu-Jamal called into our news hour mid-broadcast to be interviewed. As he began to speak, a prison guard yanked the phone out of the wall. Abu-Jamal called back a month later and recounted that "another guard appeared at the cell hollering at the top of his lungs, 'This call is terminated!' I immediately called to the sergeant standing by and looking on and said, 'Sergeant, where did this order come from?' He shrugged his shoulders and said: 'I don't know. We just got a call to cut you off.'" Abu-Jamal sued over the violation of his rights and won.

Despite his solitary confinement, Abu-Jamal has continued his work as a journalist. His weekly radio commentaries are broadcast from coast to coast. He is the author of six books. He was recently invited to present to a conference on racial imprisonment at Princeton University. He said (through a cell phone held up to a microphone): "Vast numbers of men, women, and juveniles . . . populate the prison industrial complex here in America. As many of you know, the U.S., with barely 5 percent of the world's population, imprisons 25 percent of the world's prisoners . . . the numbers of imprisoned blacks here rivals and exceeds South Africa's hated apartheid system during its height."

The United States clings to the death penalty, alone in the industrialized world. It stands with China, Iran, North Korea, Saudi Arabia, and Yemen as the world's most frequent executioners. This week's decision in Mumia Abu-Jamal's case stands as one more clear reason why the death penalty should be abolished.

September 14, 2011

Troy Davis and the Politics of Death

Death brings cheers these days in America. In the most recent Republican presidential debate in Tampa, Florida, when CNN's Wolf Blitzer asked, hypothetically, if a man who chose to carry no medical insurance, then was stricken with a grave illness, should be left to die, cheers of "Yeah!" filled the hall. When, in the prior debate, Gov. Rick Perry was asked about his enthusiastic use of the death penalty in Texas, the crowd erupted into sustained applause and cheers. The reaction from the audience prompted debate moderator Brian Williams of NBC News to follow up with the question, "What do you make of that dynamic that just happened here, the mention of the execution of 234 people drew applause?"

That "dynamic" is why challenging the death sentence to be carried out against Troy Davis by the state of Georgia on September 21 is so important. Davis has been on Georgia's death row for close to twenty years after being convicted of killing off-duty police officer Mark MacPhail in Savannah. Since his conviction, seven of the nine nonpolice witnesses have recanted their testimony, alleging police coercion and intimidation in obtaining the testimony. There is no physical evidence linking Davis to the murder.

Last March, the U.S. Supreme Court ruled that Davis should receive an evidentiary hearing, to make his case for innocence. Several witnesses have identified one of the remaining witnesses who has not recanted, Sylvester "Redd" Coles, as the shooter. U.S. District Judge William T. Moore Jr. refused, on a technicality, to allow the testimony of witnesses who claimed that, after Davis had been convicted, Coles admitted to shooting MacPhail. In his August court order, Moore summarized, "Mr. Davis is not innocent."

One of the jurors, Brenda Forrest, disagrees. She told CNN in 2009, recalling the trial of Davis, "All of the witnesses—they were able to ID him as the person who actually did it." Since the seven witnesses recanted, she says: "If I knew then what I know now, Troy Davis would not be on death row. The verdict would be not guilty."

Troy Davis has three major strikes against him. First, he is an African-American man. Second, he was charged with killing a white police officer. And third, he is in Georgia.

More than a century ago, the legendary muckraking journalist Ida B. Wells risked her life when she began reporting on the epidemic of lynchings in the Deep South. She published *Southern Horrors: Lynch Law in All Its Phases* in 1892 and followed up with *The Red Record* in 1895, detailing hundreds of lynchings. She wrote: "In Brooks County, Ga., Dec. 23, while this Christian country was preparing for Christmas celebration, seven Negroes were lynched in twenty-four hours because they refused, or were unable to tell the whereabouts of a colored man named Pike, who killed a white man . . . Georgia heads the list of lynching states."

The planned execution of Davis will not be at the hands of an unruly mob, but in the sterile, fluorescently lit confines of Georgia Diagnostic and Classification Prison in Butts County, near the town of Jackson.

The state doesn't intend to hang Troy Davis from a tree with a rope or a chain, to hang, as Billie Holiday sang, like a strange fruit: "Southern trees bear a strange fruit / Blood on the leaves and blood at the root / Black body swinging in the Southern breeze / Strange fruit hanging from the poplar trees." The state of Georgia, unless its Board of Pardons and Paroles intervenes, will administer a lethal dose of pentobarbital. Georgia is using this new execution drug because the federal Drug Enforcement Administration seized its supply of sodium thiopental last March, accusing the state of illegally importing the poison.

"This is our justice system at its very worst," said Ben Jealous, president of the National Association for the Advancement of Colored People. Amnesty International has called on the State Board of Pardons and Paroles to commute Davis' sentence. "The Board stayed Davis' execution in 2007, stating that capital punishment was not an option when doubts about guilt remained," said Larry Cox, executive director of Amnesty International USA. "Since then two more execution dates have come and gone, and there is still little clarity, much less proof, that Davis committed any crime. Amnesty International respectfully asks the Board to commute Davis' sentence to life and prevent Georgia from making a catastrophic mistake."

But it's not just the human rights groups the parole board should listen to. Pope Benedict XVI and Nobel Peace Prize laureates President Jimmy Carter and South African Archbishop Desmond Tutu, among others, also have called for clemency. Or the board can listen to mobs who cheer for death.

September 28, 2011

Troy Davis and the Machinery of Death

On September 21 at 7 p.m., Troy Anthony Davis was scheduled to die. I was reporting live from outside Georgia's death row in Jackson, awaiting news about whether the Supreme Court would spare his life.

Davis was sentenced to death for the murder of off-duty Savannah police officer Mark MacPhail in 1989. Seven of the nine nonpolice witnesses later recanted or changed their testimony, some alleging police intimidation for their original false statements. One who did not recant was the man who many have named as the actual killer. No physical evidence linked Davis to the shooting.

Davis, one of more than 3,200 prisoners on death row in the U.S., had faced three prior execution dates. With each one, global awareness grew. Amnesty International took up his case, as did the National Association for the Advancement of Colored People. Calls for clemency came from Pope Benedict XVI, former FBI Director William Sessions, and former Republican Georgia Congressman Bob Barr. The Georgia State Board of Pardons and Paroles, in granting a stay of execution in 2007, wrote that it "will not allow an execution to proceed in this state unless . . . there is no doubt as to the guilt of the accused."

But it is just that doubt that has galvanized so much global outrage over this case. As we waited, the crowd swelled around the prison, with signs saying "Too Much Doubt" and "I Am Troy Davis." Vigils were being held around the world, in places such as Iceland, England, France, and Germany. Earlier in the day, prison authorities handed us a thin press kit. At 3 p.m., it said, Davis would be given a "routine physical."

Routine? Physical? At a local church down the road, Edward DuBose, the president of Georgia's NAACP chapter, spoke, along with human rights leaders, clergy, and family members who had just left Davis. DuBose questioned the physical, "so that they could make sure he's physically fit, so that they can strap him down, so that they could put the murder juice in his arm? Make no mistake: They call it an execution. We call it murder."

Davis had turned down a special meal. The press kit described the standard fare Davis would be offered: "grilled cheeseburgers, oven-browned potatoes, baked beans, coleslaw, cookies and grape beverage." It also listed the lethal cocktail that would follow: "Pentobarbital. Pancuronium bromide. Potassium chloride. Ativan (sedative)." The pentobarbital anesthetizes, the pancuronium bromide paralyzes, and the potassium chloride stops the heart. Davis refused the sedative, and the last supper.

By 7 p.m., the U.S. Supreme Court was reportedly reviewing Davis' plea for a stay. The case was referred to Supreme Court Justice Clarence Thomas, who hails from Pin Point, Georgia, a community founded by freed slaves that is near Savannah, where Davis had lived.

The chorus for clemency grew louder. Allen Ault, a former warden of Georgia's death row prison who oversaw five executions there, sent a letter to Georgia Gov. Nathan Deal, co-signed by five other retired wardens or directors of state prisons. They wrote: "While most of the prisoners whose executions we participated in accepted responsibility for the crimes for which they were punished, some of us have also executed prisoners who maintained their innocence until the end. It is those cases that are most haunting to an executioner."

The Supreme Court denied the plea. Davis' execution began at 10:53 p.m. A prison spokesperson delivered the news to the reporters outside: time of death, 11:08 p.m.

The eyewitnesses to the execution stepped out. According to an Associated Press reporter who was there, these were Troy Davis' final words: "I'd like to address the MacPhail family. Let you know, despite the situation you are in, I'm not the one who personally killed your son, your father, your brother. I am innocent. The incident that happened that night is not my fault. I did not have a gun. All I can ask . . . is that you look deeper into this case so that you really can finally see the truth. I ask my family and friends to continue to fight this fight. For those about to take my life, God have mercy on your souls. And may God bless your souls."

The state of Georgia took Davis' body to Atlanta for an autopsy, charging his family for the transportation. On Troy Davis' death certificate, the cause of death is listed simply as "homicide."

As I stood on the grounds of the prison, just after Troy Davis was executed, the Department of Corrections threatened to pull the plug on our broadcast. The show was over. I was reminded what Gandhi reportedly answered when asked what he thought of Western civilization: "I think it would be a good idea."

WIKILEAKS AND THE CRACKDOWN ON DISSENT

May 31, 2012

WikiLeaks, War Crimes, and the Pinochet Principle

WikiLeaks founder Julian Assange's protracted effort to fight extradition to Sweden suffered a body blow this week. Britain's Supreme Court upheld the arrest warrant, issued in December 2010. After the court announced its split 5–2 decision, the justices surprised many legal observers by granting Assange's lawyers an opportunity to challenge their decision—the first such reconsideration since the high-profile British extradition case from more than a decade ago against former Chilean dictator Augusto Pinochet. The decision came almost two years to the day after Pvt. Bradley Manning was arrested in Iraq for allegedly leaking hundreds of thousands of classified U.S. government documents to WikiLeaks. The cases remind us that all too often whistle-blowers suffer, while war criminals walk.

Assange has not been charged with any crime, yet he has been under house arrest in England for close to two years, ever since a "European Arrest Warrant" was issued by Sweden (importantly, by a prosecutor, not by a judge). Hoping to question Assange, the prosecutor issued the warrant for suspicion of rape, unlawful coercion, and sexual molestation. Assange offered to meet the Swedish authorities in their embassy in London, or in Scotland Yard, but was refused.

Assange and his supporters allege that the warrant is part of an attempt by the U.S. government to imprison him, or even execute him, and to shut down WikiLeaks. In April 2010, WikiLeaks released a U.S. military video that it named "Collateral Murder," with graphic video showing an Apache helicopter unit killing of at least twelve Iraqi civilians, including a Reuters cameraman and his driver. In July 2010, WikiLeaks released the Afghan War Logs, tens of thousands of secret U.S. military communications that laid out the official record of the violent occupation of Afghanistan, the scale of civilian deaths and likely war crimes. The Swedish arrest warrant followed just weeks later.

So many public figures have called for Assange's assassination that a website was created to catalog the threats. Former Arkansas governor, presidential candidate and Fox News commentator Mike Huckabee said, "Anything less than execution is too kind a penalty." Prominent conservative Bill Kristol said, "Why can't we use our various assets to harass, snatch or neutralize Julian Assange and his collaborators, wherever they are?"

Death threats from right-wing ideologues are one thing. The main concern with an extradition to Sweden is that Assange will then be extradited to the United States. In another prominent document release by WikiLeaks, called the Global Intelligence Files, a portion of up to 5 million emails were released from a private, global intelligence firm called Stratfor, based in Austin, Texas. The firm's vice president for intelligence, Fred Burton, wrote in a January 26, 2011, email: "Not for Pub—We have a sealed indictment on Assange. Pls protect." If an indictment has been issued in secret, then Assange could find himself in U.S. custody shortly after landing in Sweden. He could be charged with espionage (the Obama administration has already invoked the law more than all previous U.S. administrations combined), and could be imprisoned for life or executed.

The United Kingdom carefully considers extradition requests, as famously demonstrated when crusading Spanish Judge Baltasar Garzón hoped to prosecute former Chilean dictator Pinochet for torture committed under his rule from 1973 to 1990. Based on Garzón's indictment, Pinochet was arrested in 1998 while traveling in London. After sixteen months of hearings, the British courts finally decided that Pinochet could be extradited to Spain. The British government intervened, overruling the court, and allowed him to return to Chile.

Garzón is known for taking on global human-rights cases under the doctrine of universal jurisdiction, indicting Osama bin Laden for the 9/11 attacks, and probing the abuse of U.S. prisoners at Guantánamo Bay. When he began investigating abuses under the fascist government of General Francisco Franco, who ruled Spain for forty years, Garzón became the target of the right in Spain and was disbarred in early 2012, effectively ending his legal career.

Judge Garzón and Julian Assange have taken on entrenched power, whether government, military, or corporate. Bradley Manning stands accused of the same. In differing degrees, their lives have forever changed, their careers, their freedoms, and their reputations threatened or destroyed. This week, Hillary Clinton will be making the first official trip to Sweden in years. Why? What role is the U.S. government playing in Assange's case? This week's developments bear crucially on the public's right to know, and why whistle-blowers must be protected.

December 21, 2011

Bradley Manning and the Fog of War

Accused whistle-blower Pvt. Bradley Manning turned twenty-four Saturday. He spent his birthday in a pretrial military hearing that could ultimately lead to a sentence of life … or death. Manning stands accused of causing the largest leak of government secrets in United States history.

More on Manning shortly. First, a reminder of what he is accused of leaking. In April 2010, the whistle-blower website WikiLeaks released a video called "Collateral Murder." It was a classified U.S. military video from July 2007, from an Apache attack helicopter over Baghdad. The video shows a group of men walking, then the systematic killing of them in a barrage of high-powered automatic fire from the helicopter. Soldiers' radio transmissions narrate the carnage, varying from cold and methodical to cruel and enthusiastic. Two of those killed were employees of the international news agency Reuters: Namir Noor-Eldeen, a photojournalist, and Saeed Chmagh, his driver.

Renowned whistle-blower Daniel Ellsberg, who released the Pentagon Papers that helped end the war in Vietnam and who himself is a Marine veteran who trained soldiers on the laws of war, told me: "Helicopter gunners hunting down and shooting an unarmed man in civilian clothes, clearly wounded … that shooting was murder. It was a war crime. Not all killing in war is murder, but a lot of it is. And this was."

The WikiLeaks release of the Afghan War Logs followed months later, with tens of thousands of military field reports. Then came the Iraq War Diaries, with close to 400,000 military records of the U.S. war in Iraq. Next was Cablegate, WikiLeaks' rolling release (with prominent print-media partners, including the *New York Times* and the *Guardian* in Britain) of classified U.S. State Department cables, more than a quarter-million of them, dating from as far back as 1966 up to early 2010. The contents of these cables proved highly embarrassing to the U.S. government and sent shock waves around the world.

Among the diplomatic cables released were those detailing U.S. support for the corrupt Tunisian regime, which helped fuel the uprising there. Noting that *Time* magazine named "The Protester," generically, as Person of the Year, Ellsberg said Manning should be the face of that protester, since the leaks for which he is accused, following their impact in Tunisia, "in turn sparked the uprising in Egypt ... which stimulated Occupy Wall Street and the other occupations in the Middle East and elsewhere. So, one of those 'persons of the year' is now sitting in a courthouse."

Another recently revealed Cablegate release exposed details of an alleged 2006 massacre by U.S. troops in the Iraqi town of Ishaqi, north of Baghdad. Eleven people were killed, and the cable described eyewitness accounts in which the group, including five children and four women, was handcuffed, then executed with bullets to the head. The U.S. military then bombed the house, allegedly to cover up the incident. Citing attacks like these, the Iraqi government said it would no longer grant immunity to U.S. soldiers in Iraq. President Barack Obama responded by announcing he would pull the troops out of Iraq. Like a modern-day Ellsberg, if Manning is guilty of what the Pentagon claims, he helped end the war in Iraq.

Back in the Fort Meade, Maryland, hearing room, defense attorneys painted a picture of a chaotic forward operating base with little to no supervision, no controls whatsoever on soldiers' access to classified data, and a young man in uniform struggling with his sexual identity in the era of "Don't Ask, Don't Tell." Manning repeatedly flew into rages, throwing furniture and once even punching a superior in the face, without punishment. His peers at the base said he should not be in a war zone. Yet he stayed, until his arrest eighteen months ago.

Since his arrest, Manning has been in solitary confinement, for much of the time in Quantico, Virginia, under conditions so harsh that the U.N. special rapporteur on torture is investigating. Many believe the U.S. government is trying to break Manning in order to use him in its expected case of espionage against WikiLeaks founder Julian Assange. It also sends a dramatic message to any potential whistle-blower: "We will destroy you."

For now, Manning sits attentively, reports say, facing possible death for "aiding the enemy." The prosecution offered words Manning allegedly wrote to Assange as evidence of his guilt. In the email, Manning described the leak as "one of the more significant documents of our time, removing the fog of war and revealing the true nature of 21st century asymmetrical warfare." History will no doubt use the same words as irrefutable proof of Manning's courage.

October 7, 2009

Watch What You Tweet

A social worker from New York City was arrested last week while in Pittsburgh for the G-20 protests, then subjected to an FBI raid this week at home—all for using Twitter. Elliot Madison faces charges of hindering apprehension or prosecution, criminal use of a communication facility, and possession of instruments of crime. He was posting to a Twitter feed (or tweeting, as it is called) publicly available information about police activities around the G-20 protests, including information about where police had issued orders to disperse.

While alerting people to public information may not seem to be an arrestable offense, be forewarned: Many people have been arrested for the same "crime"—in Iran, that is.

Last June 20, as Iranians protested against the conduct and results of their national election, President Barack Obama said in a statement, "The universal rights to assembly and free speech must be respected, and the United States stands with all who seek to exercise those rights."

His statement was released in English, Farsi, and Arabic and posted on the White House's very own Twitter feed. His tweet read, "We call on the Iranian government to stop all violent and unjust actions against its own people."

U.S. Sens. Charles Schumer, D-N.Y., and Lindsey Graham, R-S.C., wrote to Secretary of State Hillary Clinton, urging her to pressure European nations to restrict sales of eavesdropping technology to Iran. They wrote: "Following recent elections, the Iranian government has used a new communications monitoring center to interfere with and suppress Internet and cell phone communications as part of efforts to crackdown on Iranian citizens peacefully demonstrating... including voice calls, email, text messaging, instant messages, and Web traffic, as well as posts to social networking sites such as Twitter, MySpace and Facebook."

The U.S. State Department, impressed with the importance of Twitter to Iranian protests, asked Twitter to delay system maintenance that might have interrupted the service during the Iranian protests.

While Madison optimistically mused, "I'm expecting the State Department will come out and support us also," his lawyer, respected civil rights attorney

Martin Stolar, said: "This is just unbelievable. It is the thinnest, silliest case that I've ever seen. It tends to criminalize support services for people who are involved in lawful protest activity. And it's just shocking that somebody could be arrested for essentially walking next to somebody and saying: 'Hey, don't go down that street, because the police have issued an order to disperse. Stay away from there.'"

Madison, his wife, and housemates were roused from sleep during the weekend when the Joint Terrorism Task Force swept into their house, handcuffing them for hours, searching the house and removing computers and other property from everyone in the house. Madison said the FBI "for 16 hours, proceeded to take everything, from plush toys to kitchen magnets and lots of books . . . they took Curious George stuffed animals."

Rather than encourage and support the use of distributed, decentralized social networks to strengthen our democracy and dissent (remember, the Obama campaign itself relied extensively on these online and mobile tools), the government seems headed in the opposite direction. Los Angeles Chief of Police William Bratton recently won acclaim at the annual meeting of the Major Cities Chiefs Association, a professional organization of police executives representing sixty-three of the largest cities in the United States and Canada. Bratton has launched "iWatchLA," described as "a community awareness program created to educate the public about behaviors and activities that may have a connection to terrorism." The iWatch program, despite Bratton's assertion otherwise, is about spying on your neighbors and turning them in to the police.

One Iranian tweeter for the virtual news hub Tehran Bureau recalled the June protests in an essay: "An officer spoke to us through a loud speaker: 'Disperse: This is your last warning.' The sight of them made my knees tremble, but the wave pushed on and so I went along." He was beaten, bloodied, arrested, and held for twenty days. While Elliot Madison was not physically harmed, his legal battles are just beginning, and his case could prove central to the future of free speech in the mobile, digital age.

November 25, 2009

Books, Not Bombs

California campuses have been rocked by protests this past week, provoked by massive student fee increases voted on by the University of California Board of Regents. After a year of sequential budget cuts, faculty and staff dismissals and furloughs, and the elimination of entire academic departments, the 32 percent fee increase proved to be the trigger for statewide actions of an unprecedented scale. With President Barack Obama's Afghanistan war strategy—which, according to one leak, will include a surge of 35,000 troops—soon to be announced, the juxtaposition of education cuts and military increases is incensing many, and helping to build a movement.

As I traveled throughout California this past week on a book tour, I was, coincidentally, in the midst of the regents' vote and the campus protests. At UC Berkeley, UC Santa Cruz, UC Santa Barbara, UCLA, Cal State Fresno, UC Davis, and Cal State Chico, students approached me with stories of how the fee increases were going to price them out of school. Students were occupying buildings, marching, and holding teach-ins. At UC Davis, several young women, among the fifty-two arrested, described to me how they had been attacked by campus police, shot with Tasers. Students there also protested the Saturday closure of the libraries, showing up at the president's university-provided house to study there, since the library was closed. He let them in to study rather than spark a confrontation that probably would have ended with police action and arrests.

Blanca Misse, a UC Berkeley graduate student and organizer with the Student Worker Action Team, was among those who've been organizing. She told me, "We are striking because we care a lot about public education, and we care about another kind of public education, maybe, than the one they offer, a real public education out of the corporate model."

Laura Nader (Ralph Nader's sister) is a professor of social cultural anthropology at UC Berkeley, where she has taught for nearly fifty years. Earlier this year she co-authored a measure approved by the UC Berkeley Academic Senate calling on the school's athletics program to become self-sufficient and stop receiving subsidies from student fees. She is a critic of the increasing power that corporations such as BP and Novartis have over the universities, and she has a long personal history fighting for public education. She teaches general-education classes that attract hundreds of students—noting that students these days, taught to take tests, "are great at choosing answers on a multiple-choice test, but have never heard of Hiroshima and Nagasaki." Her focus on the basics reflects her concern of the attack on public education in this country: "It isn't something that just happened, and it isn't something that was unplanned," she told me. "People really do adhere to the model that this shouldn't be a public good. And if we continue in this direction, there's going to be a two-class system: those who go to college are going to be those who can afford it, and those who don't are going to be the middle class."

The movement's centerpiece is a strong coalition that includes students, workers, and faculty. Bob Samuels is president of the University Council–American Federation of Teachers, the union representing non-senate faculty and librarians of the University of California. Although California is facing a serious budget crisis, Samuels told me the UC system has more than sufficient funds: "It doesn't have to raise student fees. It doesn't have to fire faculty. It doesn't have to cut courses. They're talking about eliminating minors and majors. They're talking about moving classes online. They're doing these drastic things. And what we're seeing is just basically undergraduate students are subsidizing research, they're subsidizing administrators, they're subsidizing things that have nothing to do with undergraduate instruction."

During the Bush administration, military recruiting faced an all-time low. Now, after the economic collapse of late 2008, recruiters are having no problems. President Obama seems committed to increasing the size, and thus necessarily the duration, of the war and occupation in Afghanistan. One of the most popular university professors in California, Anaya Roy of UC Berkeley, offers a summary that Obama should heed: "In this context of inequality, one doesn't need radical instruments of redistribution. One only needs a few things, like decent public education or access to health care or some sort of reasonable approach that says enough of this massive spending on war."

December 2, 2009

Canada's Olympic Crackdown

Going to Canada? You may be detained at the border and interrogated. I was, last week. I was heading from Seattle to give a talk at the Vancouver Public Library. My detention provoked outrage across Canada, making national news. It has serious implications for the freedom of the press in North America.

I drove to the border with two colleagues. We showed our passports to the Canadian guard and answered standard questions about our purpose for entering Canada. No visas are necessary for U.S. citizens to enter.

The guard promptly told us to pull over, leave the car, and enter the border crossing building.

What followed was a flagrant violation of freedom of the press and freedom of speech. A guard first demanded the notes for my talk. I was shocked. I explained that I speak extemporaneously. He would not back off. He demanded notes. I went out to the car and brought in a copy of my new book, a collection of my weekly columns called *Breaking the Sound Barrier*. I handed him a copy and said I start with the last column in it.

"I begin each talk with the story of Tommy Douglas," I explained, "the late premier of Saskatchewan, father of Canada's universal health care system." Considered the greatest Canadian, Douglas happens to be actor Kiefer Sutherland's grandfather, but I didn't get that far.

"What else?" the armed guard demanded as we stood in the Douglas border facility.

"I'll be talking about global warming and the Copenhagen climate summit."

"What else?"

"I'll address the wars in Iraq and Afghanistan."

"What else?" The interrogator was hand-writing notes, while another guard was typing at a computer terminal.

"Well, that's about it."

He looked at me skeptically. "Are you going to talk about the Olympics?" he asked.

I was puzzled. "Do you mean how President Obama recently traveled to Copenhagen to lobby for the Olympic Games to be held in Chicago?"

He shot back, "You didn't get those. I am talking about the Vancouver 2010 Olympics." Again, stunned, I said I wasn't planning to.

The guard looked incredulous. "Are you telling me you aren't going to be talking about the Olympics?" I repeatedly asserted that I was not.

Clearly not believing me, the guard and others combed through our car.

When I went out to check, he was on my colleague's computer, poring through it.

Afterward, they pulled me in a back room and took my photo, then called in the others, one by one. Then they handed us back our passports with "control documents" stapled inside. The forms said we had to leave Canada within two days and had to check in with their border agency upon leaving. We went to the car—and discovered that they had rifled through our belongings and our papers and had gone into at least two of our three laptops. We raced to the event, where people had been told about our detention. We were ninety minutes late, but the room remained packed, the crowd incensed at their government.

It was then that I started learning about what was going on. The crackdown is widespread, it turns out. David Eby, executive director of the British Columbia Civil Liberties Association, told me, "We have a billion dollars being spent on security here; protesters and activists have been identified as the No. 1 security threat to the Olympic Games . . . we have new city bylaws that restrict the content of people's signs." According to critics, the police can raid your home if you place an anti-Olympic sign in your window. There are concerns that homeless people may be swept from Vancouver, about how much public funding the Games are receiving while vital social services are financially starved. Anti-Olympic activists— and their families and friends—are being followed, detained, and questioned.

Our detention and interrogation were not only a violation of freedom of the press but also a violation of the public's right to know. Because if journalists feel there are things they can't report on, that they'll be detained, that they'll be arrested or interrogated, this is a threat to the free flow of information. And that's the public's loss, an Olympic loss for democracy.

April 7, 2010

Collateral Murder in Iraq

A United States military video was released this week showing the indiscriminate targeting and killing of civilians in Baghdad. The nonprofit news organization WikiLeaks obtained the video and made it available on the Internet. The video was made July 12, 2007, by a U.S. military Apache helicopter gunship, and includes audio of military radio transmissions.

Two Reuters employees—a journalist and his driver—were killed in the attack, along with at least eight other people, and two children were injured. The radio transmissions show not only the utter callousness of the soldiers, laughing and swearing as they kill, but also the strict procedure they follow, ensuring that all of their attacks are clearly authorized by their chain of command. The leaked video is a grim depiction of how routine the killing of civilians has become, and is a stark reminder of how necessary journalism is, and how dangerous its practice has become.

After photographer Namir Noor-Eldeen, twenty-two, and his driver, Saeed Chmagh, forty, were killed, Reuters demanded a full investigation. Noor-Eldeen, despite his youth, had been described by colleagues as one of the pre-eminent war photographers in Iraq. Chmagh was a father of four.

The video shows a group of men in an open square in Baghdad, leading the two Reuters employees to a building nearby. Noor-Eldeen and Chmagh are shown, each carrying a camera with a telephoto lens. A U.S. soldier in the helicopter says: "OK, we got a target 15 coming at you. It's a guy with a weapon." There is much back and forth between two helicopters and ground troops in armored vehicles nearby:

"Have five to six individuals with AK-47s. Request permission to engage."

"Roger that. Uh, we have no personnel east of our position. So, uh, you are free to engage. Over."

The helicopter circles around, with the cross hairs squarely in the center of the group of about eight men. WikiLeaks and its partner for this story, the Icelandic National Broadcasting Service, added subtitles to the video, as well as arrows indicating the Reuters employees.

Sustained automatic-weapon fire erupts, and most of the men are killed instantly. Noor-Eldeen runs away, and the cross hairs follow him, shooting non-stop, until he falls, dead.

The radio transmission continues, "All right, hahaha, I hit 'em . . ." and then, "Yeah, we got one guy crawling around down there. . . ."

Chmagh, seriously wounded, was dragging himself away from the other bodies. A voice in the helicopter, seeking a rationale to shoot, said: "Come on, buddy. All you gotta do is pick up a weapon. . . . If we see a weapon, we're gonna engage."

A van pulled up, and several men, clearly unarmed, came out and lifted Chmagh, ostensibly to carry him to medical care. The soldiers on the Apache sought and received permission to "engage" the van and opened fire, tearing apart the front of the van and killing the men. The weapon used was a 30-millimeter machine gun, used to pierce armor. With everyone in sight apparently dead, U.S. armored vehicles moved in. When a vehicle drove over Noor-Eldeen's corpse, an observer in the helicopter said, laughing, "I think they just drove over a body." The troops discovered two children in the van, who had miraculously survived. One voice on the military radio requests permission to evacuate them to a U.S. military hospital. Another voice commands them to hand over the wounded children to Iraqi police for delivery to a local clinic, ensuring delayed and less-adequate treatment.

The U.S. military inquiry into the killings cleared the soldiers of any wrong-doing, and Reuters' Freedom of Information requests for the video were denied. Despite the Pentagon's whitewash, the attack was brutal and might have involved a war crime, since those removing the wounded are protected by the Geneva Conventions. WikiLeaks says it obtained the video "from a number of military whistle-blowers." WikiLeaks.org, founded in late 2006 as a secure site for whistle-blowers to safely release documents, has come under attack from the U.S. and other governments.

WikiLeaks has broken numerous stories and has received awards. It and members of the Icelandic Parliament are working together to make Iceland a world center of investigative journalism, putting solid free speech and privacy protections into law. The words of legendary journalist I. F. Stone still hold true: "Governments lie." Because of that, we need courageous journalists and media workers, like Namir Noor-Eldeen and Saeed Chmagh, and we need whistle-blowers and news organizations that will carefully protect whistle-blowers' identities while bringing their exposés to public scrutiny.

July 28, 2010

WikiLeaks' Afghan War Diary

WikiLeaks.org has done it again, publishing thousands of classified documents about the U.S. war in Afghanistan. The website provides a secure platform for whistle-blowers to deliver documents, videos, and other electronic media while maintaining anonymity. Last March it released a video shot from a U.S. military helicopter over Baghdad, exposing the Army's indiscriminate killing of at least twelve people, two of whom worked for the Reuters news agency. This week, WikiLeaks, along with three mainstream media partners—the *New York Times*, the *Guardian* of London, and *Der Spiegel* in Germany—released 91,000 classified reports from the United States military in Afghanistan. The reports, mostly written by soldiers on the ground immediately after military actions, represent a true diary of the war from 2004 to 2009, detailing everything from the killing of civilians, including children, to the growing strength of the Taliban insurgency, to Pakistan's support for the Taliban.

After the documents were released, WikiLeaks founder and editor in chief Julian Assange told me: "Most civilian casualties occur in instances where one, two, 10 or 20 people are killed—they really numerically dominate the list of events. . . . The way to really understand this war is by seeing that there is one killed after another, every day, going on and on."

Assange described a massacre, what he called a "Polish My Lai." On August 16, 2007, Polish troops returned to a village where they had suffered an IED roadside bomb that morning. The Poles launched mortars into the village, striking a house where a wedding party was under way. Assange suspects that the Poles, retaliating for the IED, committed a war crime, concealed in the dry bureaucratic language in the report: "Current Casualty list: 6x KIA (1x male, 4 female, one baby) 3x WIA (all female, one of which was 9 months pregnant)."

KIA means "Killed in Action," and the tens of thousands of classified reports are dense with KIAs. Assange says that there are 2,000 civilian deaths detailed in the reports. Other entries describe "Task Force 373," a U.S. Army assassination unit that allegedly captures or kills people believed to be members of the Taliban or al-Qaida.

The Obama administration is running for cover, and its response has been confused. National security adviser Gen. James Jones condemned the disclosure of classified information, saying it "could put the lives of Americans and our partners at risk, and threaten our national security." At the same time, White House press secretary Robert Gibbs said "there's no broad new revelations in this."

The threat posed by this historic leak is not a threat to the lives of American soldiers at war, but rather to a policy that puts those lives at risk. With public support already waning, this leak can only strengthen the call for the war's end.

"I've been waiting for it for a long time," tweeted Daniel Ellsberg, the most famous whistle-blower in America. Ellsberg is the former military analyst who famously leaked the Pentagon Papers in 1971, thousands of pages of a top-secret government study revealing the secret history of the Vietnam War. Many credit Ellsberg's action with helping to end the Vietnam War. Ellsberg told me this week: "I'm very impressed by the [WikiLeaks] release. It is the first release in 39 years on the scale of the Pentagon Papers. How many times in these years should there have been the release of thousands of pages showing our being lied into war in Iraq, as in Vietnam, and the nature of the war in Afghanistan?"

Assange has been advised by his lawyers not to enter the United States.

Homeland Security agents descended on a recent hacker conference in New York where he was scheduled to speak. He had canceled. He said the Obama administration also tried to get the Australian government to arrest him. Speaking to me from London, Assange said: "We are not pacifists. We are transparency activists who understand that transparent government tends to produce just government. That is our modus operandi behind our whole organization: to get out suppressed information into the public where the press and the public and our nations' politics can work on it to produce better outcomes."

September 29, 2010

FBI Raids and the Criminalization of Dissent

Early in the morning on Friday, September 24, FBI agents in Chicago and Minnesota's Twin Cities kicked in the doors of anti-war activists, brandishing guns, spending hours rifling through their homes. The FBI took away computers, photos, notebooks, and other personal property. Residents were issued subpoenas to appear before a grand jury in Chicago. It was just the latest in the ongoing crackdown on dissent in the U.S., targeting peace organizers as supporters of "foreign terrorist organizations."

Coleen Rowley knows about the FBI. She was a career special agent with the FBI who blew the whistle on the bureau's failures in the lead-up to the 9/11 attacks. *Time* magazine named her Person of the Year in 2002. A few days after the raids in her hometown of Minneapolis, she told me, "This is not the first time that you've seen this Orwellian turn of the war on terror onto domestic peace groups and social justice groups . . . we had that begin very quickly after 9/11, and there were Office of Legal Counsel opinions that said the First Amendment no longer controls the war on terror."

Jess Sundin's home was raided. She was the lead organizer of the St. Paul, Minnesota, anti-war march on Labor Day 2008 that occurred as the Republican National Convention began. She described the raid: "They spent probably about four hours going through all of our personal belongings, every book, paper, our clothes, and filled several boxes and crates with our computers, our phones, my passport . . . with which they left my house."

They smashed activist Mick Kelly's fish tank when they barged into his home. The net cast by the FBI that morning included not only anti-war activists, but those who actively support a changed foreign policy toward Israel-Palestine and Colombia. The warrant for Kelly sought all records of his travel, not only to those countries, but also all his domestic U.S. travel since 2000, and all his personal contacts.

No one was arrested. No one was charged with a crime. Days later, hundreds of protesters rallied outside FBI offices nationally.

The raids happened just days after the U.S. Department of Justice's inspector general released a report, "A Review of the FBI's Investigations of Certain Domestic Advocacy Groups." The IG looked at FBI surveillance and investigation of, among others, the environmental group Greenpeace, People for the Ethical Treatment of Animals, and the Pittsburgh-based Thomas Merton Center. Founded in 1972 to support opposition to the war in Vietnam, the Merton Center continues to be a hub of anti-war activism in Pittsburgh. In 2002, the FBI spied on a Merton-organized rally, claiming "persons with links to international terrorism would be present." As the IG reports, this claim was a fabrication, which was then relayed to FBI Director Robert Mueller, who repeated it, under oath, to the Senate Judiciary Committee.

The illegal surveillance trickles down, through "Joint Terrorism Task Forces" that bring together federal, state, and local law enforcement; Homeland Security; and military agencies, often under the roof of a "fusion center," the name given to shadowy trans-jurisdictional intelligence centers. There, it seems, slapping the "domestic terror" tag on activists is standard.

Pennsylvania Gov. Ed Rendell recently apologized when it was revealed that his state Homeland Security director, James Powers, had contracted with a private company to research and distribute information about citizen groups engaged in legal activity. Groups opposed to the environmentally destructive extraction of natural gas known as "fracking," for example, were referred to as "environmental extremists."

Their crime: holding a screening of the Sundance-winning documentary *Gasland*.

Back in the Twin Cities, the state has been forced to back off eight other activists, dubbed the "RNC 8," who were part of organizing the protests at the Republican National Convention. They all were pre-emptively arrested, before the convention started, and charged, under Minnesota state law, as terrorists. The prosecution has since dropped all terrorism charges (four of them will go to trial on other charges).

This is all happening while the Obama administration uses fear of terrorism to seek expanded authority to spy on Internet users, and as another scandal is brewing: The Justice Department also revealed this week that FBI agents regularly cheated on an exam testing knowledge of proper rules and procedures governing domestic surveillance. This is more than just a cheating scandal. It's about basic freedoms at the core of our democracy, the abuse of power and the erosion of civil liberties.

December 1, 2010

WikiLeaks and the End of U.S. "Diplomacy"

WikiLeaks is again publishing a trove of documents, in this case classified U.S. State Department diplomatic cables. The whistle-blower website will gradually be releasing more than 250,000 of these documents in the coming months so that they can be analyzed and gain the attention they deserve. The cables are internal, written communications among U.S. embassies around the world and also to the U.S. State Department. WikiLeaks described the leak as "the largest set of confidential documents ever to be released into the public domain [giving] an unprecedented insight into U.S. government foreign activities."

Critics argue, as they did with earlier leaks of secret documents regarding Iraq and Afghanistan, that lives will be lost as a result. Rather, lives might actually be saved, since the way that the U.S. conducts diplomacy is now getting more exposure than ever—as is the apparent ease with which the U.S. government lives up (or down) to the adage used by pioneering journalist I. F. Stone: "Governments lie."

Take the case of Khaled el-Masri. El-Masri was snatched in Macedonia as part of the CIA's secret extraordinary rendition program, in which people are taken by the U.S. government and sent to other countries, where they can be subjected to torture. He was held and tortured in a secret prison in Afghanistan for months before being dropped by the CIA on an isolated road in Albania, even though the CIA had long established that it had grabbed the wrong man. El-Masri, a German citizen, sought justice through German courts, and it looked like thirteen CIA agents might be charged. Then the U.S. Embassy in Berlin stepped in, threatening, according to one cable, that "issuance of international arrest warrants would have a negative impact on our bilateral relationship." No charges were ever filed in Germany, suggesting the diplomatic threat worked. The thirteen agents are, however, still facing charges in Spain, where prosecutors enjoy some freedom from political pressures.

Or so we thought. In fact, Spain figures prominently in the leaked documents as well. Among the cables is one from May 14, 2007, authored by Eduardo Aguirre, a conservative Cuban-American banker appointed U.S. ambassador to Spain by George W. Bush. Aguirre wrote: "For our side, it will be important to continue to raise the Couso case, in which three U.S. servicemen face charges related to the 2003 death of Spanish cameraman Jose Couso during the battle for Baghdad."

Couso was a young cameraman with the Spanish TV network Telecinco. He was filming from the balcony of the Palestine Hotel in Baghdad on April 8, 2003, when a U.S. Army tank fired on the hotel packed with journalists, killing Couso and a Reuters cameraman. Ambassador Aguirre was trying to quash the lawsuit brought by the Couso family in Spain.

The U.S. ambassador was also pressuring the Spanish government to drop a precedent-setting case against former Defense Secretary Donald Rumsfeld and other Bush administration officials. In that same memo, Aguirre writes, "The Deputy Justice Minister also said the GOS [government of Spain] strongly opposes a case brought against former Secretary Rumsfeld and will work to get it dismissed. The judge involved in that case has told us he has already started the process of dismissing the case."

These revelations are rocking the Spanish government, as the cables clearly show U.S. attempts to disrupt the Spanish justice system.

Ambassador Aguirre told Spain's *El País* newspaper several years ago, "I am George Bush's plumber, I will solve all the problems George gives me."

In another series of cables, the U.S. State Department instructs its staff around the world and at the U.N. to spy on people, and, remarkably, to collect biometric information on diplomats. The cable reads, "Data should include e-mail addresses, telephone and fax numbers, fingerprints, facial images, DNA and iris scans."

WikiLeaks is continuing its partnership with a global group of media outlets: Britain's the *Guardian*, *El País*, the *New York Times*, German magazine *Der Spiegel*, and France's *Le Monde*. David Leigh, investigations editor of the *Guardian*, told me, "We haven't seen anything yet," with literally almost a quarter million cables still not publicly revealed.

A renowned political analyst and linguist, MIT professor Noam Chomsky helped Daniel Ellsberg, America's premier whistle-blower, release the Pentagon Papers forty years ago. I asked Chomsky about the latest cables released by WikiLeaks. "What this reveals," he reflected, "is the profound hatred for democracy on the part of our political leadership."

December 15, 2010

"Assangination": From Character Assassination to the Real Thing

Despite being granted bail, WikiLeaks founder and editor Julian Assange remains imprisoned in London, awaiting extradition proceedings to answer a prosecutor's questions in Sweden. He hasn't been formally charged with any crime. His lawyers have heard that a grand jury in the United States has been secretly empaneled, and that a U.S. federal indictment is most likely forthcoming.

Politicians and commentators, meanwhile, have been repeatedly calling for Assange to be killed.

Take Democratic strategist and commentator Bob Beckel, who said on a Fox Business show: "We've got special ops forces. A dead man can't leak stuff.... This guy's a traitor, he's treasonous, and he has broken every law of the United States. And I'm not for the death penalty, so ... there's only one way to do it: illegally shoot the son of a bitch." U.S. Rep. Peter King, R-N.Y., called WikiLeaks a "foreign terrorist organization" and said that the website "posed a clear and present danger to the national security of the United States." He went on: "This is worse even than a physical attack on Americans; it's worse than a military attack."

One of Assange's lawyers in London, Jennifer Robinson, told me, in response to the flood of threats: "Obviously we take these sorts of very public pronouncements incredibly seriously. And people making these statements ought to be reported to the police for incitement to violence."

One of Beckel's co-panelists on Fox said what needed to be done was to "cut the head off the snake," a phrase which, ironically, gained more significance when it appeared days later in one of the leaked cables. In the cable, Saudi Ambassador to the U.S. Adel al-Jubeir "recalled the King's frequent exhortations to the U.S. to attack Iran and so put an end to its nuclear weapons program. 'He told you to cut off the head of the snake.'"

Assange has found support in some surprising quarters. Conservative Harvard Law professor Jack Goldsmith blogged: "I find myself agreeing with those who think Assange is being unduly vilified ... it is not obvious what law he has violated.... I do not understand why so much ire is directed at Assange and so little at the *New York Times*." (WikiLeaks has partnered with several news organizations, including the *New York Times*, in its document releases.)

Col. Lawrence Wilkerson, the former chief of staff of Secretary of State Colin Powell, joined a group of former government officials in a letter of support for Assange, writing, "WikiLeaks has teased the genie of transparency out of a very opaque bottle, and powerful forces in America, who thrive on secrecy, are trying desperately to stuff the genie back in."

Likewise from a feminist group in Britain. Since the principal, public reason for Assange's arrest relates to questions about potential sexual crimes in Sweden, Katrin Axelsson, from the group Women Against Rape, wrote in a letter to the British newspaper the *Guardian*: "Many women in both Sweden and Britain will wonder at the unusual zeal with which Julian Assange is being pursued for rape allegations. . . . Women don't take kindly to our demand for safety being misused, while rape continues to be neglected at best or protected at worst."

Assange, in an op-ed piece published in *The Australian* newspaper shortly after his arrest, wrote there is a chorus in the U.S. State Department of 'You'll risk lives! National Security! You'll endanger troops!' by releasing information, and then they say there is nothing of importance in what WikiLeaks publishes. It can't be both."

In a statement released to Australian television, Assange said: "My convictions are unfaltering. I remain true to the ideals I have expressed. . . . If anything, this process has increased my determination that they are true and correct."

Extradition proceedings are complex, lengthy affairs. WikiLeaks, for that matter, is not just Julian Assange, but a geographically distributed network of people and servers, and it has promised that the work of facilitating the release of documents from governments and corporations will continue. The U.S. Justice Department, if it pursues a case, will have to answer the question: If WikiLeaks is a criminal organization, what of its media partners, like the *New York Times*?

December 22, 2010

President Obama's Christmas Gift to AT&T (and Comcast and Verizon)

One of President Barack Obama's signature campaign promises was to protect the freedom of the Internet. He said, in November 2007, "I will take a back seat to no one in my commitment to network neutrality, because once providers start to privilege some applications or websites over others, then the smaller voices get squeezed out and we all lose."

Jump ahead to December 2010, where Obama is clearly in the back seat, being driven by Internet giants like AT&T, Verizon, and Comcast. With him is his appointed chairman of the Federal Communications Commission, Julius Genachowski, his Harvard Law School classmate and basketball pal who just pushed through a rule on network neutrality that Internet activists consider disastrous.

Free Press managing director Craig Aaron told me, "This proposal appears to be riddled with loopholes that would open the door to all kinds of future abuses, allowing companies like AT&T, Comcast, Verizon, the big Internet service providers, to decide which websites are going to work, which aren't, and which are going to be able to get special treatment."

For comedian-turned-senator Al Franken, D-Minn., the new rules on Net neutrality are no joke. He offered this example, writing:

> Verizon could prevent you from accessing Google Maps on your phone, forcing you to use their own mapping program, Verizon Navigator, even if it costs money to use and isn't nearly as good. Or a mobile provider with a political agenda could prevent you from downloading an app that connects you with the Obama campaign (or, for that matter, a Tea Party group in your area).

AT&T is one of the conglomerates that activists say practically wrote the FCC rules that Genachowski pushed through. We've seen this flip-flop before. Weeks before his 2007 Net neutrality pledge, then Sen. Obama took on AT&T, which was exposed for engaging in warrantless wiretapping of U.S. citizens at the request of the Bush administration. AT&T wanted retroactive immunity from prosecution. Obama campaign spokesman Bill Burton told *Talking Points Memo*: "To be clear: Barack will support a filibuster of any bill that includes retroactive immunity for telecommunications companies."

But by July 2008, a month before the Democratic National Convention, with Obama the presumptive presidential nominee, he not only didn't filibuster, but voted for a bill that granted telecoms retroactive immunity from prosecution. AT&T had gotten its way, and showed its appreciation quickly. The official tote bag issued to every DNC delegate was emblazoned with a large AT&T logo. AT&T threw an opening-night bash for delegates that was closed to the press, celebrating the Democratic Party for its get-out-of-jail-free card.

AT&T, Verizon, cable giant Comcast, and other corporations have expressed support for the new FCC rule. Genachowski's Democratic Party allies on the commission, Michael Copps and Mignon Clyburn (the daughter of House Majority Whip James Clyburn), according to Aaron, "tried to improve these rules, but the chairman refused to budge, apparently because he had already reached an agreement with AT&T and the cable lobbyists about how far these rules were going to go." Clyburn noted that the rules could allow mobile Internet providers to discriminate, and that poor communities, particularly African-American and Latino, rely on mobile Internet services more than wired connections.

Aaron laments the power of the telecom and cable industry lobbyists in Washington, D.C.: "In recent years, they've deployed 500 lobbyists, basically one for every member of Congress, and that's just what they report. AT&T is the biggest campaign giver in the history of campaign giving, as long as we have been tracking it. So they have really entrenched themselves. And Comcast, Verizon, the other big companies, are not far behind."

Aaron added: "When AT&T wants to get together all of their lobbyists, there's no room big enough. They had to rent out a movie theater. People from the public interest who are fighting for the free and open Internet here in D.C. can still share a cab."

Campaign money is now more than ever the lifeblood of U.S. politicians, and you can be sure that Obama and his advisers are looking to the 2012 election, which will likely be the costliest in U.S. history. Vigorous and innovative use of the Internet and mobile technologies is credited with helping Obama secure his victory in 2008. As the open Internet becomes increasingly stifled in the U.S., and the corporations that control the Internet become more powerful, we may not see such democratic participation for much longer.

- -

May 11, 2011

Tony Kushner and the Angels of Dissent

Tony Kushner will be receiving an honorary degree from John Jay College of criminal justice in New York City. This shouldn't be big news. Kushner is a renowned playwright who won the Pulitzer Prize for drama, along with an Emmy award and two Tonys. The degree became big news when it was abruptly shelved by the City University of New York board of trustees during its May 2 meeting, after a trustee accused Kushner of being anti-Israel.

A campaign grew almost immediately, first calling on previous recipients of honorary degrees from CUNY colleges (of which John Jay College is one) to return them. Within days, what would have been a quickly forgotten bestowal of an honorary degree erupted into an international scandal. The chair of the board, Benno Schmidt, former president of Yale University, convened an emergency executive session of the board, which voted unanimously to restore the honor to Kushner.

The controversy exposed the extreme polarity that increasingly defines the Israel/Palestine conflict, and the willingness by some to suppress free speech and vigorous dialogue to further rigid, political dogma. The trustee who attacked Kushner, Jeffrey Wiesenfeld, began his tirade at the original board meeting with an attack on Mary Robinson, who was formerly both the president of Ireland and the United Nations high commissioner for human rights. He then went on: "There is a lot of disingenuous and nonintellectual activity directed against the state of Israel on campuses throughout the country, the west generally, and oftentimes the United States, as well."

He presented several quotes that he attributed to Kushner to make his case, ending with, "I don't want to bore you all with the details."

Tony Kushner told me: "[W]hat he's doing is sparing them not boring details, but the full extent of the things that I've said about the state of Israel that would in fact make it clear to the board that I am in no way an enemy of the state of Israel, that I am, in fact, a vocal and ardent supporter of the state of Israel, but I don't believe that criticism of state policy means that one seeks the destruction of a state. I've been very critical of the policies of my own government."

First, a little history on Kushner's work. He won the Pulitzer for his play *Angels in America*. The play is subtitled *A Gay Fantasia on National Themes*, and addresses the HIV/AIDS epidemic and the struggle that many gay and lesbian people endure in the United States. A key character in the play is a fictionalized version of Roy Cohn, a prominent attorney, who, early in his career, was a key adviser to Sen. Joseph McCarthy. Cohn helped McCarthy with his fanatical pursuit of suspected communists in the U.S. government and beyond. He was considered a lifelong closeted gay man, despite the fact that he helped target people for political persecution for being gay. Cohn died in 1986 of complications due to AIDS, although he publicly described his illness as liver cancer. Thus, in a dramatic, real-life turn of events, Kushner, who has written extensively on the witchhunts of the McCarthy era, has now become the object of such a witch hunt himself.

The CUNY Board of Trustees' version of Roy Cohn here is Wiesenfeld, appointed by a former Republican governor of New York, George Pataki.

I interviewed Tony Kushner soon after he got word that his honorary degree had been restored. He said U.S. policy toward the Middle East "based on rightwing fantasies and theocratic fantasies and scripture-based fantasies of what history and on-the-ground reality is telling us, is catastrophic and is going to lead to the destruction of the state of Israel." He went on: "These people are not defending it. They're not supporting it. They're, in fact, causing a distortion of U.S. policy regarding Israel and a distortion of the internal politics of Israel itself, because they exert a tremendous influence in Israel and support rightwing politicians who, I think, have led the country into a very dark and dangerous place."

During the McCarthy era, the U.S. was a dark and dangerous place as well. Now, amid the uprisings in the Arab and Muslim world, the recent rapprochement between Fatah and Hamas, and the likely recognition of Palestinian statehood by the United Nations general assembly, there is no more urgent time for vigorous and informed debate.

The future of peace in the Middle East depends on dissent. Those, like Tony Kushner, with the courage to speak out are the true angels in America.

• •

May 18, 2011

Andrew Breitbart's "Electronic Brownshirts"

Judy Ancel, a Kansas City, Missouri, professor, and her St. Louis colleague were teaching a labor history class together this spring semester. Little did they know, video recordings of the class were making their way into the thriving sub rosa world of rightwing attack video editing, twisting their words in a way that resulted in the loss of one of the professors' jobs amid a wave of intimidation and death threats. Fortunately, reason and solid facts prevailed, and the videos ultimately were exposed for what they are: fraudulent, deceptive, sloppily edited hit pieces.

Rightwing media personality Andrew Breitbart is the forceful advocate of the slew of deceptively edited videos that target and smear progressive individuals and institutions. He promoted the videos that purported to catch employees of the community organization ACORN assisting a couple in setting up a prostitution ring. He showcased the edited video of Shirley Sherrod, an African-American employee of the U.S. Department of Agriculture, which completely convoluted her speech, making her appear to admit to discriminating against a white farmer. She was fired as a result of the cooked-up controversy. Similar video attacks have been waged against Planned Parenthood.

Judy Ancel has been the director of the University of Missouri–Kansas City's institute for labor studies since 1988. Using a live video link, she co-teaches a course on the history of the labor movement with Professor Don Giljum, who teaches at University of Missouri–St. Louis. The course comprises seven day-long, interactive sessions throughout the semester. They are video-recorded and made available through a password-protected system to students registered in the class.

One of those students, Philip Christofanelli, copied the videos and, he admits on one of Breitbart's sites, that he did "give them out in their entirety to a number of my friends." At some point, a series of highly and very deceptively edited renditions of the classes appeared on Breitbart's website. It was then that Ancel's and Giljum's lives were disrupted, and the death threats started. A post on Breitbart's BigGovernment.com summarized the video: "The professors not only advocate the occasional need for violence and industrial sabotage, they outline specific tactics that can be used."

Ancel told me, "I was just appalled, because I knew it was me speaking, but it wasn't saying what I had said in class." She related the attack against her and Giljum to the broader attack on progressive institutions currently: "These kinds of attacks are the equivalent of electronic brownshirts. They create so much fear, and they are so directed against anything that is progressive—the right to an education, the rights of unions, the rights of working people—I see, are all part of an overall attack to silence the majority of people and create the kind of climate of fear that allows for us to move very, very sharply to the right. And it's very frightening."

Ancel's contact information was included in the attack video, as was Giljum's. She received a flurry of threatening emails. Giljum received at least two death threats over the phone. The University of Missouri conducted an investigation into the charges prompted by the videos, during which time they posted uniformed and plainclothes police in the classrooms. Giljum is an adjunct professor, with a full-time job working as the business manager for Operating Engineers Local 148, a union in St. Louis. Meanwhile, the union acceded to pressure from the Missouri AFL-CIO, and asked Giljum to resign, just days before his May 1 retirement, after working there for twenty-seven years.

Gail Hackett, provost of the University of Missouri–Kansas City, released a statement after the investigation, clearing the two professors of any wrongdoing: "It is clear that edited videos posted on the internet depict statements from the instructors in an inaccurate and distorted manner by taking their statements out of context and reordering the sequence in which those statements were actually made so as to change their meaning."

The University of Missouri–St. Louis also weighed in with similar findings, and stated that Giljum was still eligible to teach there.

On April 18, Andrew Breitbart appeared on Sean Hannity's Fox News show, declaring, "We are going to take on education next, go after the teachers and the union organizers." It looks as if Ancel and Giljum were the first targets of that attack.

In this case, the attack failed. While ACORN was ultimately exonerated by a congressional investigation, the attack took its toll, and the organization lost its funding and collapsed. President Barack Obama and Agriculture Secretary Tom Vilsack apologized to Shirley Sherrod, and Vilsack begged her to return to work. Sherrod has a book coming out and a lawsuit pending against Breitbart.

Let's hope this is a sign that deception, intimidation, and the influence of the rightwing echo chamber are on the decline.

* *

July 6, 2011

WikiLeaks, Wimbledon, and War

Last Saturday was sunny in London, and the crowds were flocking to Wimbledon and to the annual Henley Regatta. Julian Assange, the founder of the whistle-blower website WikiLeaks.org, was making his way by train from house arrest in Norfolk, three hours away, to join me and Slovenian philosopher Slavoj Zizek for a public conversation about WikiLeaks, the power of information, and the importance of transparency in democracies. The event was hosted by the Frontline Club, an organization started by war correspondents in part to memorialize their many colleagues killed covering war. Frontline Club co-founder Vaughan Smith looked at the rare sunny sky fretfully, saying, "Londoners never come out to an indoor event on a day like this." Despite years of accurate reporting from Afghanistan to Kosovo, Smith was, in this case, completely wrong.

Close to 1,800 people showed up, evidence of the profound impact WikiLeaks has had, from exposing torture and corruption to toppling governments.

Assange is in England awaiting a July 12 extradition hearing, as he is wanted for questioning in Sweden related to allegations of sexual misconduct. He has not been charged. He has been under house arrest for more than six months, wears an electronic ankle bracelet, and is required to check in daily at the Norfolk police station.

WikiLeaks was officially launched in 2007 in order to receive leaked information from whistle-blowers, using the latest technology to protect the anonymity of the sources. The organization has increasingly gained global recognition with the successive publication of massive troves of classified documents from the U.S. government relating to the wars in Iraq and Afghanistan, and thousands of cables from the U.S. embassies around the world.

Of the logs from the two wars, Assange said that they "provided a picture of the everyday squalor of war. From children being killed at roadside blocks to over a thousand people being handed over to the Iraqi police for torture, to the reality of close air support and how modern military combat is done . . . men surrendering, being attacked."

The State Department cables are being released over time, creating a steady stream of embarrassment for the U.S. government and inspiring outrage and protests globally, as the classified cables reveal the secret, cynical operations behind U.S. diplomacy. "Cablegate," as the largest State Department document release in U.S. history has been dubbed, has been one of the sparks of the Arab Spring. People living under repressive regimes in Tunisia and Yemen, for example, knew their governments were corrupt and brutal. But to read the details, and see the extent of U.S. government support for these dictators, helped ignite a firestorm.

Likewise, thousands of Haiti-related cables analyzed by independent newspaper *Haïti Liberté* and the *Nation* magazine revealed extensive U.S. manipulation of the politics and the economy of that country. (This column was mentioned in one of the Haiti cables, referencing our reporting on those critical of the Obama administration's post-earthquake denial of visas to 70,000 Haitians who had already been approved.) One series of cables details U.S. efforts to derail delivery of subsidized petroleum from Venezuela in order to protect the business interests of Chevron and ExxonMobil. Other cables show U.S. pressure to prevent an increase in Haiti's minimum wage at the behest of U.S. apparel companies. This, in the poorest country in the Western Hemisphere.

For his role as editor in chief of WikiLeaks, Assange has faced numerous threats, including calls for his assassination. U.S. Vice President Joe Biden called him a "high-tech terrorist," while Newt Gingrich said: "Julian Assange is engaged in terrorism. . . . He should be treated as an enemy combatant, and WikiLeaks should be closed down permanently and decisively."

Indeed, efforts to shut down WikiLeaks to date have failed. Bank of America has reportedly hired several private intelligence firms to coordinate an attack on the organization, which is said to hold a large cache of documents revealing the bank's potentially fraudulent activities. WikiLeaks has also just sued MasterCard and Visa, which have stopped processing credit-card donations to the website.

The extradition proceedings hold a deeper threat to Assange: He fears Sweden could then extradite him to the U.S. Given the treatment of Pvt. Bradley Manning, accused of leaking many of the documents to WikiLeaks, he has good reason to be afraid. Manning has been kept in solitary confinement for close to a year, under conditions many say are tantamount to torture.

At the London event, support for WikiLeaks ran high. Afterward, Julian Assange couldn't linger to talk. He had just enough time to get back to Norfolk to continue his house arrest. No matter what happens to Assange, WikiLeaks has changed the world forever.

• •

August 17, 2011

San Francisco Bay Area's BART Pulls a Mubarak

What does the police killing of a homeless man in San Francisco have to do with the Arab Spring uprisings from Tunisia to Syria? The attempt to suppress the protests that followed. In our digitally networked world, the ability to communicate is increasingly viewed as a basic right. Open communication fuels revolutions—it can take down dictators. When governments fear the power of their people, they repress, intimidate, and try to silence them, whether in Tahrir Square or downtown San Francisco.

Charles Blair Hill was shot and killed on the platform of the Bay Area Rapid Transit (BART) system's Civic Center platform on July 3, by BART police officer

James Crowell. BART police reportedly responded to calls about a man drinking on the underground subway platform. According to police, Hill threw a vodka bottle at the two officers and then threatened them with a knife, at which point Crowell shot him. Hill was pronounced dead at the hospital.

Hill's killing sparked immediate and vigorous protests against the BART police, similar to those that followed the BART police killing of Oscar Grant on New Year's Day 2009. Grant was handcuffed, facedown on a subway platform, and restrained by one officer when another shot and killed him with a point-blank shot to the back. The execution was caught on at least two cell phone videos. The shooter, BART officer Johannes Mehserle, served just over seven months in jail for the killing.

On July 11, major protests shut down the Civic Center BART station. As another planned protest neared on August 11, BART officials took a measure unprecedented in U.S. history: They shut down cell phone towers in the subway system.

"It's the first known incident that we've heard of where the government has shut down a cell phone network in order to prevent people from engaging in political protest," Catherine Crump of the ACLU told me. "Cellphone networks are something we've all come to rely on. People use them for all sorts of communication that have nothing to do with protest. And this is really a sweeping and overbroad reaction by the police."

The cellular-service shutdown, which was defended by BART authorities who claimed it was done to protect public safety, immediately drew fire from free-speech activists around the globe. On Twitter, those opposed to BART's censorship started using the hashtag #muBARTak to make the link to Egypt.

When the embattled Egyptian dictator Hosni Mubarak shut down cell service and the Internet, those in Tahrir Square innovated workarounds to get the word out. An activist group called Telecomix, a volunteer organization that supports free speech and an open Internet, organized 300 dial-up phone accounts that allowed Egyptian activists and journalists to access the Internet to post tweets, photos, and videos of the revolution in progress.

"We were very active—Tunisia, Egypt, Libya, Syria—trying to keep the Internet running in these countries in the face of really almost overwhelming efforts by governments to shut them down," Telecomix activist Peter Fein told me. "Telecomix believes that the best way to support free speech and free communication is by building, by building tools that we can use to provide ourselves with those rights, rather than relying on governments to respect them."

Expect hacktivist groups to support revolutions abroad, but also to assist protest movements here at home. In retaliation for BART's cell phone shutdown, a decentralized hacker collective called Anonymous shut down BART's website. In a controversial move, Anonymous also released the information of more than 2,000 BART passengers, to expose the shoddy computer security standards maintained by BART.

The BART police say the FBI is investigating Anonymous' attack. I interviewed an Anonymous member who calls himself "Commander X" on the *Democracy Now!* news hour. His voice disguised to protect his anonymity, he told me over the phone: "We're filled with indignation, when a little organization like BART … kills innocent people, two or three of them in the last few years, and then has the nerve to also cut off the cell phone service and act exactly like a dictator in the Mideast. How dare they do this in the United States of America."

• •

March 1, 2012

WikiLeaks vs. Stratfor: Pursue the Truth, Not Its Messenger

WikiLeaks, the whistle-blower website, has again published a massive trove of documents, this time from a private intelligence firm known as Stratfor. The source of the leak was the hacker group "Anonymous," which took credit for obtaining more than 5 million emails from Stratfor's servers. Anonymous obtained the material on December 24, 2011, and provided it to WikiLeaks, which in turn partnered with twenty-five media organizations globally to analyze the emails and publish them.

Among the emails was a short one-liner that suggested the U.S. government has produced, through a secret grand jury, a sealed indictment against WikiLeaks founder Julian Assange. In addition to painting a picture of Stratfor as a runaway, rogue private intelligence firm with close ties to government-intelligence agencies serving both corporate and U.S. military clients, the emails support the growing awareness that the Obama administration, far from diverging from the secrecy of the Bush/Cheney era, is obsessed with secrecy, and is aggressively opposed to transparency.

I traveled to London last Independence Day weekend to interview Assange. When I asked him about the grand-jury investigation, he responded: "There is no judge, there is no defense counsel, and there are four prosecutors. So, that is why people that are familiar with grand-jury inquiries in the United States say that a grand jury would not only indict a ham sandwich, it would indict the ham and the sandwich."

As I left London, the *Guardian* newspaper exposed more of Rupert Murdoch's News Corp. phone-hacking scandal, which prompted the closing of his tabloid newspaper, the largest circulation Sunday newspaper in the U.K., *News of the World.* The coincidence is relevant, as *News of the World* reported anything but what its title claimed, focusing instead on salacious details of the private lives of celebrities, sensational crimes, and photos of scantily clad women. For this and his other endeavors, Murdoch amassed a reported personal fortune of $7.6 billion.

Meanwhile, Assange—who, like Murdoch, was born in Australia (Murdoch abandoned his nationality for U.S. citizenship in order to purchase more U.S. broadcast licenses)—had engaged in one of largest and most courageous acts of publishing in history by founding WikiLeaks.org, which allows people to safely and securely deliver documents using the Internet in ways that make it almost impossible to trace. He and his colleagues at WikiLeaks had published millions of leaked documents, most notably about the U.S. wars and occupations in Iraq and Afghanistan, and thousands of U.S. diplomatic cables, true "news of the world." The Sydney Peace Foundation awarded Assange a gold medal for "exceptional courage and initiative in pursuit of human rights." In contrast, the U.S. government targeted him, possibly under the Espionage Act. Murdoch is hailed as a pioneering newsman, while pundits on Murdoch-owned cable-television outlets openly call for Assange's murder.

The Stratfor emails will be released over time, along with context provided by WikiLeaks' media partners. Already revealed by the documents are the close, and potentially illegal, connections between Stratfor employees and government-intelligence and law-enforcement officials. *Rolling Stone* magazine reports that the U.S. Department of Homeland Security was monitoring Occupy Wall Street protests nationally, and the Texas Department of Public Safety has an undercover agent at Occupy Austin who was disclosing information to contacts at Stratfor. Stratfor also is hired by multinational corporations to glean "intelligence" about critics. Among companies using Stratfor were Dow Chemical, Lockheed Martin, Northrop Grumman, Raytheon, and Coca-Cola.

Fred Burton, Stratfor's vice president of intelligence, and a former head of counterintelligence at the U.S. State Department's diplomatic corps, wrote in an email, "Not for Pub—We have a sealed indictment on Assange. Pls protect." Burton and others at Stratfor showed intense interest in WikiLeaks starting in 2010, showing intense dislike for Assange personally. Burton wrote: "Assange is going to make a nice bride in prison. Screw the terrorist. He'll be eating cat food forever." Another Stratfor employee wanted Assange waterboarded.

Michael Ratner, legal adviser to Assange and WikiLeaks, told me, "The Obama administration has gone after six people under the Espionage Act. That's more cases than happened since the Espionage Act was actually begun in 1917.... What this is about is the United States wanting to suppress the truth."

1917 is also the year when U.S. Sen. Hiram Johnson famously said, "The first casualty when war comes is truth." The White House is holding a gala dinner this week, honoring Iraq War veterans. Bradley Manning is an Iraq War vet who won't be there. He is being court-martialed, facing life in prison or possibly death, for allegedly releasing thousands of military and diplomatic documents to WikiLeaks revealing the casualties of war. President Barack Obama would better serve the country by also honoring Assange and Manning.

We should pursue the truth, not its messengers.

July 29, 2009

Obama's Military Is Spying on U.S. Peace Groups

Anti-war activists in Olympia, Washington, have exposed Army spying and infiltration of their groups, as well as intelligence gathering by the Air Force, the federal Capitol Police, and the Coast Guard.

The infiltration appears to be in direct violation of the Posse Comitatus Act preventing U.S. military deployment for domestic law enforcement and may strengthen congressional demands for a full-scale investigation of U.S. intelligence activities, like the Church Committee hearings of the 1970s.

Brendan Maslauskas Dunn asked the city of Olympia for documents or emails about communications between the Olympia police and the military relating to anarchists, Students for a Democratic Society (SDS), or the Industrial Workers of the World (Dunn's union). Dunn received hundreds of documents. One email contained reference to a "John J. Towery II," who activists discovered was the same person as their fellow activist "John Jacob."

Dunn told me: "John Jacob was actually a close friend of mine, so this week has been pretty difficult for me. He said he was an anarchist. He was really interested in SDS. He got involved with Port Militarization Resistance (PMR), with Iraq Vets Against the War. He was a kind person. He was a generous person. So it was really just a shock for me."

"Jacob" told the activists he was a civilian employed at Fort Lewis Army Base and would share information about base activities that could help the PMR organize rallies and protests against public ports being used for troop and Stryker military vehicle deployment to Iraq and Afghanistan. Since 2006, PMR activists have occasionally engaged in civil disobedience, blocking access to the port.

Larry Hildes, an attorney representing Washington activists, says the U.S. attorney prosecuting the cases against them, Brian Kipnis, specifically instructed the Army not to hand over any information about its intelligence-gathering activities, despite a court order to do so.

Which is why Dunn's request to Olympia and the documents he obtained are so important.

The military is supposed to be barred from deploying on U.S. soil, or from spying on citizens. Christopher Pyle, now a professor of politics at Mount Holyoke College, was a military intelligence officer. He recalled: "In the 1960s, Army intelligence had 1,500 plainclothes agents [and some would watch] every demonstration of 20 people or more. They had a giant warehouse in Baltimore full of information on the law-abiding activities of American citizens, mainly protest politics." Pyle later investigated the spying for two congressional committees: "As a result of those investigations, the entire U.S. Army Intelligence Command was abolished, and all of its files were burned. Then the Senate Intelligence Committee wrote the Foreign Intelligence Surveillance Act of 1978 to stop the warrantless surveillance of electronic communications."

Reps. Barbara Lee, D-Calif., Rush Holt, D-N.J., and others are pushing for a new, comprehensive investigation of all U.S. intelligence activities, of the scale of the Church Committee hearings, which exposed widespread spying on and disruption of legal domestic groups, attempts at assassination of foreign heads of state, and more.

Demands mount for information on and accountability for Vice President Dick Cheney's alleged secret assassination squad, President George W. Bush's warrantless wiretapping program, and the CIA's alleged misleading of Congress. But the spying in Olympia occurred well into the Obama administration (and may continue today). President Barack Obama supports retroactive immunity for telecom companies involved in the wiretapping, and has maintained Bush-era reliance on the state secrets privilege. Lee and Holt should take the information uncovered by Brendan Dunn and the Olympia activists and get the investigations started now.

April 26, 2012

The NSA Is Watching You

Three targeted Americans: a career government intelligence official, a film-maker, and a hacker. None of these U.S. citizens was charged with a crime, but they have been tracked, surveilled, detained—sometimes at gunpoint—and interrogated, with no access to a lawyer. Each remains resolute in standing up to the increasing government crackdown on dissent.

The intelligence official: William Binney worked for almost forty years at the secretive National Security Agency (NSA), the U.S. spy agency that dwarfs the CIA. As technical director of the NSA's World Geopolitical and Military Analysis Reporting Group, Binney told me, he was tasked to "see how we could solve collection, analysis and reporting on military and geopolitical issues all around the world, every country in the world." Throughout the 1990s, the NSA developed a massive eavesdropping system code-named ThinThread, which, Binney says, maintained crucial protections on the privacy of U.S. citizens demanded by the U.S. Constitution. He recalled, "After 9/11, all the wraps came off for NSA," as massive domestic spying became the norm. He resigned on October 31, 2001.

Along with several other NSA officials, Binney reported his concerns to Congress and to the Department of Defense. Then, in 2007, as then Attorney General Alberto Gonzales was being questioned on Capitol Hill about the very domestic spying to which Binney objected, a dozen FBI agents charged into his house, guns drawn. They forced aside his son and found Binney, a diabetic amputee, in the shower. They pointed their guns at his head, then led him to his back porch and interrogated him.

Three others were raided that morning. Binney called the FBI raid "retribution and intimidation so we didn't go to the Judiciary Committee in the Senate and tell them, 'Well, here's what Gonzales didn't tell you, OK.'" Binney was never charged with any crime.

The filmmaker: Laura Poitras is an Academy Award–nominated documentary filmmaker, whose recent films include *My Country, My Country*, about the U.S. occupation of Iraq, and *The Oath*, which was filmed in Yemen. Since 2006, Poitras has been detained and questioned at airports at least forty times. She has had her computer and reporter's notebooks confiscated and presumably copied, without a warrant. The most recent time, April 5, she took notes during her detention. The agents told her to stop, as they considered her pen a weapon.

She told me: "I feel like I can't talk about the work that I do in my home, in my place of work, on my telephone, and sometimes in my country. So the chilling effect is huge. It's enormous."

The hacker: Jacob Appelbaum works as a computer security researcher for the nonprofit organization the Tor Project (torproject.org), which is a free software package that allows people to browse the Internet anonymously, evading government surveillance. Tor was actually created by the U.S. Navy, and is now developed and maintained by Appelbaum and his colleagues. Tor is used by dissidents around the world to communicate over the Internet. Tor also serves as the main way that the controversial WikiLeaks website protects those who release documents to it. Appelbaum has volunteered for WikiLeaks, leading to intense U.S. government surveillance.

Appelbaum spoke in place of Julian Assange, the WikiLeaks founder, at a conference called Hackers on Planet Earth, or HOPE, as people feared Assange would be arrested. He started his talk by saying: "Hello to all my friends and fans in domestic and international surveillance. I'm here today because I believe that we can make a better world." He has been detained at least a dozen times at airports. "I was put into a special room, where they frisked me, put me up against the wall.... Another one held my wrists.... They implied that if I didn't make a deal with them, that I'd be sexually assaulted in prison.... They took my cellphones, they took my laptop. They wanted, essentially, to ask me questions about the Iraq War, the Afghan War, what I thought politically."

I asked Binney if he believed the NSA has copies of every email sent in the U.S. He replied, "I believe they have most of them, yes."

Binney said two senators, Ron Wyden and Mark Udall, have expressed concern, but have not spoken out, as, Binney says, they would lose their seats on the Senate Select Committee on Intelligence. Meanwhile, Congress is set to vote on the Cyber Intelligence Sharing and Protection Act, or CISPA. Proponents of Internet freedom are fighting the bill, which they say will legalize what the NSA is secretly doing already.

Members of Congress, fond of quoting the country's founders, should recall these words of Benjamin Franklin before voting on CISPA: "They who can give up essential liberty to obtain a little temporary safety, deserve neither liberty nor safety."

UPRISINGS:
FROM THE ARAB SPRING
TO OCCUPY WALL STREET

July 12, 2012

The Pain in Spain Falls Mainly on the Plain (Folk)

As Spain's prime minister announced deep austerity cuts Wednesday in order to secure funds from the European Union to bail out Spain's failing banks, the people of Spain have taken to the streets once again for what they call "Real Democracy Now." This comes a week after the government announced it was launching a criminal investigation into the former CEO of Spain's fourth-largest bank, Bankia. Rodrigo Rato is no small fish: Before running Bankia he was head of the International Monetary Fund. What the U.S. media don't tell you is that this official government investigation was initiated by grassroots action.

The Occupy movement in Spain is called M-15, for the day it began, May 15, 2011. I met with one of the key organizers in Madrid last week on the day the Rato investigation was announced. He smiled, and said, "Something is starting to happen." The organizer, Stéphane Grueso, is an activist filmmaker who is making a documentary about the May 15 movement. He is a talented professional, but, like 25 percent of the Spanish population, he is unemployed:

> We didn't like what we were seeing, where we were going. We felt we were losing our democracy, we were losing our country, we were losing our way of life. . . . We had one slogan: *"Democracia real YA!"*—we want a "real democracy, now!" Fifty people stayed overnight in Puerta del Sol, this public square. And then the police tried to take us out, and so we came back. And then this thing began to multiply in other cities in Spain. In three, four days' time, we were like tens of thousands of people in dozens of cities in Spain, camped in the middle of the city—a little bit like we saw in Tahrir in Egypt.

The occupation of Puerta del Sol and other plazas around Spain continued, but, as with Occupy Wall Street encampments around the U.S., they were eventually broken up. The organizing continued, though, with issue-oriented working groups and neighborhood assemblies. One M-15 working group decided to sue Rodrigo Rato, and recruited pro bono lawyers and identified more than fifty plaintiffs, people who felt they'd been personally defrauded by Bankia. While the lawyers were volunteers, a massive lawsuit costs money, so this movement, driven by social media, turned to "crowd funding," to the masses of supporters in their movement for small donations. In less than a day, they raised more than $25,000. The lawsuit was filed in June of this year.

Olmo Gálvez is another M-15 organizer I met with in Madrid. A young businessman with experience around the world, Gálvez was profiled in *Time* magazine when they chose "The Protester" as the Person of the Year. Rato's alleged fraud at Bankia involved the sale of Bankia "preferred stock" to regular account holders, so-called retail investors, since sophisticated investors were not buying it. Gálvez explained: "They were selling it to people—some of them couldn't read, many were elderly. That was a big scandal that wasn't in the media." Some who invested in Bankia's scheme had to sign the contract with a fingerprint because they couldn't write, nor could they read about, let alone understand, what they were sinking their savings into.

This week, thousands of coal miners marched to Madrid, some walking 240 miles from Asturias, on Spain's northern coast. When the miners arrived in Madrid Tuesday night, according to the online publication ElDiario.es, they chanted *"somos el 99 percent"* ("we are the 99 percent") and were greeted like heroes. Wednesday morning, Prime Minister Mariano Rajoy, of the right-wing Partido Popular, made his latest pronouncement on austerity measures: an increase in the sales tax, cuts to the public-sector payroll, and shortening the period of unemployment support to six months.

As Rajoy was making his announcement in parliament, the miners were in the streets, joined by thousands of regular citizens, all demanding that government cuts be halted. The marchers were met by riot police, who fired rubber-coated steel balls and tear gas at them. Some protesters returned with volleys of firecrackers and other projectiles, and, in the ensuing melee, at least seventy-six were injured and eight arrested.

Stéphane Grueso sums up the movement: "We are not a party. We are not a union. We are not an association. We are people. We want to expel corruption from public life ... now, today, maybe it is starting to happen."

June 23, 2010

Another World Is Possible, Another Detroit Is Happening

DETROIT—"I have a dream." Ask anyone where the Rev. Martin Luther King Jr. first proclaimed those words, and the response will most likely be at the March on Washington in August 1963. In fact, he delivered them two months earlier, on June 23, in Detroit, leading a march down Woodward Avenue. King said:

> I have a dream that one day, right down in Georgia and Mississippi and Alabama, the sons of former slaves and the sons of former slave owners will be able to live together as brothers....
>
> I have a dream this afternoon that my four little children ... will be judged on the basis of the content of their character, not the color of their skin.
>
> I have a dream this afternoon that one day right here in Detroit, Negroes will be able to buy a house or rent a house anywhere that their money will carry them and they will be able to get a job.

Forty-seven years later, thousands of people, of every hue, religion, class, and age, might not have used those words exactly, but they marched down that same avenue here in Detroit in the same spirit, opening the U.S. Social Forum. More than 10,000 citizens, activists, and organizers have come from around the world for four days of workshops, meetings, and marches to strengthen social movements and advance a progressive agenda. Far larger than any Tea Party convention, it has gotten very little mainstream-media coverage. Not a tightly scripted, staged political convention, or a multiday music festival, the U.S. Social Forum defines itself as "an open meeting place for reflective thinking, democratic debate of ideas, formulation of proposals, free exchange of experiences." It is appropriate that the U.S. Social Forum should be held here, in this city that has endured the collapse of the auto industry and the worst of the foreclosure crisis. In Detroit, one is surrounded, simultaneously, by stark failures of capitalism and by a populace building an alternative, just, and greener future.

Environmental writer Rebecca Solnit says of the decay of Detroit, "the continent has not seen a transformation like Detroit's since the last days of the

Maya." The core of modern Detroit, the automobile industry, helped facilitate the creation of suburbs that ultimately spelled doom for vibrant inner cities. Detroit, which had 2 million residents in the mid-1950s, now has dwindled to around 800,000. Poverty, joblessness, depopulation, and decay have created an almost post-apocalyptic scene here.

Carried within this dystopic, urban disaster, though, are the seeds of Detroit's potential rebirth. Legendary Detroit organizer/philosopher Grace Lee Boggs helped organize the 1963 King march in Detroit. She turns ninety-five this week, and will be celebrated here at the U.S. Social Forum. We visited her at her home, which might well become a Detroit historic site because of the many organizations that were born there. She has lived in that same house for more than half a century, much of that time with her husband, the late political activist and autoworker Jimmy Boggs. Smiling, she says, "It's really wonderful that the Social Forum decided to come to Detroit, because Detroit, which was once the symbol of miracles of industrialization and then became the symbol of the devastation of deindustrialization, is now the symbol of a new kind of society, of people who grow their own food, of people who try and help each other, to how we begin to think, not so much of getting jobs and advancing our own fortunes, but how we depend on each other. I mean, it's another world that we're creating here in Detroit."

She reflects on the two delegations of young people attending the USSF with whom she has already met: "I hope they understand from Detroit that all of us, each of us, can become a cultural creative.... We are creating a new culture. And we're not doing it because we are such wonderful people. We're doing it because we had to, not only to survive materially, but to survive as human beings."

From urban gardens to collective businesses to electric cars, Detroit is beginning to chart an alternative path. As the great Indian writer Arundhati Roy has said, "Another world is not only possible, she's on the way, and, on a quiet day, if you listen very carefully, you can hear her breathe."

February 9, 2011

Egypt's Youth Will Not Be Silenced

"In memoriam, Christoph Probst, Hans Scholl, Sophie Scholl" reads the banner at the top of Kareem Amer's popular Egyptian dissident blog. "Beheaded on Feb. 22, 1943, for daring to say no to Hitler, and yes to freedom and justice for all." The young blogger's banner recalls the courageous group of anti-Nazi pamphleteers who called themselves the White Rose Collective. They secretly produced and distributed six pamphlets denouncing Nazi atrocities, proclaiming, in one, "We will not be silent." Sophie and her brother Hans Scholl were captured by the Nazis, tried, convicted, and beheaded.

Kareem Amer, who spent four years in prison in Egypt for his blogging, has disappeared off the streets of Cairo after leaving Tahrir Square with a friend, according to CyberDissidents.org. The group assumes Amer is now among the hundreds of journalists and human rights activists snatched by the regime of Egyptian dictator Hosni Mubarak, and has launched a campaign to demand his release.

Amer disappeared just before Wael Ghonim was released. Ghonim is a thirty-year-old Google executive who helped administer a Facebook page instrumental to organizing the January 25 protests in Egypt. The page, called "We are all Khaled Said," is named in memory of a young man killed by police in Alexandria in June 2010. A photo of Khaled Said's corpse appeared on the Internet, his face savagely beaten. Ghonim traveled to Egypt to participate in the protests, and was arrested and secretly held by the Egyptian government for twelve days. He was interviewed on Egyptian TV channel Dream 2 upon his release. He broke down and cried on camera when shown the photos of many who had been killed so far in the protests. Ghonim said: "I'm not a hero. I was only using the keyboard, on the Internet. I never put my life in danger. The real heroes are the ones on the ground."

Ghonim's release swelled the crowds in Tahrir Square, still demanding an end to Mubarak's thirty-year regime. Tahrir, which means *liberation* in Arabic, is the heart and soul of the pro-democracy movement in Egypt, but it is not the only place where spirited, defiant people gather. As this is written, a new encampment is being established outside the Egyptian Parliament. Six thousand workers are reportedly striking at the Suez Canal. As the entrenched dictator-ship claimed to be making concessions, its shock troops unleashed a wave of vi-olence, intimidation, arrest, and murder.

Egypt's burgeoning youth population is driving the revolution. The April 6 Youth Movement was formed last year to support textile strikers in the Egyptian city of Mahalla. One of the founders of the movement, Asmaa Mahfouz, who has just turned twenty-six, posted a video to Facebook January 18, days after the Tunisian revolution forced the ouster of that country's dictator. She said:

> Four Egyptians have set themselves on fire to protest humiliation and hunger and poverty and degradation they had to live with for 30 years. Four Egyptians have set themselves on fire thinking maybe we can have a revolu-tion like Tunisia, maybe we can have freedom, justice, honor and human dig-nity.... I'm making this video to give you one simple message: We want to go down to Tahrir Square on January 25. If we still have honor and want to live in dignity on this land, we have to go down on January 25.

Her call to action was another spark. From the Internet, people began or-ganizing in the neighborhoods, bridging the digital divide with printed fliers and word of mouth. Following January 25, the epic first day of protest, she posted another video message: "What we learned yesterday is that power be-longs to the people, not to the thugs. Power is in unity, not in division. Yesterday, we truly lived the best moments of our lives."

The first week of protests breached what many are calling "the fear barrier." Since the government-backed violence of January 28, according to Human Rights Watch, at least 302 people have been killed in the cities of Cairo, Alexan-dria, and Suez.

President Barack Obama continues to insist that the U.S. can't choose the leader of Egypt, but that the people of Egypt must. That is true. But the Obama administration continues to supply the Mubarak regime with economic and military aid. The "Made in U.S.A." stamped on the tear gas canisters used against protesters in Tahrir Square enraged the people there. In the past thirty years, the U.S. has spent tens of billions of dollars to shore up the Mubarak regime. It is time to turn off the cash and weapons spigot now.

February 23, 2011

Uprisings:
From the Middle East to the Midwest

As many as 80,000 people marched to the Wisconsin state capitol in Madison on Saturday as part of an ongoing protest against newly elected Republican Gov. Scott Walker's attempt to not just badger the state's public employee unions, but to break them. The Madison uprising follows on the heels of those in the Middle East. A sign held by one university student, an Iraq War vet, read, "I went to Iraq and came home to Egypt?" Another read, "Walker: Mubarak of the Midwest." Likewise, a photo has circulated in Madison of a young man at a rally in Cairo, with a sign reading, "Egypt supports Wisconsin workers: One world, one pain." Meanwhile, Libyans continue to defy a violent government crackdown against masses seeking to oust longtime dictator Moammar Gaddafi, and more than 10,000 marched Tuesday in Ohio to oppose Republican Gov. John Kasich's attempted anti-union legislative putsch.

Just a few weeks ago, solidarity between Egyptian youth and Wisconsin police officers, or between Libyan workers and Ohio public employees, might have elicited a raised eyebrow.

The uprising in Tunisia was sparked by the suicide of a young man named Mohamed Bouazizi, a twenty-six-year-old university graduate who could not find professional work. Selling fruits and vegetables in the market, he was repeatedly harassed by Tunisian authorities who eventually confiscated his scale. Unbearably frustrated, he set himself on fire, a spark that ignited the protests that became the wave of revolution in the Middle East and North Africa. For decades in the region, people have lived under dictatorships—many that receive U.S. military aid—suffering human-rights abuses along with low income, high unemployment, and almost no freedom of speech. All this, while the elites amassed fortunes.

Similar grievances underlie the conflicts in Wisconsin and Ohio. The "Great Recession" of 2008, according to economist Dean Baker, is now in its thirty-seventh month, with no sign of relenting. In a recent paper, Baker says that, due to the financial crisis, "many political figures have argued the need to drastically reduce the generosity of public sector pensions, and possibly to default on pension obligations already incurred. Most of the pension shortfall . . .

is attributable to the plunge in the stock market in the years 2007–2009."

In other words, Wall Street hucksters, selling the complex mortgage-backed securities that provoked the collapse, are the ones who caused any pension shortfall. Pulitzer Prize–winning journalist David Cay Johnston said recently: "The average Wisconsin state employee gets $24,500 a year. That's not a very big pension . . . 15 percent of the money going into it each year is being paid out to Wall Street to manage the money. That's a really huge high percentage to pay out to Wall Street to manage the money."

So, while investment bankers skim a huge percentage off pension funds, it's the workers who are being demonized and asked to make the sacrifices. Those who caused the problem, who then got lavish bailouts and now are treated to huge salaries and bonuses, are not being held accountable. Following the money, it turns out Walker's campaign was funded by the notorious Koch brothers, major backers of the Tea Party organizations. They also gave $1 million to the Republican Governors Association, which gave substantial support to Walker's campaign. Is it surprising that Walker supports corporations with tax breaks, and has launched a massive attack on unionized, public-sector employees?

One of the unions being targeted by Walker, and by Kasich in Ohio, is AFSCME, the American Federation of State, County and Municipal Employees. The union was founded in 1932, in the midst of the Great Depression, in Madison. Its 1.6 million members are nurses, corrections officers, child-care providers, EMTs, and sanitation workers. It is instructive to remember, in this Black History Month, that it was the struggle of the sanitation workers of AFSCME local No. 1733 that brought Dr. Martin Luther King Jr. to Memphis, Tennessee, back in April 1968. As Jesse Jackson told me as he marched with students and their unionized teachers in Madison on Tuesday: "Dr. King's last act on earth, marching in Memphis, Tennessee, was about workers' rights to collective bargaining and rights to dues checkoff. You cannot remove the roof for the wealthy and remove the floor for the poor."

The workers of Egypt were instrumental in bringing down the regime there, in a remarkable coalition with Egypt's youth. In the streets of Madison, under the capitol dome, another demonstration of solidarity is taking place. Wisconsin's workers have agreed to pay and pension concessions, but will not give up their right to collective bargaining. At this point, Walker would be wise to negotiate. It is not a good season to be a tyrant.

April 13, 2011

Barack Obama Must Speak Out on Bahrain Bloodshed

Three days after Hosni Mubarak resigned as the longstanding dictator in Egypt, people in the small Gulf state of Bahrain took to the streets, marching to their version of Tahrir: Pearl Square, in the capital city of Manama. Bahrain has been ruled by the same family, the House of Khalifa, since the 1780s—more than 220 years. Bahrainis were not demanding an end to the monarchy, but for more representation in their government.

One month into the uprising, Saudi Arabia sent military and police forces over the sixteen-mile causeway that connects the Saudi mainland to Bahrain, an island. Since then, the protesters, the press, and human-rights organizations have suffered increasingly violent repression.

One courageous young Bahraini pro-democracy activist, Zainab al-Khawaja, has seen the brutality up close. To her horror, she watched her father, Abdulhadi al-Khawaja, a prominent human-rights activist, be beaten and arrested. She described it to me from Manama:

> Security forces attacked my home. They came in without prior warning. They broke down the building door, and they broke down our apartment door, and instantly attacked my father without giving him a chance to speak and without giving any reason for his arrest. They dragged my father down the stairs and started beating him in front of me. They beat him until he was unconscious. The last thing I heard my father say was that he couldn't breathe. When I tried to intervene, when I tried to tell them: "Please stop beating him. He will go with you voluntarily. You don't need to beat him this way," they told me to shut up, basically, and they grabbed me . . . and dragged me up the stairs back into the apartment. By the time I had got out of the room again, the only trace of my father was his blood on the stairs.

Human Rights Watch has called for the immediate release of al-Khawaja. Zainab's husband and brother-in-law have also been arrested. Tweeting as "angryarabiya" she has commenced a water-only fast in protest. She also has written a letter to President Barack Obama:

If anything happens to my father, my husband, my uncle, my brother-in-law, or to me, I hold you just as responsible as the Al-Khalifa regime. Your support for this monarchy makes your government a partner in crime. I still have hope that you will realize that freedom and human rights mean as much to a Bahraini person as it does to an American.

Obama condemned the Gaddafi government in his speech, justifying the recent military attacks in Libya, saying: "Innocent people were targeted for killing. Hospitals and ambulances were attacked. Journalists were arrested." Now that the same things are happening in Bahrain, Obama has little to say.

As with the uprisings in Egypt and Tunisia, the sentiment is nationalist, not religious. The country is 70 percent Shia, ruled by the Sunni minority. Nevertheless, a central rallying cry of the protests has been "Not Shia, Not Sunni: Bahraini." This debunks the argument used by the Bahraini government that the current regime is the best bulwark against increased influence of Iran, a Shia country, in the oil-rich Gulf. Add to that Bahrain's strategic role: it is where the U.S. navy's fifth fleet is based, tasked with protecting "U.S. interests" like the Strait of Hormuz and the Suez Canal, and supporting the wars in Iraq and Afghanistan. Surely, U.S. interests include supporting democracy over despots.

Nabeel Rajab is the president of the Bahrain Centre for Human Rights—the organization formerly run by the recently abducted Abdulhadi al-Khawaja. Rajab is facing a possible military trial for publishing the photograph of a protester who died in custody. Rajab told me: "Hundreds of people are in jail for practicing their freedom of expression. People are tortured for expressing their freedom of expression. Thousands of people sacked from their jobs . . . And all that, because one day, a month ago, almost half of the Bahraini population came out in the street demanding democracy and respect for human rights."

Rajab noted that democracy in Bahrain would lead to democracy in neighboring Gulf dictatorships, especially Saudi Arabia, so most regional governments have a stake in crushing the protests. Saudi Arabia is well positioned for the task, as the recent beneficiary of the largest arms deal in U.S. history. Despite the threats, Rajab was resolute: "As far as I'm breathing, as far as I'm alive, I am going to continue. I believe in change. I believe in democracy. I believe in human rights. I'm willing to give my life. I'm willing to give anything to achieve this goal."

June 9, 2010

The Gaza Freedom Flotilla: Framing the Narrative

They called it "Operation Sea Breeze." Despite the pleasant-sounding name, Israel's violent commando raid on a flotilla of humanitarian aid ships, which left nine civilians dead, has sparked international outrage. The raid occurred in the early-morning hours of May 31, as the six vessels laden with humanitarian aid were still in international waters, bound for Gaza, where 1.5 million Palestinian residents are in their third year of an Israeli-imposed blockade. Israel has, from the outset, sought to limit the debate over the attack, and to control the images.

Israeli military boats and helicopters raided the vessels and took control of the flotilla. Nine of the activists on board the largest vessel, the *Mavi Marmara*, were killed at close range by Israeli commandos firing live ammunition. Nineteen-year-old U.S. citizen Furkan Dogan was shot once in the chest and four times in the head. Israel commandeered the six vessels and arrested the roughly 700 activists and journalists, hauled them to the Israeli port of Ashdod, and kept them out of meaningful communication with family, press, and lawyers for days. The Israeli government confiscated every recording and communication device it could find—devices containing almost all the recorded evidence of the raid—thus allowing the state to control what the world learned about the assault. The Israelis selected, edited, and released footage they wanted the world to see.

Four days after their capture, most of the detainees were deported by the Israeli government, well after the story had been framed.

I caught up with two veteran journalists who were covering the Gaza Freedom Flotilla for Australia's *Sydney Morning Herald*, chief correspondent Paul McGeough and his photographer, Kate Geraghty. They were in Istanbul, where they had been deported from Israel. They had spent time on most of the ships of the flotilla, but were aboard the smaller, U.S.-flagged *Challenger 1* when the raid occurred.

Geraghty described how she was shot with a Taser: "I was photographing Israeli commandos coming up a ladder. There was a white flash, this thing hit my arm. I was thrown a meter and a half. It hurt, and I immediately became sick, began throwing up." She yelled that she and McGeough were from the *Sydney*

Morning Herald, and one of the commandos responded, in English with an Australian accent, "We know you're from the *Herald.*" Despite her breadth of experience covering conflict zones around the world, she found her maltreatment by the Israelis "more personal. They knew who we were, they stole my gear, they falsely imprisoned us when we were in international waters covering a legitimate story."

I pointed out to McGeough the Rasmussen poll that found 49 percent of U.S. voters believe pro-Palestinian activists on the aid ships are to blame for what happened. He replied, "If ordinary Americans had seen below deck, the men with zip ties on their wrists, on their knees for hours, denied permission to go to the toilet, forced to soil their pants, women pleading to be able to give drinks to men, that may have changed their sense of what happened on the ships."

When journalists are free to function, they can report the truth. The Israeli military has been forced to retract its claim that passengers aboard the flotilla were agents of al-Qaida. An Israel Defense Forces press release sent out two days after the assault says approximately forty flotilla passengers "are mercenaries belonging to the Al Qaeda terror organization." The independent journalist Max Blumenthal says both he and an Israeli colleague asked the Israeli military press office to substantiate its claim. No evidence was provided, and one day later the press release was modified. The original headline was changed from "Attackers of the IDF Soldiers Found to be Al Qaeda Mercenaries" to "Attackers of the IDF Soldiers Found Without Identification Papers."

McGeough told me: "This is what we do: We embed with U.S. forces in Iraq, and with Australian forces in Afghanistan. I've spoken to Israeli officials, and in the West Bank and Gaza I've spoken to Hamas, to young would-be suicide bombers, because that's how we get stories. If you just tell one side of the story then people can't have a sensible view of a dynamic conflict, in order to understand how it might be resolved."

McGeough and Geraghty and all the other journalists have yet to receive their laptops, cameras, videos, photos, and other possessions from the Israelis. And Israel has said it will not accept an independent investigation of its raid. Israel's continued attempts to hide the truth only further imperil the security of Israelis, Palestinians, and all those working for a just peace in the Middle East.

September 21, 2011

99 Percenters Occupy Wall Street

If 2,000 Tea Party activists descended on Wall Street, you would probably have an equal number of reporters there covering them. Yet 2,000 people did occupy Wall Street on Saturday. They weren't carrying the banner of the Tea Party, the Gadsden flag with its coiled snake and the threat "Don't Tread on Me." Yet their message was clear: "We are the 99 percent that will no longer tolerate the greed and corruption of the 1 percent." They were there, mostly young, protesting the virtually unregulated speculation of Wall Street that caused the global financial meltdown.

One of New York's better-known billionaires, Mayor Michael Bloomberg, commented on the protests: "You have a lot of kids graduating college, can't find jobs. That's what happened in Cairo. That's what happened in Madrid. You don't want those kinds of riots here." Riots? Is that really what the Arab Spring and the European protests are about?

Perhaps to the chagrin of Mayor Bloomberg, that is exactly what inspired many who occupied Wall Street. In its most recent communique, the Wall Street protest umbrella group said: "On Saturday we held a general assembly, two thousand strong. . . . By 8 p.m. on Monday we still held the plaza, despite constant police presence. . . . We are building the world that we want to see, based on human need and sustainability, not corporate greed."

Speaking of the Tea Party, Texas Gov. Rick Perry has caused a continuous fracas in the Republican presidential debates with his declaration that the United States' revered Social Security system is a "Ponzi scheme." Charles Ponzi was the con artist who swindled thousands in 1920 with a fraudulent promise for high returns on investments. A typical Ponzi scheme involves taking money from investors, then paying them off with money taken from new investors, rather than paying them from actual earnings. Social Security is actually solvent, with a trust fund of more than $2.6 trillion. The real Ponzi scheme threatening the U.S. public is the voracious greed of Wall Street banks.

I interviewed one of the "Occupy Wall Street" protest organizers. David Graeber teaches at Goldsmiths, University of London, and has authored several books, most recently *Debt: The First 5,000 Years.* Graeber points out that, in the midst of the financial crash of 2008, enormous debts between banks were renegotiated. Yet only a fraction of troubled mortgages have gotten the same treatment. He said: "Debts between the very wealthy or between governments can always be renegotiated and always have been throughout world history. . . . It's when you have debts owed by the poor to the rich that suddenly debts become a sacred obligation, more important than anything else. The idea of renegotiating them becomes unthinkable."

President Barack Obama has proposed a jobs plan and further efforts to reduce the deficit. One is a so-called millionaire's tax, endorsed by billionaire Obama supporter Warren Buffett. The Republicans call the proposed tax "class warfare." Graeber commented: "For the last 30 years we've seen a political battle being waged by the super-rich against everyone else, and this is the latest move in the shadow dance, which is completely dysfunctional economically and politically. It's the reason why young people have just abandoned any thought of appealing to politicians. We all know what's going to happen. The tax proposals are a sort of mock populist gesture, which everyone knows will be shot down. What will actually probably happen would be more cuts to social services."

Outside in the cold Tuesday morning, the demonstrators continued their fourth day of the protest with a march amidst a heavy police presence and the ringing of an opening bell at 9:30 a.m. for a "people's exchange," just as the opening bell of the New York Stock Exchange is rung. While the bankers remained secure in their bailed-out banks, outside the police began arresting protesters. In a just world, with a just economy, we have to wonder, who would be out in the cold? Who would be getting arrested?

• •

October 12, 2011

A New Bush Era or a Push Era?

Back when Barack Obama was still just a U.S. senator running for president, he told a group of donors in a New Jersey suburb, "Make me do it." He was borrowing from President Franklin D. Roosevelt, who used the same phrase (according to Harry Belafonte, who heard the story directly from Eleanor Roosevelt) when responding to legendary union organizer A. Philip Randolph's demand for civil rights for African-Americans.

While President Obama has made concession after concession to both the corporate-funded Tea Party and his Wall Street donors, now that he is again in campaign mode, his progressive critics are being warned not to attack him, as that might aid and abet the Republican bid for the White House.

Enter the 99 percenters. The Occupy Wall Street ranks continue to grow, inspiring more than 1,000 solidarity protests around the country and the globe. After weeks, and one of the largest mass arrests in U.S. history, Obama finally commented: "I think people are frustrated, and the protesters are giving voice to a more broad-based frustration about how our financial system works." But neither he nor his advisers—nor the Republicans—know what to do with this burgeoning mass movement.

Following the controversial Citizens United v. Federal Election Commission decision by the U.S. Supreme Court, which allows unlimited corporate donations to support election advertising, the hunger for campaign cash is insatiable. The Obama re-election campaign aims to raise $1 billion. According to the Center for Responsive Politics, the financial industry was Obama's second-largest source of 2008 campaign contributions, surpassed only by the lawyers/lobbyists industry sector.

The suggestion that a loss for Obama would signal a return to the Bush era has some merit: The Associated Press reported recently that "almost all of [Mitt] Romney's 22 special advisers held senior Bush administration positions in diplomacy, defense or intelligence. Two former Republican senators are included as well as Bush-era CIA chief Michael Hayden and former Homeland Security Secretary Michael Chertoff." But so is the Obama presidency an expansion of the Bush era, unless there is a new "Push era."

The organic strength of Occupy Wall Street defies the standard dismissals from the corporate media's predictably stale stable of pundits. For them, it is all about the divide between the Republicans and the Democrats, a divide the protesters have a hard time seeing. They see both parties captured by Wall Street. Richard Haass, head of the establishment Council on Foreign Relations, said of the protesters, "They're not serious." He asked why they are not talking about entitlements. Perhaps it is because, to the 99 percent, Social Security and

Medicare are not the problem, but rather growing inequality, with the 400 richest Americans having more wealth than half of all Americans combined. And then there is the overwhelming cost and toll of war, first and foremost the lives lost, but also the lives destroyed, on all sides.

It's why, for example, Jose Vasquez, executive director of Iraq Veterans Against the War, was down at Occupy Wall Street on Monday night. He told me: "It's no secret that a lot of veterans are facing unemployment, homelessness and a lot of other issues that are dealing with the economy. A lot of people get deployed multiple times and are still struggling.... I've met a lot of veterans who have come here. I just met a guy who is active duty, took leave just to come to Occupy Wall Street."

The historic election of Barack Obama was achieved by millions of people across the political spectrum. For years during the Bush administration, people felt they were hitting their heads against a brick wall. With the election, the wall had become a door, but it was only open a crack. The question was, would it be kicked open or slammed shut? It is not up to one person. Obama had moved from community organizer in chief to commander in chief. When forces used to having the ear of the most powerful person on earth whisper their demands in the Oval Office, the president must see a force more powerful outside his window, whether he likes it or not, and say, "If I do that, they will storm the Bastille." If there's no one out there, we are all in big trouble.

• •

October 19, 2011

The Arc of the Moral Universe, from Memphis to Wall Street

The national memorial to Martin Luther King Jr. was dedicated last Sunday. President Barack Obama said of Dr. King, "If he were alive today, I believe he would remind us that the unemployed worker can rightly challenge the excesses of Wall Street without demonizing all who work there." The dedication occurred amidst the increasingly popular and increasingly global Occupy Wall Street movement. What Obama left unsaid is that King, were he alive, would most likely be protesting Obama administration policies.

Not far from the dedication ceremony, Cornel West, preacher, professor, writer, and activist, was being arrested on the steps of the U.S. Supreme Court. He said, before being hauled off to jail: "We want to bear witness today that we know the relation between corporate greed and what goes on too often in the Supreme Court decisions. . . . We will not allow this day of Martin Luther King Jr.'s memorial to go without somebody going to jail, because Martin King would be here right with us, willing to throw down out of deep love."

West was arrested with eighteen others, declaring "solidarity with the Occupy movement all around the world, because we love poor people, we love working people, and we want Martin Luther King Jr. to smile from the grave that we haven't forgot his movement."

Over the same weekend as the dedication, the U.S. military/CIA's drone campaign, under Commander in Chief Obama, launched what the independent, nonprofit Bureau of Investigative Journalism, based in London, called the 300th drone strike, the 248th since Obama took office. According to the BIJ, of the at least 2,318 people killed by drone strikes, between 386 and 775 were civilians, including 175 children. Imagine how Obama's fellow Nobel Peace Prize laureate, Dr. King, would respond to those grim statistics.

Back in 1963, King published a collection of sermons titled "Strength to Love." His preface began, "In these turbulent days of uncertainty the evils of war and of economic and racial injustice threaten the very survival of the human race." Three of the fifteen sermons were written in Georgia jails, including "Shattered Dreams." In that one, he wrote, "To cooperate passively with an unjust system makes the oppressed as evil as the oppressor." King revisited the idea of shattered dreams four years later, eight months before his assassination, in his speech called "Where Do We Go from Here," saying: "Our dreams will sometimes be shattered and our ethereal hopes blasted. . . . Let us realize the arc of the moral universe is long but it bends toward justice."

Earlier in that year, 1967, a year to the day before he was killed, King gave his oft-overlooked "Beyond Vietnam" speech at Riverside Church in New York City. King preached, "I knew that I could never again raise my voice against the violence of the oppressed in the ghettos without having first spoken clearly to the greatest purveyor of violence in the world today, my own government."

With those words, with that speech, King set the tone for his final, fateful year. Despite death threats, and his close advisers urging him not to go to Memphis, King went to march in solidarity with that city's sanitation workers. On April 4, 1968, he was shot and killed on the balcony of the Lorraine Motel.

Deeply impacted at the time by the assassination, we can follow two young men along King's arc of moral justice all the way to Occupy Wall Street. One was John Carlos, a U.S. Olympic track star. Carlos won the bronze medal in the 200 meter race at the 1968 Summer Olympics in Mexico City. Carlos and his teammate Tommie Smith, who won the gold, raised their black-gloved fists in the power salute on the medal stand, instantly gaining global fame. They both stood without shoes, protesting black children in poverty in the United States. Last week, John Carlos spoke at Occupy Wall Street, and he told me after, "I'm just so happy to see so many people who are standing up to say: 'We're not asking for change. We demand change.'"

The other person is the Rev. Jesse Jackson. He was with King when he was assassinated. Late Monday night, the New York Police Department seemed to be making a move on Occupy Wall Street's first-aid tent. Jackson was there. Just days past his seventieth birthday, Jackson joined arms with the young protesters, defying the police. The police backed off. And the arc of the moral universe bent a bit more toward justice.

. . . .

October 26, 2011

Globalizing Dissent, from Tahrir Square to Liberty Plaza

The winds of change are blowing across the globe. What triggers such change, and when it will strike, is something that no one can predict.

Last January 18, a courageous young woman in Egypt took a dangerous step. Asmaa Mahfouz was twenty-five years old, part of the April 6 Youth Movement, with thousands of young people engaging online in debate on the future of their country. They formed in 2008 to demonstrate solidarity with workers in the industrial city of Mahalla, Egypt. Then, in December 2010, a young man in Tunisia, Mohamed Bouazizi, set himself on fire to protest the frustration of a generation. His death sparked the uprising in Tunisia that toppled the long-reigning dictator, President Zine el-Abidine Ben Ali.

Similar acts of protest spread to Egypt, where at least four men attempted self-immolation. One, Ahmed Hashem el-Sayed of Alexandria, died. Asmaa Mahfouz was outraged and posted a video online, staring directly into the camera, her head covered, but not her face. She identified herself and called for people to join her on January 25 in Tahrir Square. She said (translated from Arabic): "I'm making this video to give you one simple message: We want to go down to Tahrir Square on January 25. If we still have honor and want to live in dignity on this land, we have to go down on January 25. We'll go down and demand our rights, our fundamental human rights.... I won't even talk about any political rights. We just want our human rights and nothing else. This entire government is corrupt—a corrupt president and a corrupt security force. These self-immolators were not afraid of death but were afraid of security forces. Can you imagine that?"

Nine months later, Asmaa Mahfouz was giving a teach-in at Occupy Wall Street. Standing on steps above the crowd Monday night, she had a huge smile on her face as she looked out on a sea of faces. After she finished, I asked her what gave her strength. She answered with characteristic humility, speaking English: "I can't believe it when I saw a million people join in the Tahrir Square. I'm not more brave, because I saw my colleagues, Egyptian, were going towards the policemen, when they just pushing us, and they died for all of us. So they are the one who are really brave and really strong. ... I saw people, really, died in front of me, because they were protecting me and protecting others. So, they were the most brave, bravest men."

I asked how it felt to be in the United States, which had for so long supported the Mubarak regime in Egypt. She replied: "While they giving money and power and support to Mubarak regime, our people, Egyptian people, can success against all of this, against the U.S. power. So, the power to the people, not for the U.S. bullets or bombs or money or anything. The power to the people. So that I am here to be in solidarity and support the Wall Street Occupy protesters, to say them 'the power to the people,' and to keep it on and on, and they will success in the end."

The Egyptian revolution has not been without consequences for her. Last August, she was arrested by the Egyptian military. As my colleague Sharif Abdel Kouddous reported from Cairo, Asmaa sent two controversial tweets that prompted the arrest by the Supreme Council of the Armed Forces, the military government that has ruled Egypt since Mubarak's fall.

Her arrest provoked a worldwide response, with groups ranging from the Muslim Brotherhood to Amnesty International condemning it. She was released, but, as Sharif noted at the time, Asmaa was only one of 12,000 civilians arrested since the revolution.

The arrests are happening here in the U.S. now, at many of the protest sites across the country. As Asmaa was preparing to head back to Egypt, hundreds of riot police descended on Occupy Oakland, firing beanbag rounds and tear gas. The University of New Mexico is threatening to evict the encampment there, which is called "(Un)occupy Albuquerque" to highlight that the land there is occupied native land.

Asmaa Mahfouz is running for a seat in the Egyptian Parliament, and maybe someday, she says, the presidency. When I asked her what she had to say to President Barack Obama, who had given his speech to the Muslim world in Cairo, she replied: "You promised the people that you are the change and 'yes, we can.' So we are here from the Wall Street Occupy, and we are saying the same word: 'yes, we can.' We can make the freedom, and we can get our freedom, even if it's from you."

November 2, 2011

Call of Duty: Veterans Join the 99 Percent

11–11–11 is not a variant of Herman Cain's much-touted 9–9–9 tax plan, but rather the date of this year's Veterans Day. This is especially relevant, as the U.S. has now entered its second decade of war in Afghanistan, the longest war in the nation's history. U.S. veterans of the Iraq and Afghanistan wars are appearing more and more on the front lines—the front lines of the Occupy Wall Street protests, that is.

Video from the Occupy Oakland march on Tuesday, October 25, looks and sounds like a war zone. The sound of gunfire is nearly constant in the video. Tear-gas projectiles were being fired into the crowd when the cry of "Medic!" rang out. Civilians raced toward a fallen protester lying on his back on the pavement, mere steps from a throng of black-clad police in full riot gear, pointing guns as the civilians attempted to administer first aid.

The fallen protester was Scott Olsen, a twenty-four-year-old former U.S. Marine who had served two tours of duty in Iraq. The publicly available video shows Olsen standing calmly alongside a Navy veteran holding an upraised Veterans for Peace flag. Olsen was wearing a desert camouflage jacket and sun hat, and his Iraq Veterans Against the War (IVAW) T-shirt. He was hit in the head by a police projectile, most likely a tear-gas canister, suffering a fractured skull. As the small group of people gathered around him to help, a police officer lobbed a flashbang grenade directly into the huddle, and it exploded.

Four or five people lifted Olsen and raced with him away from the police line. At the hospital, he was put into an induced coma to relieve brain swelling. He is now conscious but unable to speak. He communicates using a notepad.

I interviewed one of Olsen's friends, Aaron Hinde, also an Iraq War veteran. He was at Occupy San Francisco when he started getting a series of frenzied tweets about a vet down in Oakland. Hinde raced to the hospital to see his friend. He later told me a little about him: "Scott came to San Francisco about three months ago from Wisconsin, where he actually participated in the holding of the State Capitol over there. Scott's probably one of the warmest, kindest guys I know. He's just one of those people who always has a smile on his face and never has anything negative to say. . . . And he believed in the Occupy movement, because it's very obvious what's happening in this country, especially to us veterans. We've had our eyes opened by serving and going to war overseas. So, there's a small contingency of us out here, and we're all very motivated and dedicated."

As I was covering one of the Occupy Wall Street rallies in Times Square on October 15, I saw Sgt. Shamar Thomas become deeply upset. Police on horseback had moved in on protesters, only to be stopped by a horse that went down on its knees. Other officers had picked up metal barricades, squeezing the frightened crowd against steam pipes. Sgt. Thomas was wearing his desert camouflage, his chest covered with medals from his combat tour in Iraq. He shouted at the police, denouncing their violent treatment of the protesters. Thomas later wrote of the incident: "There is an obvious problem in the country and PEACE-FUL PEOPLE should be allowed to PROTEST without Brutality. I was involved in a RIOT in Rutbah, Iraq 2004 and we did NOT treat the Iraqi citizens like they are treating the unarmed civilians in our OWN Country."

A group calling itself Veterans of the 99 Percent has formed and, with the New York City Chapter of IVAW, set Wednesday as the day to march to Liberty Plaza to formally join and support the movement. Their announcement read: "'Veterans of the 99 Percent' hope to draw attention to the ways veterans have been impacted by the economic and social issues raised by Occupy Wall Street. They hope to help make veterans' and service members' participation in this movement more visible and deliberate."

When I stopped by Occupy Louisville in Kentucky last weekend, the first two people I met there were veterans. One of them, Gary James Johnson, told me: "I served in Iraq for about a year and a half. I joined the military because I thought it was my obligation to help protect this country. . . . And right here, right now, this is another way I can help."

Pundits predict the cold weather will crush the Occupy movement. Ask any veteran of Afghanistan and Iraq about surviving outdoors in extreme weather. And consider the sign at Liberty Plaza, held by yet another veteran: "2nd time I've fought for my country. 1st time I've known my enemy."

November 16, 2011

The Brave New World of Occupy Wall Street

We got word just after 1 a.m. Tuesday that New York City police were raiding the Occupy Wall Street encampment. I raced down with the *Democracy Now!* news team to Zuccotti Park, renamed Liberty Square. Hundreds of riot police had already surrounded the area. As they ripped down the tents, city sanitation workers were throwing the protesters' belongings into dump trucks. Beyond the barricades, back in the heart of the park, 200 to 300 people locked arms, refusing to cede the space they had occupied for almost two months. They were being handcuffed and arrested, one by one.

The few of us members of the press who managed to get through all the police lines were sent to a designated area across the street from Zuccotti Park. As our cameras started rolling, they placed two police buses in front of us, blocking our view. My colleagues and I managed to slip between them and into the park, climbing over the trashed mounds of tents, tarps, and sleeping bags. The police had almost succeeded in enforcing a complete media blackout of the destruction.

We saw a broken bookcase in one pile. Deeper in the park, I spotted a single book on the ground. It was marked "OWSL," for Occupy Wall Street Library, also known as the People's Library, one of the key institutions that had sprung up in the organic democracy of the movement. By the latest count, it had accumulated 5,000 donated books. The one I found, amidst the debris of democracy that was being hauled off to the dump, was *Brave New World Revisited*, by Aldous Huxley.

As the night progressed, the irony of finding Huxley's book grew. He wrote it in 1958, almost thirty years after his famous dystopian novel, *Brave New World*. The original work described society in the future where people had been stratified into haves and have-nots. The *Brave New World* denizens were plied with pleasure, distraction, advertisement, and intoxicating drugs to lull them into complacency, a world of perfect consumerism, with lower classes doing all the work for an elite.

Brave New World Revisited was Huxley's nonfiction response to the speed with which he saw modern society careening to that bleak future. It seemed relevant, as the encampment, motivated in large part by the opposition to the supremacy of commerce and globalization, was being destroyed.

Huxley wrote in the book: "Big Business, made possible by advancing technology and the consequent ruin of Little Business, is controlled by the State—that is to say, by a small group of party leaders and the soldiers, policemen and civil servants who carry out their orders. In a capitalist democracy, such as the United States, it is controlled by what Professor C. Wright Mills has called the Power Elite." Huxley goes on to write, "This Power Elite directly employs several millions of the country's working force in its factories, offices and stores, controls many millions more by lending them the money to buy its products, and, through its ownership of the media of mass communication, influences the thoughts, the feelings and the actions of virtually everybody."

One of the People's Library volunteers, Stephen Boyer, was there as the park was raided. After avoiding arrest and helping others with first aid, he wrote: "Everything we brought to the park is gone. The beautiful library is gone. Our collection of 5,000 books is gone. Our tent that was donated is gone. All the work we've put into making it is gone."

New York City Mayor Michael Bloomberg's office later released a photo of a table with some books stacked on it, claiming the books had been preserved. As the People's Library tweeted: "We're glad to see some books are OK. Now, where are the rest of the books and our shelter and our boxes?" The shelter, by the way, was donated to the library by National Book Award–winner Patti Smith, the rock 'n' roll legend.

Many other Occupy protest sites have been raided recently. Oakland Mayor Jean Quan admitted to the BBC that she had been on a conference call with eighteen cities, discussing the situation. Another report noted that the FBI and Homeland Security have been advising the cities.

A New York state judge ruled late Tuesday that the eviction will stand, and that protesters cannot return to Zuccotti Park with sleeping bags or tents. After the ruling, a constitutional attorney sent me a text message: "Just remember: the movement is in the streets. Courts are always last resorts." Or, as Patti Smith famously sings, "People Have the Power."

November 23, 2011

Pulling Accounts from the Unaccountable

Less than a month after Occupy Wall Street began, a group was gathered in New York's historical Washington Square Park, in the heart of Greenwich Village. This was a moment of critical growth for the movement, with increasing participation from the thousands of students attending the cluster of colleges and universities there. A decision was made to march on local branches of the too-big-to-fail banks, so participants could close their accounts, and others could hold "teach-ins" to discuss the problems created by these unaccountable institutions.

Heather Carpenter, according to the federal lawsuit filed this week in New York, is studying to be a certified nursing assistant, working to pay for school as a counselor for mentally disabled people at a group home on Long Island. Her fiancé, Julio Jose Jimenez-Artunduaga, is a Colombian immigrant, pursuing the American Dream and working part time as a bartender. They marched from Washington Square Park to a nearby Citibank branch, where she went to the teller to close her account, explaining her frustration with the bank's new monthly $17 fee for accounts with balances below $6,000.

As described in the lawsuit, the teach-in began with participants "announcing the amount of their debt, discussing their student loan experience, and reciting sobering statistics related to the debt of college graduates." The bank staff called the police, and Julio went outside to avoid any conflict. Heather closed her account and left as well. By that time, a large group of NYPD officers, including Chief of Department Joseph J. Esposito, as well as several plainclothes officers showed up. The police stormed into the bank, locked the doors, and began arresting those involved with the teach-in.

Even though Heather was outside, a plainclothes officer identified her as a protester and told her to get back in the bank. She said she was a customer and showed her receipt. To her shock, as documented by video, Heather was grabbed from behind by a plainclothes officer who began forcing her into the bank. She screamed, but within seconds disappeared into the vestibule, surrounded by a dozen cops, where she was roughly handcuffed and arrested. Julio was roughed up and arrested as well—all for closing an account at Citibank.

They spent over thirty hours in police custody and were charged with resisting arrest and criminal trespass. A month later, the New York District Attorney's office indicated it would drop the charges at their court appearances. Heather and Julio still want to see Chief Esposito and the other arresting officers in court, though, for an explanation of the officers' excessive force and unlawful arrest of the two.

Just weeks after their arrest, on November 5, thousands around the U.S. participated in Bank Transfer Day. Kristen Christian was upset with the announcement that Bank of America was going to charge a monthly $5 debit card fee. She created a Facebook event and shared it with her friends. Before long, Bank Transfer Day had 85,000 online supporters.

She reported that 40,000 new accounts were created at nonprofit credit unions across the country that day. She said that the $5 fee, which Bank of America has since scrapped, "illustrates how out of touch the executives of the large banks can be . . . with Bank of America, the fee only applied to account holders with less than $20,000 in combined accounts. I couldn't support a business that would directly target the impoverished and working class."

Just after the financial crash in late 2008, activists in Oregon started looking into the creation of a state bank, modeled after the only state-owned bank in the United States, in North Dakota. The cities of Portland and Seattle are now looking into shifting their massive municipal accounts away from the Wall Street banks. According to one report, Bank of America may lose upward of $185 billion from customers closing accounts.

In January 2010, the Move Your Money Project formed, encouraging individuals to shift their funds to local and nonprofit credit unions, to defund the Wall Street megabanks. Its organizers released a video based on the classic 1946 film of bank malfeasance, *It's a Wonderful Life*, in which protagonist George Bailey fights to protect consumers from the greedy bank president, Mr. Potter. As Bailey exhorted in the film, "This town needs this measly one-horse institution, if only to have some place for people to come without crawling to Potter." The Move Your Money video ends with this message: "If you leave your money with the big banks, they will use it to pay lobbyists to keep Congress from fixing the system . . . don't just watch 'It's a Wonderful Life' . . . move your money."

January 18, 2012

The SOPA Blackout Protest Makes History

January 18 marked the largest online protest in the history of the Internet. Websites from large to small "went dark" in protest of proposed legislation before the U.S. House and Senate that could profoundly change the Internet. The two bills, SOPA in the House and PIPA in the Senate, ostensibly aim to stop the piracy of copyrighted material over the Internet on websites based outside the United States. Critics—among them, the founders of Google, Wikipedia, the Internet Archive, Tumblr, and Twitter—counter that the laws will stifle innovation and investment, hallmarks of the free, open Internet. The Obama administration has offered muted criticism of the legislation, but, as many of his supporters have painfully learned, what President Barack Obama questions one day, he signs into law the next.

First, the basics. SOPA stands for the Stop Online Piracy Act, while PIPA is the Protect IP Act. The two bills are very similar. SOPA would allow copyright holders to complain to the U.S. attorney general about a foreign website they allege is "committing or facilitating the commission of criminal violations" of copyright law. This relates mostly to pirated movies and music. SOPA would allow the movie industry, through the courts and the U.S. attorney general, to send a slew of demands that Internet service providers (ISPs) and search engine companies shut down access to those alleged violators, and even to prevent linking to those sites, thus making them "unfindable." It would also bar Internet advertising providers from making payments to websites accused of copyright violations.

SOPA could, then, shut down a community-based site like YouTube if just one of its millions of users was accused of violating one U.S. copyright. As David Drummond, Google's chief legal officer and an opponent of the legislation, blogged, "Last year alone, we acted on copyright takedown notices for more than 5 million webpages. PIPA and SOPA will censor the web, will risk our industry's track record of innovation and job creation, and will not stop piracy."

Corynne McSherry, intellectual property director at the Electronic Frontier Foundation, told me, "These bills propose new powers for the government and for private actors to create, effectively, blacklists of sites . . . then force service providers to block access to those sites. That's why we call these the censorship bills."

The bills, she says, are the creation of the entertainment, or "content," industries: "SOPA, in particular, was negotiated without any consultation with the technology sector. They were specifically excluded." The exclusion of the tech sector has alarmed not only Silicon Valley executives, but also conservatives like Utah Republican Congressman Jason Chaffetz, a Tea Party favorite. He said in a December House judiciary committee hearing, "We're basically going to reconfigure the Internet and how it's going to work, without bringing in the nerds."

PIPA sponsor Sen. Patrick Leahy, D-Vt., said in a press release, "Much of what has been claimed about [PIPA] is flatly wrong and seems intended more to stoke fear and concern than to shed light or foster workable solutions." Sadly, Leahy's ire sounds remarkably similar to that of his former Senate colleague Christopher Dodd, who, after retiring, took the job of chairman and CEO of the powerful lobbying group Motion Picture Association of America (at a reported salary of $1.2 million annually), one of the chief backers of SOPA/PIPA. Said Dodd of the broad-based, grassroots Internet protest, "It's a dangerous and troubling development when the platforms that serve as gateways to information intentionally skew the facts to incite their users in order to further their corporate interests."

EFF's McSherry said, "No one asked the Internet—well, the Internet is speaking now. People are really rising up and saying: 'Don't interfere with basic Internet infrastructure. We won't stand for it.'"

As the Internet blackout protest progressed January 18, and despite Dodd's lobbying, legislators began retreating from support for the bills. The Internet roared, and the politicians listened, reminiscent of the popular uprising against media consolidation in 2003 proposed by then Federal Communications Commission chairman Michael Powell, the son of General Colin Powell. Information is the currency of democracy, and people will not sit still as moneyed interests try to deny them access.

When Internet users visited the sixth-most popular website on the planet during the protest blackout, the English-language section of Wikipedia, they found this message: "Imagine a World Without Free Knowledge. For over a decade, we have spent millions of hours building the largest encyclopedia in human history. Right now, the U.S. Congress is considering legislation that could fatally damage the free and open Internet."

In a world with fresh, Internet-fueled revolutions, it seems that U.S. politicians are getting the message.

February 8, 2012

America's Pro-Choice Majority Speaks Out

The leadership of the Catholic Church has launched what amounts to a holy war against President Barack Obama. Archbishop Timothy Dolan appealed to church members, "Let your elected leaders know that you want religious liberty and rights of conscience restored and that you want the administration's contraceptive mandate rescinded," he said. Obama is now under pressure to reverse a health-care regulation that requires Catholic hospitals and universities, like all employers, to provide contraception to insured women covered by their health plans. Bill Donohue of the Catholic League said, "This is going to be fought out with lawsuits, with court decisions, and, dare I say it, maybe even in the streets." In the wake of the successful pushback against the Susan G. Komen Race for the Cure's decision to defund Planned Parenthood, the Obama administration should listen to the majority of Americans: The United States, including Catholics, is strongly pro-choice.

Rick Santorum most likely benefited from the twenty-four-hour news cycle this week with his three-state win. Exactly one week before the caucus/primary voting, on January 31, the Associated Press broke the story that Susan G. Komen Race for the Cure, a $2 billion-per-year breast-cancer fundraising and advocacy organization, had enacted policies that would effectively lead it to deny funding to Planned Parenthood clinics to conduct breast-cancer screenings, especially for women with no health insurance. Linked to the decision was a recently hired Komen vice president, Karen Handel, who, as a candidate for governor of Georgia in 2010, ran on a platform to defund Planned Parenthood. The backlash was immediate, broad-based, and unrelenting. By February 3, Komen reversed its decision. On February 7, Handel resigned from Komen.

Adding fuel to the ire was news that the U.S. Department of Health and Human Services had issued the regulation requiring employer insurance plans to provide contraception. The coup de grace, on primary/caucus day, was the decision handed down by the Ninth U.S. Circuit Court of Appeals overturning California's controversial Proposition 8, which banned same-sex marriages.

For Santorum, in a primary battle with Mitt Romney, it was "three strikes, you're in." As a conservative Catholic and father of seven, Santorum has long waged the culture war, with a focus on marriage, abortion, and sex. He once likened homosexuality to bestiality.

According to the nonpartisan Guttmacher Institute, which studies reproductive health issues globally, in the United States, "among all women who have had sex, 99 percent have used a contraceptive method other than natural family planning. This figure is virtually the same among Catholic women (98 percent)." According to a Public Religion Research Institute poll, 58 percent of Catholics believe that employers should provide employees with health-care plans that include contraception.

Catholic activists who acknowledge the broad use of contraception among their church members, despite its official prohibition, suggest women can "go elsewhere" to get the preventive care. And if they can't afford to? Loretta Ross, national coordinator of the SisterSong Women of Color Reproductive Justice Collective in Atlanta, told me: "This rule really allows low-income women, women who are dependent on their health care, to access birth control—women of color, in particular ... if you don't want to use birth control, don't buy it, don't use it. But don't block others who do want to use it, who cannot afford it, from accessing it."

One possible solution to the debate came from a surprising quarter. Michael Brendan Dougherty, a Catholic commentator, was in church a couple of weeks ago when he heard the priest read out a letter from Archbishop Dolan encouraging Catholics to oppose the president. Dougherty, who supports the church's opposition to the regulation, suggested to me that a single-payer health-care option could solve the problem: "It would solve this particular problem of conscience, as it has in Europe. The bishops don't like that the government subsidizes abortion or contraception, but they are not in full mode of fury, because they are not being asked to formally cooperate with things they view as sinful."

Loretta Ross agrees with the single-payer solution, but says the current contraception controversy masks a "war on women with all this rhetoric about religious freedom and care for not only the pre-born, but now, with the attack on contraception, you're attacking the preconceived. . . . We're not going to take it lying down. And as the fight with the Komen Foundation proved, we are a force to be reckoned with. And we're actually going to work to strengthen President Obama's stand in supporting contraceptive access."

June 21, 2012

A Movement Built by Dreamers

Undocumented immigrants in the United States number around 12 million people, a group larger than the populations of most countries on the planet. Among those are as many as 800,000 young people who are now most likely eligible for limited legal status, thanks to executive action taken last week by President Barack Obama. In a Rose Garden speech, Obama said that he and Secretary of Homeland Security Janet Napolitano were working "to mend our nation's immigration policy, to make it more fair, more efficient and more just—specifically for certain young people sometimes called 'Dreamers.'" Behind the speech was a movement for social change, built by millions, each with their own story.

The "Dreamers" are those who are here without legal documentation, often derogatorily referred to as "illegals," but who came to this country as children, in some cases as infants. As he said in his speech: "These are young people who study in our schools, they play in our neighborhoods, they're friends with our kids, they pledge allegiance to our flag. They are Americans in their heart, in their minds, in every single way but one: on paper." For ten years, people have pushed for an act of Congress to give these young people legal status, through a bill called the DREAM Act, short for the Development, Relief, and Education for Alien Minors Act.

People in the movement don't consider themselves "alien." They call themselves "undocumented Americans." One of those who stands to directly benefit from White House's decision is Lorella Praeli, from New Haven, Connecticut, a member of the United We Dream national coordinating committee. She fought for passage of the Connecticut version of the DREAM Act. The bill was signed into law last year, making undocumented students eligible for in-state tuition at state colleges. Praeli is a 2011 graduate of Quinnipiac University, which she attended on a scholarship.

"I had a car accident when I was two and a half, which resulted in the amputation of my right leg," she explained. "My family and I sought treatment at Shriners Hospital. So for many years, we spent time between Peru and Tampa, Florida, which is where the hospital is. When I was ten, my family decided to move to Connecticut. That's how I ended up here."

She went on, "I didn't know I was undocumented until toward the end of my high school career, applying to colleges. . . . You need to fill out FAFSA [Free Application for Federal Student Aid], and you need a Social Security number. That was kind of my introduction to what being undocumented really meant and to start to internalize what it meant to be undocumented, feeling very isolated."

She was invited by the New Haven mayor's office to speak at a press conference. She recalled: "I didn't have anything prepared. I got up, and I said something like 'I am done standing on the sidelines.' And that was my coming out, very publicly. And that, I think, just changed my life for the better."

They call them "coming out" stories. Another young immigrant, Jose Antonio Vargas, said it was, for him, less daunting to come out as a gay teenager than to come out as an undocumented American. He came from the Philippines at the age of twelve, to stay with his grandparents in California. He didn't learn that he was "illegal" until he applied for his driving permit at the age of sixteen. Vargas ultimately became a reporter at the *Washington Post*. There he was part of a team that won the Pulitzer Prize for reporting on the Virginia Tech massacre in 2007. By 2011, after hiding his immigration status for almost fifteen years, Vargas "came out" in a *New York Times Sunday Magazine* article.

He explained what prompted his decision: "Watching United We Dream and watching these four activists from Miami, [who] walked from Miami to Washington, D.C., to fight for the DREAM Act, the Trail of Dreams. I felt like a coward, and I felt accountable. And that's when I decided that, you know what? I've got to go do this."

Movements—whether they are civil rights, gay rights, or immigration rights—are built on a foundation of innumerable small acts of courage. Like the four undocumented students who marched from Miami to D.C., or those who sat in at four of Obama's campaign offices around the country, immediately before his announcement last week (risking arrest and thus, potentially, deportation), these "Dreamers" are committed, and organizing. As the anthropologist Margaret Mead said: "Never doubt that a small group of thoughtful, committed people can change the world; indeed, it's the only thing that ever has."

WHEN
CORPORATIONS RULE

August 25, 2009

Who Is Obama Playing Ball With?

It looked like it was business as usual for President Barack Obama on the first day of his Martha's Vineyard vacation, as he spent five hours golfing with Robert Wolf, president of UBS Investment Bank and chairman and CEO of UBS Group Americas. Wolf, an early financial backer of Obama's presidential campaign, raised $250,000 for him back in 2006, and in February was appointed by the president to the White House's Economic Recovery Advisory Board. Economic recovery for whom?

Interestingly, Wolf's appointment came in the same month that UBS agreed to pay the U.S. $780 million to settle civil and criminal charges related to helping people in the U.S. avoid taxes. Not to worry. UBS, an ailing bank with a preexisting condition, had great insurance coverage. It was actually receiving $2.5 billion in a backdoor bailout from bailed-out insurance giant AIG. Sen. Olympia Snowe, R-Maine, said, "It looks like we're simply laundering this money through AIG." UBS, this bank that shelters wealthy tax dodgers, was actually being bailed out by hardworking U.S. taxpayers.

UBS, which once stood for Union Bank of Switzerland, was founded more than a century ago. Its success hinges on Switzerland's famous banking secrecy laws, allowing people to squirrel money away in untraceable "numbered accounts." Secret Swiss bank accounts have become a favorite way for wealthy people in the U.S. to dodge taxes. According to the U.S. Senate's Permanent Subcommittee on Investigations, in a July 2008 report, "From at least 2000 to 2007, UBS made a concerted effort to open accounts in Switzerland for wealthy U.S. clients, employing practices that could facilitate, and have resulted in, tax evasion by U.S. clients."

As part of the settlement, UBS agreed to share client account information with the U.S. government. While there may be as many as 52,000 such accounts, UBS is releasing around 4,450 client names. Internal Revenue Service Commissioner Doug Shulman said in a press release, "We will be receiving an unprecedented amount of information on taxpayers who have evaded their tax obligation by hiding money offshore at UBS." UBS will be sending account holders notification that their names may be among those delivered to the IRS, and the IRS, in turn, is granting leniency to tax dodgers who turn themselves in before

September 23. Account holders won't know if their names are included, though, so gamblers among them may keep quiet and hope their accounts stay secret.

Last Friday, as Wolf was preparing for his golf game with Obama, UBS whistle-blower Bradley Birkenfeld was sentenced to forty months in prison for facilitating offshore tax evasion through UBS banking schemes, despite assisting federal investigators in exposing the secretive bank.

Above the entrance to UBS's headquarters in Zurich is a bust of the Greek god Hermes—not only the fleet-footed messenger of the gods, but also the god of thieves and merchants. The symbolism is striking. Whether or not Wolf won his golf game against Obama, UBS has clearly scored a hole-in-one.

•••

October 20, 2010

When Banks Are the Robbers

The big banks that caused the collapse of the global finance market, and received tens of billions of dollars in taxpayer-funded bailouts, have likely been engaging in wholesale fraud against homeowners and the courts. But in a promising development this week, attorneys general from all fifty states announced a bipartisan joint investigation into foreclosure fraud.

Bank of America, JPMorgan Chase, GMAC, and other big mortgage lenders recently suspended most foreclosure proceedings, following revelations that thousands of their foreclosures were being conducted like "foreclosure mills," with tens of thousands of legal documents signed by low-level staffers with little or no knowledge of what they were signing.

Then the Obama administration signaled that it was not supporting a foreclosure moratorium. Not long after, Bank of America announced it was restarting its foreclosure operations. GMAC followed suit, and others will likely join in. So much for the voluntary moratorium.

GMAC Mortgage engaged in mass document processing, dubbed "robo-signing." In several cases, GMAC Mortgage filed documents with courts that were signed by Jeffrey Stephan. Stephan presided over a staff of twelve in suburban Philadelphia. Ohio Attorney General Richard Cordray filed a lawsuit against GMAC Mortgage, Stephan, and the bank that owns GMAC, Ally Financial (itself a subsidiary of General Motors).

According to one report, Stephan received 10,000 mortgage foreclosure documents to process in one month. Based on an eight-hour workday, he would have had to read, verify, and sign, in the presence of a notary, about one document per minute. He admitted to signing documents without reading them or checking the facts about homeowners said to be in default. And Stephan was just one of many "robo-signers."

Recall that GM received $51 billion in taxpayer bailouts; its subsidiary, GMAC, received $16.3 billion; and Ally Financial subsidiary GMAC Mortgage received $1.5 billion as an "incentive payment for home loan modification."

So you as a taxpayer may have bailed out a bank that is fraudulently foreclosing on you. What recourse do you have?

Back in February 2009, Ohio Rep. Marcy Kaptur advised homeowners to force lenders to "produce the note." People facing foreclosure were being taken to court while the bank alleging default couldn't even prove it owned the mortgage. The mortgage document often had been lost in the tangled web of financial wheeling and dealing. Kaptur told me: "Millions and millions of families are getting foreclosure notices. They don't have proper legal representation . . . possession is nine-tenths of the law; therefore, stay in your property."

If you stay in your home, your mortgage lender may break in. Nancy Jacobini of Orange County, Florida, was inside her home when she heard an intruder. Thinking she was being burglarized, she called 911. Police determined the intruder was actually someone sent by JPMorgan Chase to change the locks. And Jacobini wasn't even in foreclosure!

Most banks that suspended foreclosure efforts only did so in twenty-three states—because it is only in those twenty-three states that courts actually adjudicate over foreclosure proceedings. One judge who oversees foreclosures is New York State Supreme Court Justice Arthur Schack. He has made national headlines for rejecting dozens of foreclosure filings. He told *Democracy Now!* news hour, "My job is to do justice . . . we run into numerous problems with assignments of mortgages, questionable affidavits of merit and just sloppy paperwork in general."

Bruce Marks runs Neighborhood Assistance Corporation of America (NACA), a national nonprofit that helps people avoid foreclosure. He told me: "When President Obama was running for president, he said one of the first things he'll do is put a moratorium on foreclosures. He never did. He never backed bankruptcy reform so people could have the right to go in front of a bankruptcy judge."

He went on: "And where is President Obama? When he says, 'Well, you know, we don't want to upset the market,' what is good about a market when someone is foreclosed on and ... you've got a vacant building? We have to have a national moratorium to give ourselves a window of opportunity to restructure mortgages ... to look at homeowners as people, not as a commodity to make money."

According to RealtyTrac, banks repossessed 102,134 properties in September, a home roughly every thirty seconds. Every thirty seconds, banks—many that received funds from the Bush administration's TARP, and that may be using fraudulent practices—foreclose on an American family's dream of home ownership. Meanwhile, GMAC Mortgage has reported increased profits for the first half of 2010.

• •

February 2, 2011

When Corporations Choose Despots over Democracy

"People holding a sign 'To: America. From: the Egyptian People. Stop supporting Mubarak. It's over!" So tweeted my brave colleague, *Democracy Now!* senior producer Sharif Abdel Kouddous, from the streets of Cairo.

More than 2 million people rallied throughout Egypt on Tuesday, most of them crowded into Cairo's Tahrir Square. *Tahrir*, which means *liberation* in Arabic, has become the epicenter of what appears to be a largely spontaneous, leaderless, and peaceful revolution in this, the most populous nation in the Middle East. Defying a military curfew, this incredible uprising has been driven by young Egyptians, who compose a majority of the 80 million citizens. Twitter and Facebook, and SMS text messaging on cell phones, have helped this new generation to link up and organize, despite living under a U.S.-supported dictatorship for the past three decades. In response, the Mubarak regime, with the help of U.S. and European corporations, has shut down the Internet and curtailed cellular service, plunging Egypt into digital darkness. Despite the shutdown, as media activist and professor of communications C. W. Anderson told me, "people make revolutions, not technology."

The demands are chanted through the streets for democracy, for self-determination. Sharif headed to Egypt Friday night, into uncertain terrain. The hated Interior Ministry security forces, the black-shirted police loyal to President Hosni Mubarak, were beating and killing people, arresting journalists, and smashing and confiscating cameras.

On Saturday morning, Sharif went to Tahrir Square. Despite the SMS and Internet blackout, Sharif, a talented journalist and technical whiz, figured out a workaround, and was soon tweeting out of Tahrir: "Amazing scene: three tanks roll by with a crowd of people riding atop each one. Chanting 'Hosni Mubarak out!'"

Egypt has been the second-largest recipient of U.S. foreign aid for decades, after Israel (not counting the funds expended on the wars and occupations of Iraq and Afghanistan). Mubarak's regime has received roughly $2 billion per year since coming to power, overwhelmingly for the military.

Where has the money gone? Mostly to U.S. corporations. I asked William Hartung of the New America Foundation to explain:

"It's a form of corporate welfare for companies like Lockheed Martin and General Dynamics, because it goes to Egypt, then it comes back for F-16 aircraft, for M-1 tanks, for aircraft engines, for all kinds of missiles, for guns, for tear-gas canisters [from] a company called Combined Systems International, which actually has its name on the side of the canisters that have been found on the streets there."

Hartung just published a book, *Prophets of War: Lockheed Martin and the Making of the Military-Industrial Complex*. He went on: "Lockheed Martin has been the leader in deals worth $3.8 billion over that period of the last 10 years; General Dynamics, $2.5 billion for tanks; Boeing, $1.7 billion for missiles, for helicopters; Raytheon for all manner of missiles for the armed forces. So, basically, this is a key element in propping up the regime, but a lot of the money is basically recycled. Taxpayers could just as easily be giving it directly to Lockheed Martin or General Dynamics."

Likewise, Egypt's Internet and cell phone "kill switch" was enabled only through collaboration with corporations. U.K.-based Vodafone, a global cellular-phone giant (which owns 45 percent of Verizon Wireless in the U.S.), attempted to justify its actions in a press release: "It has been clear to us that there were no legal or practical options open to Vodafone . . . but to comply with the demands of the authorities."

Narus, a U.S. subsidiary of Boeing Corp., sold Egypt equipment to allow "deep packet inspection," according to Tim Karr of the media policy group Free Press. Karr said the Narus technology "allows the Egyptian telecommunications companies . . . to look at texting via cell phones, and to identify the sort of dissident voices that are out there. . . . It also gives them the technology to geographically locate them and track them down."

Mubarak has pledged not to run for re-election come September. But the people of Egypt demand he leave now. How has he lasted thirty years? Maybe that's best explained by a warning from a U.S. Army general fifty years ago, President Dwight D. Eisenhower. He said, "We must guard against the acquisition of unwarranted influence, whether sought or unsought, by the military-industrial complex."

That deadly complex is not only a danger to democracy at home, but, by shoring up despots, to democracies abroad.

• •

October 5, 2011

Policing the Prophets of Wall Street

The Occupy Wall Street protest grows daily, spreading to cities across the United States. "We are the 99 percent," the protesters say, "that will no longer tolerate the greed and corruption of the 1 percent."

The response by the New York City Police Department has been brutal. Last

Saturday, the police swept up more than 700 protesters in one of the largest mass arrests in U.S. history. The week before, innocent protesters were pepper-sprayed in the face without warning or reason.

That is why, after receiving a landmark settlement this week from the police departments of Minneapolis and St. Paul, as well as the U.S. Secret Service, my colleagues and I went to Liberty Square, the heart of the Wall Street occupation, to announce the legal victory.

On Labor Day 2008, the *Democracy Now!* news team and I were covering the first day of the Republican National Convention in St. Paul. Thousands protested outside. I was on the convention floor, interviewing delegates from what that week was the hottest state, Alaska. Blocks away, my colleagues Sharif Abdel Kouddous and Nicole Salazar were covering a police assault on the dispersing crowd of marchers.

The riot police had hemmed the protesters into a parking lot, along with credentialed journalists. The police charged at Nicole, shouting "On your face!" She shouted back "Press, press!" holding up her press credentials in one hand and filming with the other, video-recording her own violent arrest. She screamed as they brought her down on her face, a knee or boot in her back, dragging her by her leg and bloodying her face. The first thing they then did was pull the battery from her camera, if there was any question about what they did not want documented. As Sharif tried to calm the riot(ing) police, they pushed him against a brick wall, kicked him in the chest twice, threw him down, and handcuffed him.

I got a call on my cell phone and raced from the Convention Center to the scene of the arrests. The riot police had encircled the area. I ran up to the police, my credentials hanging around my neck. I asked for the commanding officer to get my journalist colleagues released. It wasn't seconds before they tore me through the police line, twisted my arms behind my back, and handcuffed me. Finally brought to stand next to Sharif, as fully credentialed journalists, we demanded to be released, whereupon a Secret Service agent came over and ripped the credentials from around our necks.

We filed suit. This past week, the St. Paul and Minneapolis police and the Secret Service have settled with us. In addition to paying out $100,000, the St. Paul police department has agreed to implement a training program aimed at educating officers regarding the First Amendment rights of the press and public with respect to police operations—including police handling of media coverage of mass demonstrations—and to pursue implementation of the training program in Minneapolis and statewide.

As we move into the next conventions and cover protests like Occupy Wall Street, this largest settlement to come out of the 2008 RNC arrests should be a warning to police departments around the country to stop arresting and intimidating journalists, or engaging in any unlawful arrests. We shouldn't have to get a record while trying to put things on the record.

But do police actually pay the price? Before the 2008 Republican and Democratic national conventions, each party bought insurance policies to indemnify the convention cities from any damages resulting from lawsuits.

Bruce Nestor, president of the Minnesota chapter of the National Lawyers Guild, told me: "St. Paul actually negotiated a special insurance provision with the Republican host committee so that the first $10 million in liability for lawsuits arising from the convention will be covered by the host committee. . . . It basically means we (the city) can commit wrongdoing, and we won't have to pay for it."

Jump forward to today. The bailed-out Wall Street megabank JPMorgan Chase gave a tax-deductible $4.6 million donation to the New York City Police Foundation, which has protesters asking: Who is the NYPD paid to protect, the public or the corporations? The 99 percent or the 1 percent?

Marina Sitrin, part of Occupy Wall Street's legal working group, told me that the protest was going to be based at Chase Plaza, but the NYPD pre-emptively closed it. The protesters moved to Zuccotti Park, which they renamed Liberty Square.

According to an undated press release on JPMorgan Chase's website, in response to the $4.6 million donation: "New York City Police Commissioner Raymond Kelly sent CEO and Chairman Jamie Dimon a note expressing 'profound gratitude' for the company's donation." Given the size of the donation, and the police harassment and violence against the protesters, we must question how Kelly shows his gratitude.

January 26, 2012

Obama's Late Payment
to Mortgage-Fraud Victims

In his State of the Union address, many heard echoes of the Barack Obama of old, the presidential aspirant of 2007 and 2008. Among the populist pledges rolled out in the speech was tough talk against the too-big-to-fail banks that have funded his campaigns and for whom many of his key advisers have worked: "The rest of us are not bailing you out ever again," he promised.

President Obama also made a striking announcement, one that could have been written by the Occupy Wall Street General Assembly: "I'm asking my attorney general to create a special unit of federal prosecutors and leading state attorneys general to expand our investigations into the abusive lending and packaging of risky mortgages that led to the housing crisis. This new unit will hold accountable those who broke the law, speed assistance to homeowners, and help turn the page on an era of recklessness that hurt so many Americans."

Remarkably, President Obama named New York Attorney General Eric Schneiderman as co-chairperson of the Unit on Mortgage Origination and Securitization Abuses. Schneiderman was on a team of state attorneys general negotiating a settlement with the nation's five largest banks. He opposed the settlement as being too limited and offering overly generous immunity from future prosecution for financial fraud. For his outspoken consumer advocacy, he was kicked off the negotiating team. He withdrew his support of the settlement talks, along with several other key attorneys general, including California's Kamala Harris, an Obama supporter, and Delaware's Beau Biden, the vice president's son.

In an Op-Ed penned last November, Schneiderman and Biden wrote, "We recognized early this year that, though many public officials—including state attorneys general, members of Congress and the Obama administration—have delved into aspects of the bubble and crash, we needed a more comprehensive investigation before the financial institutions at the heart of the crisis are granted broad releases from liability."

When news of Schneiderman's appointment surfaced, MoveOn.org sent an email to its members declaring: "Just weeks ago, this investigation wasn't even on the table, and the big banks were pushing for a broad settlement that would have made it impossible.... This is truly a huge victory for the 99 percent movement."

The stakes are very high for the public, and for President Obama. He relied heavily on Wall Street backers to fund his massive campaign war chest in 2008. Now, in this post–*Citizens United* era, with expected billion-dollar campaign budgets, Obama could find himself out of favor with Wall Street. For the public, as noted by the Center for Responsible Lending: "More than 20,000 new families face foreclosure each month, including a disproportionate percentage of African-American and Latino households. CRL research indicates that we are only about halfway through the crisis."

Unanswered at this point is whether or not Schneiderman's appointment signals his willingness to go along with the multistate settlement now said to be nearing completion. Details are not yet public, but the deal is said to involve a $25 billion payment from the largest banks as a settlement for charges surrounding problematic mortgage-loan practices like robo-signing documents and grossly inadequate loan servicing, making foreclosures more likely. *Rolling Stone*'s Matt Taibbi, who has been doing essential investigative reporting on the financial crisis, told me: "It doesn't make sense for companies to settle without New York or California, since the potential liability from those two states alone could put them out of business, could cripple any of the too-big-to-fail banks."

Obama is aware that those at the Occupy Wall Street protests around the country include many who were his most active supporters during the 2008 campaign. Does the formation of the new task force signify a move to more progressive policies, as MoveOn suggests?

Longtime consumer advocate and former presidential candidate Ralph Nader doesn't hold much hope: "This financial crimes unit, that's like putting another label on a few doors in the Justice Department without a real expansion in the budget." Delaware's Biden expressed similar concerns about the task force, asking: "How many FBI agents are being put on it? How many investigators? How many prosecutors?"

This is the Occupy Wall Street conflict distilled. Will Eric Schneiderman's new job lead to the indictment of fraudulent financiers, or to just another indictment of our corrupt political system?

February 2, 2012

Romney's 1% Nation Under God

Although Mitt Romney has yet to win a majority in a Republican primary, he won big in Florida. After he and the pro-Romney super PACs flooded the airwaves with millions of dollars' worth of ads in a state where nearly half the homeowners are underwater, he talked about whom he wants to represent. "We will hear from the Democrat Party the plight of the poor, and there's no question, it's not good being poor," he told CNN's Soledad O'Brien. "You could choose where to focus, you could focus on the rich, that's not my focus. You could focus on the very poor, that's not my focus. My focus is on middle-income Americans." Of the very rich, Romney assures us, "They're doing just fine." With an estimated personal wealth of $250 million, Romney should know.

Romney's campaign itself is well-financed, but his success to date, especially against his current main rival, Newt Gingrich, is driven by massive cash infusions to a so-called super PAC, the new breed of political action committee that can take unlimited funds from individuals and corporations. Super PACs are legally prohibited from coordinating their activities with a candidate's campaign. Federal Election Commission filings made public January 31 reveal that the principal super PAC supporting Romney, Restore Our Future, raised close to $18 million in the second half of 2011, from just 199 donors. Among his supporters are Alice Walton, who, although listed in the report as a "rancher," is better known as an heir to the Walmart fortune, and the famously caustic venture capitalist and billionaire Samuel Zell, the man credited with driving the Tribune media company into bankruptcy. William Koch, the third of the famous Koch brothers, also gave.

Juxtapose those 199 with the number of people living in poverty in the United States. According to the most recent figures available from the U.S. Census Bureau, 46.2 million people lived in poverty in 2010, 15.1 percent of the population, the largest number in the fifty-two years the poverty estimates have been published. 2010 marked the fourth consecutive annual increase in the number of people in poverty.

Romney, in his victory speech in New Hampshire, said: "This country already has a leader who divides us with the bitter politics of envy. We must offer an alternative vision. I stand ready to lead us down a different path, where we are lifted up by our desire to succeed, not dragged down by a resentment of success.... We are one nation under God."

The next morning, NBC's Matt Lauer challenged him, asking: "Did you suggest that anyone who questions the policies and practices of Wall Street and financial institutions, anyone who has questions about the distribution of wealth and power in this country, is envious? Is it about jealousy, or fairness?" Romney doubled down, claiming: "I think it's about envy. I think it's about class warfare. When you have a president encouraging the idea of dividing America based on the 99 percent versus 1 percent—and those people who have been most successful will be in the 1 percent... [it's] entirely inconsistent with the concept of one nation under God."

And not caring for the poor is consistent? Romney presents a confusing critique of President Barack Obama and the Occupy Wall Street movement. Put aside for the moment that Occupy Wall Street is generally very critical of President Obama, and especially of his appointees like Treasury Secretary Timothy Geithner (who switched from Republican to independent in order to serve under Obama, but did not switch his politics) and former economic adviser Larry Summers. Romney clearly has no idea what the Occupy Wall Street movement is about if he thinks that the tens of thousands protesting, often facing police violence and risking arrest, are there because of envy. It is, as Lauer put it in his question, about fairness.

In the same New Hampshire speech, Romney said President Obama "wants to turn America into a European-style entitlement society." Curious words from a man who salted $3 million into a Swiss bank account. His hastily closed UBS bank account stands out as its own form of European entitlement. Coupled with investments in tax havens like Bermuda and the Cayman Islands, Romney's effective tax rate was 13.9 percent in 2010, a fraction of the 35 percent paid by average middle-class families that he claims to care so much about.

As Romney campaigns across his 1 percent nation under God, he moves from Florida, the state with the highest foreclosure rate, to Nevada, the state with the highest unemployment rate. Expect him to increasingly care, if not for the very poor, then for the votes they will likely cast against him.

February 23, 2012

New Obama Campaign Co-Chair: "The President Is Wrong"

"The president is wrong." So says one of the newly appointed co-chairs of President Barack Obama's re-election campaign.

Those four words headline the website of the organization Progressives United, founded by former U.S. senator, and now Obama campaign adviser, Russ Feingold. He is referring to Obama's recent announcement that he will accept super PAC funds for his re-election campaign. Feingold writes: "The President is wrong to embrace the corrupt corporate politics of Citizens United through the use of super PACs—organizations that raise unlimited amounts of money from corporations and the richest individuals, sometimes in total secrecy. It's not just bad policy; it's also dumb strategy." And, he says, it's "dancing with the devil."

In 1905, President Theodore Roosevelt said to Congress, "All contributions by corporations to any political committee or for any political purpose should be forbidden by law." He signed a bill into law banning such contributions in 1907. In 2012, this hundred-year history of campaign-finance controls died, thanks to five U.S. Supreme Court justices who decided, in the 2010 Citizens United case, that corporations can use their money to express free speech, most notably in their efforts to influence federal elections.

After eighteen years representing Wisconsin in the U.S. Senate, Feingold lost his re-election to self-funded Republican multimillionaire and tea-party favorite Ron Johnson. Since then, Feingold has been teaching law, started Progressives United and, while supporting the effort to recall Wisconsin's embattled Gov. Scott Walker, has steadfastly refused to run against him or for the U.S. Senate seat being vacated by retiring Democratic Sen. Herb Kohl.

Feingold was the sole member of the U.S. Senate to vote against the USA PATRIOT Act. He was a fierce critic of the Bush administration's warrantless wiretapping program. Although Obama, as a senator, originally threatened to filibuster any legislation that would grant retroactive immunity to the telecom corporations involved with the wiretapping, he reversed himself on the eve of the Democratic Convention in 2008 and voted for the bill. Feingold remained adamantly opposed. On the war in Afghanistan, Feingold told me: "I was the first member of the Senate to call for a timeline to get us out of Afghanistan. Even before Obama was elected, when it was between [John] McCain and Obama, I said, 'Why are we talking about a surge?' . . . Sending our troops over there, spending billions and billions of dollars in Afghanistan, makes no sense. And I think it was a mistake for the president to do the surge, and I think he's beginning to realize we need to get out of there."

Feingold opposed Obama's Wall Street reform bill, saying it was too weak, and supported the state attorneys general, like New York's Eric Schneiderman and another of the new campaign co-chairs, California's Kamala Harris, who, at first, opposed the proposed settlement with the five largest banks over allegations of mortgage-service fraud and "robo-signing." Feingold's reaction to the $25 billion settlement that the White House pushed through? "We were among the few that refused to do a little dance after this announcement . . . whenever it ends up being Wall Street, somehow there's always a clunker in there."

As I interviewed Feingold, just hours after he was named one of the thirty-five Obama campaign co-chairs, I asked him if he was an odd choice for the position. Feingold responded: "How about a co-chair that's proud of him for bringing us health care for the first time in seventy years? How about a co-chair who thinks that he has actually done a good thing with the economy and helped with the stimulus package, and we've had twenty-two months of positive job growth? How about a co-chair for a president that has the best reputation overseas of any president in memory, that has reversed the awful damage of the Bush administration, who in places like Cairo and in India and Indonesia has reached out to the rest of the world. Believe me, on balance, there's no question. And finally, how about a co-chair of a president who I believe will help us appoint justices who will overturn Citizens United?"

Until then, as the Obama campaign "dances with the devil" of super PACs, perhaps campaign co-chair Russ Feingold will help us follow the money.

May 10, 2012

Coal, Foreclosures, and Bank of America's "Extraordinary Event"

Shareholder meetings can be routine, unless you are Bank of America, in which case they may be declared an "extraordinary event." That is what the city of Charlotte, North Carolina, called the bank's shareholder meeting this week. Bank of America is currently the second-largest bank in the U.S. (after JPMorgan Chase), claiming more than $2 trillion in assets. It also is the "too big to fail" poster child of Occupy Wall Street, a speculative banking monstrosity that profits from, among other things, the ongoing foreclosure crisis and the exploitation of dirty coal.

North Carolina, which went for Barack Obama in 2008, is a swing state in this year's presidential election. Current polls indicate the Tar Heel State is a tossup. To boost its chances there, the Democratic Party has chosen Charlotte to host this summer's Democratic National Convention. In preparation, the Charlotte City Council passed an amendment to the city code allowing the city manager to declare so-called extraordinary events. The ordinance is clearly structured to grant police extra powers to detain, search, and arrest people who are within the arbitrarily defined "extraordinary event" zone. The ordinance reads, in part, "It shall be unlawful for any person ... to willfully or intentionally possess, carry, control, or have immediate access to any of the following" and then lists a page of items, including scarves, backpacks, duffel bags, satchels, and coolers.

Wednesday's protest outside the Bank of America headquarters, with hundreds marching, was peaceful and spirited. The colorful array of creative signs was complemented by activists inside the meeting, who, as shareholders, were entitled to address the gathering. George Goehl of National People's Action, who was inside, told CNN about Bank of America CEO Brian Moynihan's reaction: "Dozens of us were able to speak, but Moynihan mostly dodged, deflected and denied. He looked visibly uncomfortable the entire time."

Many activists expressed outrage at the bank's role in the subprime mortgage industry and the foreclosure crisis it helped spawn. As part of a federal settlement over widespread mortgage fraud, Bank of America agreed to hand over $11.8 billion. Just two days before the protest, the bank announced it was contacting the

first 5,000 of 200,000 mortgage customers who are eligible for a loan modifica-
tion, with a potential decrease in their mortgage principal of up to 30 percent.

Last week, Rainforest Action Network members climbed 100 feet to suspend
a banner on Charlotte's Bank of America Stadium, where President Obama is
scheduled to make his nomination acceptance speech on September 6. The banner read "Bank of America" with the word "America" crossed out and replaced
with "Coal." RAN is part of a broad coalition fighting the destructive practice of
mountaintop removal. RAN Executive Director Rebecca Tarbotton told me:

> Bank of America is the lead financier of mountaintop-removal mining,
> which is a practice of mining which is really the worst of the worst mining
> that we see anywhere, essentially blowing the tops off of mountains in Ap-
> palachia, destroying people's homes, polluting their water supplies. And
> that's even before it gets into the coal plants, where it's burnt and creates air
> pollution in inner-city areas and all around our country.... [It's] the canary
> in the coal mine for our reliance on fossil fuels.

The broad coalition in and out of the shareholder meeting demonstrates a
key development in Occupy Wall Street's spring revival, and also foreshadows
possible confrontations with the Obama re-election campaign this fall.

President Obama clearly responds to pressure. Look at the issue of marriage
equality. In 1996, while campaigning for state senator in Illinois, Obama wrote
that he supported same-sex marriage. While campaigning in 2008, then U.S.
Sen. Obama stated, "I believe that marriage is the union between a man and a
woman." This week, he told ABC News, "It is important for me to affirm that I
think same-sex couples should be able to get married."

Given the political climate, it certainly is brave for Obama to endorse marriage equality, especially just hours after the voters of North Carolina voted in
favor of a state constitutional amendment that bans same-sex marriage. But he
was once a community organizer, and no doubt recalls the words of Frederick
Douglass: "Power concedes nothing without a demand. It never did, and it
never will." The LGBT community was organized and vocal, and the president's
position moved.

Those gathered inside and outside the Bank of America shareholder meeting this week—homeowners fighting foreclosure, environmentalists, Occupy
Wall Street activists—will take note of the president's change. They are sure to

continue their struggles, right through the Democratic National Convention, making it truly an "extraordinary event."

•••

July 20, 2011

Rupert Murdoch Doesn't Eat Humble Pie

"People say that Australia has given two people to the world," Julian Assange told me in London recently, "Rupert Murdoch and me." Assange, the founder of the whistle-blowing website WikiLeaks, was humbly dismissing my introduction of him, to a crowd of 1,800 at East London's Troxy theater, in which I suggested he had published perhaps more than anyone in the world. He said Murdoch took that publishing prize.

Two days later, the Milly Dowler phone hacking story exploded, and Murdoch would close one of the largest newspapers in the world, his *News of the World*, within a week.

On Tuesday, Murdoch claimed before the British House of Commons Select Committee on Culture, Media and Sport that it was his "most humble day." But what does it mean for a man with no humility to suffer his most humble day? The principal takeaway from the committee hearing must be, simply, that Rupert Murdoch is not responsible for the criminal activities under investigation, from police bribery to phone hacking. When asked if he was ultimately responsible, his answer was simple: "No." Who was? "The people I trusted to run it and maybe the people they trusted."

The monosyllabic denials stood in stark juxtaposition to his rhetorically nimble son, James Murdoch. Frequently reminding the committee that he was not present at *News of the World* during the dark days of hacking and bribing, James used more words to say essentially the same thing: I know nothing.

The performance, for now, seems to have worked. No, the buck doesn't stop with Rupert Murdoch, but the money sure rolls in nicely. News Corp.'s stock price inched up throughout the day. The Murdochs' apparent success in the hearing might be attributed to the stone-faced lawyer sitting directly behind James throughout: News Corp. Executive Vice President Joel Klein.

Klein is a new addition to the executive stable at Rupert Murdoch's media empire, hired, according to a News Corp. press release, as "a senior adviser to Mr. Murdoch on a wide range of initiatives, including developing business strategies for the emerging educational marketplace." Klein formerly was deputy White House counsel to President Bill Clinton. More lately, and more likely germane to his hiring by Murdoch, was Klein's tenure as chancellor of New York City schools, the largest school system in the U.S., serving more than 1.1 million students in more than 1,600 schools. Klein, under Mayor Michael Bloomberg, undertook controversial restructuring of the school system. My colleague at the *Democracy Now!* news hour, Juan Gonzalez, who is a columnist at the New York *Daily News* (the main competitor to Murdoch's *New York Post*), consistently documented Klein's failures as chancellor, reporting on "countless parents and teachers who long ago grew weary of his autocratic and disrespectful style." Klein's attempt to shutter nineteen schools in some of the city's poorest neighborhoods was reversed by the New York State Supreme Court. Claims of improved performance on standardized tests made under Klein's direction were shown to be based on inflated scores.

Less than two weeks after his hire was announced, News Corp. bought a privately held company, Wireless Generation. Murdoch said of the $360 million purchase, "When it comes to K through 12 education, we see a $500 billion sector in the U.S. alone."

Which is why one of the leading education tweeters, Leonie Haimson, a New York public-school parent and executive director of Class Size Matters, is concerned. She told me: "With all the allegations about phone hacking, etc., we really have concerns about the privacy of New York state students. And secondly, we don't want to open up the public coffers wide for the Murdoch companies to make money off of our kids."

New York City public schools have already granted the company a $2.7 million contract, and the New York State Education Department is close to granting Wireless Generation a $27 million no-bid contract.

News Corp. has announced the formation of a Management and Standards Committee that will answer directly to Klein. Klein, who sits on the News Corp. board of directors, will report to fellow board member and former fellow Justice

Department attorney Viet Dinh. Dinh was assistant attorney general under George W. Bush and a principal author of the USA Patriot Act, the law that, among other things, prompted an unprecedented expansion of government eavesdropping. According to recent Securities and Exchange Commission filings, Dinh and other directors lined up on July 3 to sell off stock options, with Dinh netting about $25,000, just as the scandal broke.

News Corp. is far from a news corpse, though the term is sadly relevant, with the initial exposé of *News of the World*'s grotesque hacking of murder victim Milly Dowler's voice mail, giving false hope to her family that she was alive. The FBI is now investigating whether Murdoch papers tried to profit from hacking into the voice mails of victims of the 9/11 attacks. U.S. journalists must now dig into News Corp.'s operations here, to expose not only potential criminality, but also the threat to democracy posed by unbridled media conglomerates like the Murdoch empire.

UNDOING THE COUPS,
FROM HAITI TO HONDURAS

September 23, 2009

President Zelaya and the Audacity of Action

Manuel Zelaya, the democratically elected president of Honduras, is back in his country after being deposed in a military coup June 28. Zelaya appeared there unexpectedly Monday morning, announcing his presence in Tegucigalpa, the capital, from within the Brazilian Embassy, where he has taken refuge. Hondurans immediately began flocking to the embassy to show their support. Zelaya's bold move occurs during a critical week, with world leaders gathering for the annual United Nations General Assembly, followed by the G-20 meeting of leaders and finance ministers in Pittsburgh. The Obama administration may be forced, finally, to join world opinion in decisively opposing the coup.

How Zelaya got into Honduras is still unclear. He told the press Monday, "I had to travel for 15 hours, sometimes walking, other times marching in different areas in the middle of the night." One source inside the Brazilian Embassy said he may have hidden in the trunk of a car, successfully bypassing up to twenty police checkpoints.

Around dawn Tuesday, supporters who defied the government-imposed curfew outside the Brazilian Embassy were violently dispersed with tear gas and water cannons. Electricity, phone, and water service to the embassy have been shut down, and the Honduran military has reportedly set up a truck with loudspeakers there, blasting the Honduran national anthem. On Monday, the Organization of American States (OAS) reiterated its call "for the immediate signing of the San José Agreement," the accord negotiated by Costa Rican President Óscar Arias calling for Zelaya's return as president, with members of the coup regime included in the government, and amnesty for anyone involved in the coup. Zelaya has agreed to the terms, but installed coup President Roberto Micheletti has rejected them.

After the June 28 coup, the OAS immediately suspended Honduras from OAS proceedings and called for Zelaya's immediate reinstatement. On June 30, the U.N. General Assembly issued a unanimous demand for "the immediate and unconditional restoration of power" for Zelaya.

Likewise, UNASUR, the Union of South American Nations, at its summit in Quito, Ecuador, formally denounced the coup. The OAS Inter-American Commission on Human Rights traveled to Honduras in late August and reported that demonstrations in support of Zelaya "were broken up by public security forces, both police and military, resulting in deaths, cases of torture and mistreatment, hundreds of injured, and thousands of arbitrary detentions."

President Barack Obama, on June 29, said clearly, "We believe that the coup was not legal and that President Zelaya remains the president of Honduras, the democratically elected president there." But subsequent action, or inaction, by Obama and Secretary of State Hillary Clinton has sent mixed signals. While Obama originally used the word *coup*, official policy pronouncements have avoided the term, which, if used, would trigger mandatory suspension of foreign aid. Instead, the Obama administration has deployed selective punishment of the coup regime, rescinding visas for Micheletti and other key coup figures, and halting a relatively token $30 million in aid.

Clinton said Monday, at a meeting with Costa Rica's Arias: "We just want to see this matter resolved peacefully, with an understanding that there will be the remainder of President Zelaya's term to be respected." The United Nations will most likely take action this week in support of Zelaya. Zelaya said Tuesday from the Brazilian Embassy: "The U.S. should respond and respect the OAS charter. The United States should call for an emergency meeting of the United Nations Security Council. The United States should take every type of trade sanction measure in order to pressure this regime now in power in Honduras."

Obama is expected to chair a session of the U.N. Security Council, marking the first time a U.S. president has done so. Costa Rica currently has a seat on the Security Council, and could in theory bring up the issue of Honduras. Then in Pittsburgh, where the G-20 is meeting to assess and act on the global financial crisis, Brazil's support for Zelaya may be a factor. Brazil, a G-20 member, is by far the largest economy in South America, and is a key ally and trading partner of the U.S. With tear gas wafting through the Brazilian Embassy in Tegucigalpa, and a potential armed assault on it by the coup regime to arrest Zelaya, this week may force Obama and Clinton to finally help the people of Honduras undo the coup.

January 20, 2010

Tè Tremblé—The Haitian Earth Trembled

PORT-AU-PRINCE, Haiti—Tè tremblé is Haitian Creole for "earthquake." Its literal translation: "The earth trembled." After the massive earthquake that devastated Haiti, the stench of death is everywhere. At General Hospital, bodies had been stacked four feet high near the morgue. In the community house called Matthew 25, doctors laid out a plastic tablecloth to perform a kitchen-table amputation, aided by headlamps. The injured Haitian man in his twenties might be considered fortunate: He was among the minority of injured people getting medical attention. And, unlike many amputations being performed elsewhere in Haiti, the doctors who arrived Monday were using anesthesia they had brought.

While this grim amputation was happening, an unexpected delivery of food aid arrived. Matthew 25 House typically accommodates thirty-five guests. Now more than 1,000 are there, camped out in the adjoining soccer field. There has been much reporting on the concerns about possible riots and violence that aid distribution might provoke. We witnessed the polar opposite, because an established community group was empowered to distribute the food. People lined up and got their supplies, leaving undisturbed the difficult surgery being conducted nearby. This has been typical as we've traveled through the catastrophe: People with nothing—hungry, thirsty, seeking their loved ones, burying their dead, caring for their injured—have shown fortitude, civility, and compassion despite their quiet desperation.

We went to the home of Myriam Merlet, the chief of staff of the Haitian Ministry of Women. She helped draw international attention to the use of rape as a political weapon and worked with playwright and activist Eve Ensler on the V-Day movement to help end violence against women. We found her house, indeed the entire surrounding community, destroyed. "We have just pulled her body out," they told us Sunday, five days after the earthquake. There is no telling when she died, or whether she might have been rescued. Her sister Eartha brought us to her fresh grave.

We ventured beyond Port-au-Prince, to the earthquake's epicenter, past Carrefour to Léogâne. A United Nations assessment put the level of destruction in Léogâne at 80 percent to 90 percent of structures destroyed, with no remaining government buildings. On the way, a young man hailed our car, saying: "Please, we see some helicopters overhead, but they don't stop here. We have no aid. We have no food."

One man covered in dust was using a mallet to break the cement that had entombed his grandfather. A father nearby had just dug out his one-year-old baby, dead in his playpen. According to Agence France-Presse, the U.N. warned it cannot "extend their aid operation to outlying areas until security there can be confirmed." Traveling to Léogâne, we felt no threat; we only saw people in dire need of help. While we were in Léogâne, a missionary helicopter landed, then inexplicably lifted off again, and the crew began hurling loaves of bread to the ground. Young Haitian men grew incensed. One cried, tearing up the rolls and yelling, "We are not dogs for you to throw bones at!"

We spoke with the mayor of Léogâne, Alexis Santos, who seemed almost helpless before the near-total destruction around him. I asked him, in light of the unified front offered by the U.S. government, with President Barack Obama naming former Presidents Bill Clinton and George W. Bush to lead the U.S. response, what he thought about the offer of Jean-Bertrand Aristide—the ousted former president of Haiti—to return to Haiti from exile in South Africa to stand with Haitian President René Préval, a united front to help the recovery. Santos, by no means an Aristide supporter, told me he thought it would be a good idea.

Back at Matthew 25 House (named after the biblical verse "Whatever you do for my least brothers and sisters, you do for me"), I spoke with one of the surgeons. Dr. Jennifer Bruny, who flew down with other doctors from Children's Hospital in Denver, performed the amputation earlier. The nature of the disaster, with thousands of crushing injuries, and the lack of care for so much time make amputation one of the only means available now to save lives. "This amputation should not have been necessary," she told me. "This could have been easily treated earlier. These people needed help sooner."

January 27, 2010

Let the Haitians In

Jean Montrevil was shackled, imprisoned, about to be sent to Haiti. It was January 6, days before the earthquake that would devastate Haiti, the poorest nation in the Western Hemisphere. Montrevil came to the U.S. with a green card in 1986 at the age of seventeen. Twenty years ago, still a teenager, he was convicted of possession of cocaine and sent to prison for eleven years. Upon release, he married a U.S. citizen; he has four U.S.-citizen children, owns a business, pays taxes, and is a legal, permanent resident. He is a well-respected Haitian New York community activist. But because of his earlier conviction, he was on an immigration supervision program, requiring him to check in with an immigration official every two weeks. On December 30, during his routine visit, he was immediately detained and told he would be deported to Haiti. A fellow detainee bound for Haiti had a fever. That man's illness halted the flight, and then the earthquake struck.

The devastating toll of the January 12 earthquake in Haiti continues to mount. Most efforts to rescue people from the rubble have ended. More than 150,000 people have been buried, some in makeshift graves near the ruins of the homes where they died, but many in unmarked, mass graves at Titanyen, the site of massacres during previous dictatorships and coups. More than 1 million people are homeless out of Haiti's population of 9 million. The stench of decaying bodies is still pervasive in the capital city of Port-au-Prince as well as in outlying towns, which, two weeks out, have seen little outside help. It was painful to see the mass of aid stockpiled at the airport. The Haitians need it now. For example, I saw pallets with thousands of bottles of Aquafina water there. Hopeful when a truck arrived to load up, I asked where it was headed. "To the U.S. Embassy," I was told.

One of the principal sources of national income in Haiti is the flow of remittances from the Haitian diaspora, whose cash, wired to family members back in Haiti, amounts to one-third of Haiti's gross national product. For years, after four major hurricanes and massive flooding, the Haitian community has simply been asking to be treated like Nicaraguans, Hondurans, and Salvadorans in similar circumstances, to receive Temporary Protected Status (TPS). TPS allows people to stay in the U.S., and legally work, during times of armed conflict or natural disaster, and is a critical element of any humane policy. Finally, following frantic grassroots lobbying after the earthquake, the U.S. government extended TPS to Haitians.

But TPS is not enough. Haitians need to be allowed into the United States, legally, compassionately, and immediately. I visited hospitals and clinics in Port-au-Prince, with thousands of people waiting for care, and amputations happening with ibuprofen or Motrin, if patients were lucky. Ira Kurzban, a Miami-based attorney who represented Haiti for years, says the U.S. must let in those immediately who need medical care, that far too few of the injured have been brought to the U.S. In addition, he told me, the U.S. should bring many more people from Haiti, including all those people who had approved petitions by family members. It's about 70,000 people. These people have been approved, but are essentially in a multiyear waiting line to move to the U.S. Kurzban compared the historical willingness and ability of the U.S. to accept Cuban refugees with what he calls a policy of "containment" with Haiti, preventing people from leaving and blocking the shores with the Coast Guard. The first thing I saw when flying in to Port-au-Prince days after the earthquake were the Coast Guard cutters. They weren't bringing aid in, or carrying people out. They were preventing Haitians from leaving.

National Nurses United, the largest nurses union in the U.S., has 12,000 registered nurses willing to travel to Haiti to help, but they say they can't get assistance from the Obama administration. So they called filmmaker Michael Moore. He told me this week: "This is pretty pathetic if you're having to call me. I mean, you are the largest nurses union . . . and you can't get a call in to the White House?" The NNU is seeking individual sponsors through its website.

Grassroots and church groups in New York City demanded freedom for Jean Montrevil, and he was released. It is that kind of solidarity that is now needed by millions of Haitians, here and in Haiti, suffering the greatest catastrophe in their history.

February 10, 2010

Haiti, Forgive Us

The tragedy of the Haitian earthquake continues to unfold, with slow delivery of aid, the horrific number of amputations performed out of desperate medical necessity, more than a million homeless, perhaps 240,000 dead, hunger, dehydration, the emergence of infections and waterborne diseases, and the approach of the rainy season, which will be followed by the hurricane season. Haiti has suffered a massive blow, an earthquake for which its infrastructure was not prepared, after decades—no, centuries—of military and economic manipulation by foreign governments, most notably the United States and France.

Haiti was a slave plantation controlled by France. In 1804, inspired by Toussaint L'Ouverture (after whom the now barely functioning airport in Port-au-Prince is named), the slaves rebelled, founding the world's first black republic. Under military threat from France in 1825, Haiti agreed to pay reparations to France for lost "property," including slaves that French owners lost in the rebellion. It was either agree to pay the reparations or have France invade Haiti and reimpose slavery. Many Haitians believe that original debt, which Haiti dutifully paid through World War II, committed Haiti to a future of poverty that it has never been able to escape. (While France, as part of the deal, recognized Haiti's sovereignty, slave-owning politicians in the United States, like Thomas Jefferson, refused to recognize the black republic, afraid it would inspire a slave revolt here. The U.S. withheld formal recognition until 1862.)

The U.S. Marines occupied Haiti from 1915 until 1934. In 1956, François "Papa Doc" Duvalier took control in a military coup and declared himself president for life, initiating a period of brutal, bloody dictatorship, with U.S. support. Papa Doc died in 1971, at which point his nineteen-year-old son, Jean-Claude "Baby Doc" Duvalier, took over, maintaining the same violent dictatorial control until he was driven into exile by popular revolt in 1986. Jubilee USA, a network calling for elimination of debt owed by poor countries, estimates that Baby Doc alone diverted at least $500 million in public funds to his private accounts, and that 45 percent of Haiti's debt in recent decades was accumulated during the corrupt reign of the Duvaliers.

Loans from the World Bank, the International Monetary Fund (IMF), and the Inter-American Development Bank (IDB) imposed "structural adjustment" conditions on Haiti, opening its economy to cheap U.S. agricultural products. Farmers, unable to compete, stopped growing rice and moved to the cities to earn low wages, if they were lucky enough to get one of the scarce sweatshop jobs. People in the highlands were driven to deforest the hills, converting wood into salable charcoal, which created an ecological crisis—destabilizing hillsides, increasing the destructiveness of earthquakes, and causing landslides during the rainy season.

Haiti's first democratically elected president was Jean-Bertrand Aristide, a Catholic priest committed to the poor. He was elected in 1990, then ousted in a military coup in 1991. In 1994, with Haitian refugees flooding into Florida, the Clinton administration was forced to restore Aristide to power, but only with additional structural-adjustment demands. Aristide was re-elected in 2000, only to be deposed again in a U.S.-backed coup in 2004, Haiti's bicentennial.

The destruction of Haiti's rice industry, which was replaced with U.S. government-subsidized rice that Haitians refer to as "Miami rice," as well as the sale of critical state-owned enterprises, like Haiti's sole flour mill and cement factory, have left the country dependent on foreign trade and aid, keeping Haiti at a permanent disadvantage. It is critical now to cancel Haiti's ongoing foreign debt, so that the country can devote its scant resources to rebuilding and not to repaying debt. The G-7 finance ministers met in Canada this week and announced the forgiveness of the bilateral debt between member states and Haiti. But the World Bank, IMF, and IDB debts remain (the IMF controversially promised a $100 million loan after the earthquake, eliciting condemnation, and has since pledged to convert it to a grant).

Earthquakes alone do not create disasters of the scale now experienced in Haiti. The wealthy nations have for too long exploited Haiti, denying it the right to develop in a secure, sovereign, sustainable way. The global outpouring of support for Haitians must be matched by long-term, unrestricted grants of aid, and immediate forgiveness of all that country's debt. Given their role in Haiti's plight, the United States, France, and other industrialized nations should be the ones seeking forgiveness.

July 14, 2010

Haiti, Six Months After the Earthquake

PORT-AU-PRINCE, Haiti—July 12 marked the six-month anniversary of the devastating earthquake here in Haiti that killed as many as 300,000 people and left much of the country in ruins. Up to 1.8 million people are living in squalid tent cities, with inadequate sanitation, if any, no electricity and little security, or any respite from the intense heat and the worsening rains. Rape, hunger, and despair are constant threats to the people stranded in the camps. Six months ago, the world seemed united with commitments to help Haiti recover. Now, half a year later, the rubble remains in place, and misery blankets the camps, layered with heat, drenched by rain.

After landing in Haiti, we traveled to one of the more than 1,350 refugee camps, Camp Corail. It is right near Titanyen, which was used as a dumping ground for bodies during the first coup against President Jean-Bertrand Aristide, and which, after the earthquake, was used for makeshift mass graves.

Corail is on a flat expanse of white gravel, with orderly rows of tents. During the day, the camp becomes searingly hot, with no trees for protection.

Corail resident Romain Arius told me: "In the situation we're living here in the tents, we can't continue like that anymore. We would ask them as soon as possible to give us the real houses that they said they were going to give us so that our situation could improve."

Soon after we left, we heard that a storm collapsed at least ninety-four tents and sent hundreds of residents fleeing to find shelter.

Haitians are angry, questioning where the billions of dollars donated in the immediate aftermath of the earthquake have gone. The Disaster Accountability Project found that of the 197 organizations that solicited money following the earthquake, only six had publicly available reports detailing their activities.

From the "international donor community," the wealthier nations, more than $9 billion was pledged, but to date, only Brazil, Norway, and Australia have paid in full. Most of the U.S. pledge of $1.15 billion is now being held up in Congress.

Patrick Elie, a longtime Haitian democracy activist and Haiti's former secretary of state for public security, spoke with me about land ownership and the earthquake's enormous toll: "Land tenure in Haiti is in total chaos. This is also the result of the behavior of the Haitian elites over centuries. They appropriated land, especially after independence and the end of slavery, which would have been common property. And now, there is a lot of discussion about who owns what piece of land."

Elie said that in this time of emergency that gives the government the power of eminent domain, the key question is whose land will be seized—communal land that peasants have used for centuries, or the vast tracts of land owned by the elites.

I also spoke with Sean Penn. The two-time Oscar-winning actor came to Haiti after the earthquake. Having just been through a medical crisis with his own teenage son, who underwent major surgery, he was horrified at the stories he was hearing about the amputations being performed in Haiti without anesthesia. Penn founded the J/P Haitian Relief Organization (jphro.org) and has been in Haiti for five of the past six months, managing a refugee camp at the Petionville Club golf course with 55,000 Haitians displaced by the earthquake. Sitting in a large tent, Penn was frustrated. Comparing the U.S. resources being spent in Afghanistan (which he called "a ludicrous exercise") with the U.S. spending in Haiti, he said, "You have a war here, you've got a surge coming with storms, but no face to hate, no country to rail at, no natural resources, and the faces here are black."

Penn says J/P HRO will be in Haiti for the long haul: "We plan to adapt, to adjust. I think our next major new push for us will be rubble removal and working with partners to get people returned into neighborhoods and to again work with partners. Take camp management into community management and advocacy."

Patrick Elie advocates for popular Haitian leadership in the reconstruction: "We are a people who can fend for ourselves. We have a vision of where we want to go. So we do need friends, but we don't need people to think for us, or to pity us."

According to the *Washington Post*, only 2 percent of promised reconstruction aid has been delivered. The hurricane season is upon Haiti, and millions there are counting on all of us making good on our pledges.

March 23, 2011

Aristide's Return to Haiti: A Long Night's Journey into Day

The United States did its damnedest to prevent the return of the elected president it helped oust in 2004. That it failed is a turning-point.

Late at night on March 17, 2011, former Haitian President Jean-Bertrand Aristide boarded a small plane with his family in Johannesburg, South Africa. The following morning, he arrived in Haiti. It was just over seven years after he was kidnapped from his home in a U.S.-backed coup d'etat.

Haiti has been ravaged by a massive earthquake that killed more than 300,000 people and left a million and a half homeless. A cholera epidemic carried in by United Nations occupation forces could sicken almost 800,000. A majority of the population lives on less than a dollar a day.

Now, Aristide, by far the most popular figure in Haiti today, and the first democratically elected president of the first black republic in the world, has returned home.

"*Bon retou, Titid*" ("good return, Titid"—the affectionate term for Aristide) read the signs in Port-au-Prince as thousands flocked to accompany Aristide from the Toussaint L'Ouverture airport to his home. L'Ouverture led the slave uprising that established Haiti in 1804. I was able to travel with Aristide, his wife, Mildred, and their two daughters from Johannesburg to Haiti on the small jet provided by the government of South Africa.

It was my second flight with them. In March 2004, the Aristides attempted to return from forced exile in the Central African Republic, but never made it back to Haiti. Defense Secretary Donald Rumsfeld and other U.S. officials warned Aristide to stay away from the Western Hemisphere. Defying such pressure, the Aristides stopped in Jamaica before traveling to South Africa, where they remained until last weekend.

Just before this Sunday's election in Haiti, President René Préval gave Aristide the diplomatic passport he had long promised him. Earlier, on January 19, then U.S. State Department spokesman PJ Crowley tweeted, referring to Aristide: "today Haiti needs to focus on its future, not its past." Mildred was incensed. She said the U.S. had been saying that since they forced him out of the country. Sitting in the plane a few minutes before landing in Haiti, she repeated the words of an African leader who criticized the historic abuses of colonial powers by saying, "I would stop talking about the past, if it weren't so present."

Mark Toner, the new State Department spokesman, said last week: "Former President Aristide has chosen to remain outside of Haiti for seven years. To return this week could only be seen as a conscious choice to impact Haiti's elections."

Aristide did not choose to leave, or to remain outside Haiti, and the Obama administration knows that. On February 29, 2004, Luis Moreno, the No. 2 man in the U.S. embassy in Haiti, went to the Aristides' home and hustled them off to the airport. Frantz Gabriel was Aristide's personal bodyguard in 2004. I met him when he was with the Aristides in the Central African Republic then, and saw him again last Friday as the Aristides arrived home. He recalled:

> It was not willingly that the president left, because all the people that came in to accompany the president were all military. Having been in the US military myself, I know what a GI looks like, and I know what a special forces [soldier] looks like also ... when we boarded the aircraft, everybody changed their uniform into civilian clothes. And that's when I knew that it was a special operation.

The U.S. continued to prevent Aristide from returning for the next seven years. Just last week, President Barack Obama called South African President Jacob Zuma to express "deep concerns" about Aristide's potential return, and to pressure Zuma to block the trip. Zuma, to his credit, ignored the warning. U.S. diplomatic cables released by WikiLeaks reveal a concerted drive, over years, to hamper the return of Aristide to Haiti, including diplomatically punishing any country that helped Aristide, including threatening to block a U.N. Security Council seat for South Africa.

After landing in Port-au-Prince, Aristide wasted no time. He addressed the people of Haiti from the airport. His remarks touched on a key point of the current elections there: that his political party, the most popular party in Haiti, Fanmi Lavalas, is banned, excluded from the elections. He said: "The problem is exclusion, and the solution is inclusion. The exclusion of Fanmi Lavalas is the exclusion of the majority ... because everybody is a person."

Looking out on the country he hadn't seen in seven years, he concluded: "Haiti, Haiti, the further I am from you, the less I breathe. Haiti, I love you, and I will love you always. Always."

June 1, 2011

Hope and Resistance in Honduras

While most in the United States were recognizing Memorial Day with a three-day weekend, the people of Honduras were engaged in a historic event: the return of President Manuel Zelaya, twenty-three months after he was forced into exile at gunpoint in the first coup in Central America in a quarter century. While he is no longer president, his peaceful return marks a resounding success for the opponents of the coup. Despite this, the post-coup government in Honduras, under President Porfirio "Pepe" Lobo, is becoming increasingly repressive, and is the subject this week of a letter to Secretary of State Hillary Clinton, signed by eighty-seven members of the U.S. Congress, calling for suspension of aid to the Honduran military and police.

As the only U.S. journalist on Zelaya's flight home, I asked him how he felt about his imminent return. "Full of hope and optimism," he said. "Political action is possible instead of armaments. No to violence. No to military coups. Coups never more."

When Zelaya landed in Honduras, he kneeled down and kissed the ground. He was greeted by tens of thousands of people cheering and waving the black-and-red flag of the movement born after the coup, the FNRP, or National Front of Popular Resistance, "the resistance" that Zelaya now leads. His first stop: a massive rally at the memorial for nineteen-year-old Isis Obed Murillo, who was killed one week after the 2009 coup when Zelaya first attempted to fly back into the country. Murillo was with tens of thousands awaiting Zelaya's return at the airport. The military blocked the runway and dispersed the crowd with live fire, killing the teenager.

Since then, violence and impunity have been constant. Farmers, journalists, students, teachers, and anyone else in Honduras daring to dissent face intimidation, arrest, and murder. At least twelve journalists have been killed there since the coup, according to the Committee to Protect Journalists. Scores of campesinos—small farmers—have been killed. High-school students protesting teacher layoffs and the privatization of education were violently attacked by police this week, with tear gas and live ammunition.

At the rally, Zelaya, memorializing Murillo, said, "Blood was not shed in vain, because we're still standing... resistance is today the cry of victory."

The current Honduran government agreed to allow Zelaya's return to gain readmission into the Organization of American States in an attempt to shed Honduras' pariah status in Latin America for the coup.

Pariah to Latin America, but not the United States. Even though President Barack Obama early on called Zelaya's ouster "a coup," the U.S. government soon dropped the term. But there is no other word for it. On Sunday, I spoke with Zelaya in his home. He recounted what happened.

It was around 5 a.m. on June 28, 2009, when black-hooded Honduran soldiers stormed his house after shooting through the back door.

"They threatened me, that they were going to shoot," he said. "And I said to them: 'If you have orders to shoot, then shoot me. But know that you are shooting the president of the republic.' . . . They forced me to go to their vehicles outside with my pajamas on. We landed in the U.S. military base of Palmerola. . . . And then to Costa Rica."

Ultimately, more important to Honduras is not just the return of Zelaya, but the return of democracy. Zelaya was gaining popular support for policies like a 60 percent increase in the minimum wage, the plan to take over the U.S. Palmerola air base and use it as the civilian airport in place of the notoriously dangerous Toncontin International Airport, plans to distribute land to peasant farmers, and to join the Bolivarian Alliance for the Americas (ALBA), the regional cooperative bloc developed to diminish the economic domination of the United States. On the day he was deposed, Zelaya was holding a nonbinding straw poll to assess if the population wanted to hold a national constituent assembly to evaluate possible changes to the constitution. That, he explains, is why he was deposed.

Secretary of State Clinton and her close friend Lanny Davis, who is working as a powerful lobbyist for the coup regime, have pushed hard for the legitimization of the current Lobo government, despite Clinton's own State Department cable titled "Open and Shut: The Case of the Honduran Coup," released by WikiLeaks, that the coup was clearly illegal.

As I headed to the airport to leave Honduras after this historic weekend, I passed a group of teachers, one month into their hunger strike outside the Honduran Congress. They, like a broad network of civil society groups in Honduras, while celebrating the return of their ousted president, are clear in their demand, now joined by eighty-seven members of the U.S. Congress, for an end to violence and repression in Honduras.

MORE NEWS FROM
THE UNREPORTED WORLD

November 10, 2010

Obama in the Company of Killers

If a volcano kills civilians in Indonesia, it's news. When the government does the killing, sadly, it's just business as usual, especially if an American president tacitly endorses the killing, as President Barack Obama just did with his visit to Indonesia.

As the people around Mount Merapi dig out of the ash following a series of eruptions that have left more than 150 dead, a darker cloud now hangs over Indonesia in the form of renewed U.S. support for the country's notorious Kopassus, the military's special forces commando group. Journalist Allan Nairn released several secret Kopassus documents as the Obamas landed in Jakarta, showing the level of violent political repression administered by the Kopassus—now, for the first time in more than a decade, with United States support.

Last March, Nairn revealed details of a Kopassus assassination program in the Indonesian province of Aceh. These new Kopassus documents shed remarkable detail on the province of West Papua. As Nairn wrote in his piece accompanying the documents, West Papua is "where tens of thousands of civilians have been murdered and where Kopassus is most active. . . . When the U.S. restored Kopassus aid last July the rationale was fighting terrorism, but the documents show that Kopassus in fact systematically targets civilians." In the Kopassus' own words, the civilians are "much more dangerous than any armed opposition."

One document names fifteen leaders of the Papuan civil society, all "civilians, starting with the head of the Baptist Synod of Papua. The others include evangelical ministers, activists, traditional leaders, legislators, students and intellectuals as well as local establishment figures and the head of the Papua Muslim Youth organization."

President Obama lived in Indonesia from the ages of six through ten, after his mother married an Indonesian man. Obama said in Jakarta this week: "[M]uch has been made of the fact that this marks my return to where I lived as a young boy. . . . But today, as president, I'm here to focus not on the past, but on the future—the Comprehensive Partnership that we're building between the United States and Indonesia." Part of that relationship involves the renewed support of Kopassus, which has been denied since the armed forces burned then-Indonesian-occupied East Timor to the ground in 1999, killing more than 1,400 Timorese.

A series of cell-phone videos have come out of Papua showing torture being inflicted on men there at the hands of what appear to be members of the military. In one video that surfaced just two weeks ago, soldiers burn a man's genitals with a burning stick, cover his head with a plastic bag to suffocate him, and threaten him with a rifle. Another video shows a Papuan man slowly dying from a gunshot wound as the soldier with the cell-phone camera taunts him, calling him a savage.

I spoke with Suciwati Munir, the widow of the renowned Indonesian human-rights activist Munir Said Thalib, at the Bonn, Germany, reunion of Right Livelihood Award laureates. Her husband, an unflinching critic of the Indonesian military, received the award shortly before his death. In 2004, as he traveled to the Netherlands for a law fellowship, on board the Indonesian national airline Garuda, he was given an upgrade to business class. There, he was served tea laced with arsenic.

He was dead before the plane landed. Suciwati has a message for Obama: "If Obama has a commitment to human rights in the world . . . he has to pay attention to the human-rights situation in Indonesia. And the first thing that he should ask to President Susilo Bambang Yudhoyono is to resolve the Munir case." I asked her if she wanted to meet President Obama when he came to Indonesia. She replied: "Maybe yes, because I want to remind him about the human-rights situation in Indonesia. Maybe not, because of his wrong decision, he has perpetuated the impunity in Indonesia."

This was the third attempt by President Obama to visit Indonesia. His first delay was to allow him to push through health care reform. The second was canceled in the wake of the BP oil disaster. This time he made it, although the Mount Merapi eruption forced him to leave a few hours early. Speaking from Jakarta, journalist Nairn reflected: "It's nice to be able to go back to where you grew up, but you shouldn't bring weapons as a gift. You shouldn't bring training for the people who are torturing your old neighbors."

June 15, 2011

Failed War on Drugs:
Fast, Furious, and Fueled by the U.S.

The violent deaths of Brian Terry and Juan Francisco Sicilia, separated by the span of just a few months and by the increasingly bloody U.S.-Mexico border, have sparked separate but overdue examinations of the so-called War on Drugs, and how the U.S. government is ultimately exacerbating the problem.

On the night of December 14, 2010, Agent Brian Terry was in the Arizona desert as part of the highly trained and specially armed BORTAC unit, described as the elite paramilitary force within the U.S. Border Patrol. The group engaged in a firefight, and Terry was killed. While this death might have become just another violent act associated with drug trafficking along the border, one detail has propelled it into a high-stakes confrontation between the Obama administration and the U.S. Congress: Weapons found at the scene, AK-47s, were sold into likely Mexican criminal hands under the auspices of a covert operation of the federal Bureau of Alcohol, Tobacco, Firearms and Explosives (ATF).

Dubbed "Operation Fast and Furious," the secret program aimed to trace arms sold in the U.S. to so-called straw buyers, people who buy arms on behalf of others. The ATF's operation allowed gun shops to sell bulk weapons to straw buyers who the ATF suspected were buying on behalf of Mexican drug cartels. Instead of arresting the straw buyer, considered a relatively low-level criminal by the ATF, tracing the guns as they made their way into Mexico might allow the ATF to arrest more senior members of the criminal cartels. At least, that was the plan.

According to reporting by the Center for Public Integrity, 1,765 guns were knowingly sold as part of "Fast and Furious." Another 300 or so were sold before the operation started. Of these more than 2,000 guns, fewer than 800 have been recovered. Two of the guns recovered were found at the site of Terry's death, in a region known as Peck Canyon, on the U.S. side of the border between Nogales, Mexico, and Tucson, Arizona.

Special Agent John Dodson of the ATF was among many field agents who advised superiors that the covert operation was unwise. Their concerns were not acted on, and the operation continued. After Terry's murder, Dodson blew the whistle, first to the Justice Department, then to Republican Sen. Charles

Grassley. Grassley has questioned Attorney General Eric Holder, and the House Committee on Oversight and Government Reform, chaired by Republican Darrell Issa, is now engaged in hearings on the case.

South of the border, Sicilia and six other young men were brutally murdered in March, just seven more innocent victims in the raging violence in Mexico that has claimed more than 35,000 victims since December 2006, when President Felipe Calderon began his crackdown on the drug cartels. Sicilia's father is Javier Sicilia, a renowned poet and intellectual in Mexico. Soon after his son's murder, Sicilia wrote his final poem, dedicated to his son. He is now committed to the nonviolent struggle against the bloodshed in his country. He led a protest march in May from his hometown of Cuernavaca to Mexico City's famous Zócalo, the central plaza, where 200,000 people rallied. Last weekend, he led another march, all the way to the border, and then into El Paso, Texas.

Sicilia is against the cartels, for sure. But he holds Calderon, and the United States, culpable as well. He is calling for an end to the "Merida Initiative," in which the U.S. provides arms and training for the Mexican military to fight the cartels. Sicilia also is calling for the legalization of drugs, a call in which he is joined, surprisingly, by the conservative former president of Mexico, Vicente Fox, and increasingly by Calderon himself.

Calderon is traveling in the U.S. this week, and has spoken out about the U.S. arms industry that is profiting from the sales of weapons that end up in Mexico. He also has criticized the repeal of the U.S. assault-weapons ban, which has led to a massive increase in gun violence in Mexico.

A new report released by three Democratic U.S. senators finds some 70 percent of guns seized in Mexico from 2009 to 2010 came from the United States. Of the nearly 30,000 guns seized in Mexico during that period, more than 20,000 came from the U.S.

If anything should be fast and furious in the United States, it should be the push for sane and sensible gun control and drug policies. Perhaps then, Javier Sicilia will start writing poetry again.

March 28, 2012

Forget Fear of Flying, Fear Airport Screening

There was terror in the skies this week over Texas, caused not by a terrorist but by a pilot—a Flight Standards captain, no less. JetBlue Airways Capt. Clay Osbon, flying Flight 191 from New York's John F. Kennedy International Airport to Las Vegas, began moving up and down the aisle after the jet was airborne, ranting, according to several passengers, about Iraq, Israel, al-Qaida, and bombs, calling on passengers to recite the Lord's Prayer, saying that they were "all going down." An off-duty pilot in the cabin went to the cockpit to help the co-pilot with the emergency landing, while passengers and crew subdued Osbon. Osbon, who'd been with JetBlue almost since its founding, was taken to the hospital, suspended with pay, then criminally charged with interfering with a flight crew.

That's enough to inspire a fear of flying in anyone. But just getting to your airplane these days may present a greater risk to your health than the actual flight.

New airport security screening technology, primarily backscatter X-ray devices, have come under increased scrutiny, as their effectiveness is questioned amid concerns that the radiation exposure may cause cancer. Adding to health concerns are both the graphic nature of the images captured, essentially nude photos of every person passing through the machine, and the aggressive—and for some, humiliating—nature of the alternative to the scans, the "enhanced pat-down" by a Transportation Security Administration (TSA) agent.

Republican Sen. Susan Collins introduced a bill that would require independent laboratory testing of the X-ray backscatter machines, exactly what a group of University of California, San Francisco scientists called on the Obama administration to do in April 2010. Responding to the TSA claim (provided by the manufacturer, Rapiscan) that the radiation dose is less than "the dose one receives from eating one banana," professor John Sedat and others wrote: "While the dose would be safe if it were distributed throughout the volume of the entire body, the dose to the skin may be dangerously high.... There is good reason to believe that these scanners will increase the risk of cancer to children and other vulnerable populations [including pregnant women]." When this risk is multiplied over 700 million annual travelers, Michael Love, Ph.D., the manager of the Johns Hopkins School of Medicine X-ray facility, told *Discover* magazine, "someone is going to get skin cancer." The European Union has banned the machines.

While flying the past few weekends, I refused to go through the scanners, which is every passenger's right, although the option is almost never indicated anywhere (the Collins bill also requires clear signage). I was made to wait while TSA employees were clearly available to conduct what is euphemistically called an "enhanced pat-down." The agent's aggressive questioning of my decision to "opt out" was matched only by her aggressive pat-down when I would not give in. Arriving back in New York, a friend who had just flown in from Chicago's O'Hare International Airport recounted how the TSA agent had her hands down the front of my friend's pants and said, "Feels like you've lost some weight"!

Who gains? The two manufacturers of the full-body scanners have powerful friends. As reported in *The Hill* and the *Washington Post*, L-3 Communications, maker of the millimeter wave scanner, hired lobbyist Linda Daschle, wife of former Sen. Tom Daschle. Rapiscan, the maker of the X-ray backscatter machine, reportedly paid $1 million to the Chertoff Group, run by former Department of Homeland Security (DHS) Secretary Michael Chertoff, while Chertoff appeared in the media touting the value of the machines. Each machine costs the taxpayer about $150,000, but that is only the purchase; installation, then staffing, costs much more.

TSA agents themselves may face the greatest risks. A recent TSA inspector general's report recommended that "wing shields be installed to further reduce radiation exposure levels for backscatter operators." It also noted that TSA employees reported insufficient time for training on the machines. Michael Grabell, a reporter with ProPublica who has written extensively on full-body scanners, told me: "Radiation technicians have told some of the TSA screeners that 'If I were on these machines, I'd be wearing a radiation badge.' But the TSA has refused to let them."

All these concerns have led the nonprofit Electronic Privacy Information Center to sue the TSA and DHS, seeking a halt to the use of the scanners, at least until independent testing of the risks is performed, and the results made public.

Until we know that these full-body scanners are safe, I'm opting out.

April 18, 2012

Obama's Policies:
The Real Scandal in Cartagena

President Barack Obama's re-election campaign launched its first Spanish-language ads this week, just after he returned from the Summit of the Americas. He spent three days in Colombia, longer than any president in U.S. history. The trip was marred, however, by a prostitution scandal involving the U.S. military and Secret Service. Gen. Martin Dempsey, chair of the U.S. Joint Chiefs of Staff, said, "We let the boss down, because nobody's talking about what went on in Colombia other than this incident." Dempsey is right. It also served as a metaphor for the U.S. government's ongoing treatment of Latin America.

The scandal reportedly involves eleven members of the U.S. Secret Service and five members of the U.S. Army Special Forces, who allegedly met prostitutes at one or more bars in Cartagena and took up to twenty of the women back to their hotel, some of whom may have been minors. This all deserves thorough investigation, but so do the policy positions that Obama promoted while in Cartagena.

First, the war on drugs. Obama stated at the summit, "I, personally, and my administration's position is that legalization is not the answer." Ethan Nadelmann, founder and executive director of the Drug Policy Alliance, told me that, despite Obama's predictable line, this summit showed "the transformation of the regional and global dialogue around drug policy. . . . This is the first you've had a president saying that we're willing to look at the possibility that U.S. drug policies are doing more harm than good in some parts of the world." He credits the growing consensus across the political spectrum in Latin America, from key former presidents like Vicente Fox of Mexico, who supports legalization of drugs, to current leaders like Mexico's Felipe Calderon, who cited the rapacious demand for drugs in the U.S. as the core of the problem.

Nadelmann went on: "You have the funny situation of Evo Morales, the leftist leader of Bolivia, former head of the coca growers' union, lecturing the United States about—essentially, sounding like Milton Friedman—that 'How can you expect us to reduce the supply when there is a demand?' So there's the beginning of a change here. I don't think it's going to be possible to put this genie back in the bottle."

Then there is trade. Obama and Colombian President Juan Manuel Santos also announced that the U.S.-Colombian Free Trade Agreement would take full force May 15. Colombian and U.S. labor leaders decried the move, since Colombia is the worst country on Earth for trade unionists. Labor organizers are regularly murdered in Colombia, with at least thirty-four killed in the past year and a half. When Obama was first running for president, he promised to oppose the Colombia FTA, "because the violence against unions in Colombia would make a mockery of the very labor protections that we have insisted be included in these kinds of agreements." That year, fifty-four Colombian trade unionists were killed. AFL-CIO President Richard Trumka said the announcement "is deeply disappointing and troubling." Republicans, on the other hand, are offering grudging praise to Obama for pushing the FTA.

On Cuba, Obama took the globally unpopular position of defending the U.S. embargo. Even at home, polls show that a strong majority of the American people and businesses support an end to the embargo. The U.S. also succeeded, once again, in banning Cuba from the summit, prompting Ecuadorian President Rafael Correa to boycott the meeting this year.

Responding to overall U.S. intransigence, other Western Hemisphere countries are organizing themselves. Greg Grandin, professor of Latin American history at New York University, told me: "Latin Americans themselves are creating these bodies that are excluding the United States, that are deepening integration, political and economic integration. This seems to be a venue in which they come together in order to criticize Washington, quite effectively."

Grandin compared Obama's Latin America policies to those of his predecessors: "The two main pillars of U.S. foreign policy—increasing neoliberalism and increasing militarism around drugs—continue. They feed off of each other and have created a crisis in that corridor, running from Colombia through Central America to Mexico. That's been a complete disaster, and there's no change."

It will take more than a prostitution scandal to cover that up.

January 6, 2010

Sick with Terror

The media have been swamped with reports about the attempt to blow up Northwest Airlines Flight 253 on Christmas Day. When Umar Farouk Abdulmutallab, now dubbed the "underwear bomber," failed in his alleged attack, close to 300 people were spared what would have been, most likely, a horrible, violent end. Since that airborne incident, the debates about terrorism and how best to protect the American people have been reignited.

Meanwhile, a killer that has stalked the U.S. public, claiming, by recent estimates, 45,000 lives annually—one dead American about every ten minutes—goes unchecked. That's 3,750 people dead—more than the 9/11 attacks—every month who could be saved with the stroke of a pen.

This killer is the lack of adequate health care in the United States. Researchers from Harvard Medical School found in late 2009 that 45,000 people die unnecessarily every year due to lack of health insurance. Researchers also uncovered another stunning fact: In 2008, four times as many U.S. Army veterans died because they lacked health insurance than the total number of U.S. soldiers who were killed in Iraq and Afghanistan in the same period. That's right: 2,266 veterans under the age of sixty-five died because they were uninsured.

On Tuesday, President Barack Obama was fiery when he made his public statement after meeting with his national security team about the airline breach: In seeking to thwart plans to kill Americans "we face a challenge of the utmost urgency," he said. He talked about reviewing systemic failures and declared we must "save innocent lives, not just most of the time, but all of the time."

This is all very admirable. Imagine if this same urgency was applied to a broken system that causes 45,000 unnecessary deaths per year. Since stimulus funds will now be directed to supply more scanning equipment at airports, what about spending money to ensure mammograms and prostate exams at community health centers?

And then there's the investigation of who is responsible for the attempted Christmas Day attack and getting "actionable intelligence" from the alleged bomber to prevent future attacks. All good. We actually have "actionable intelligence" on why people die due to lack of health care, and how insurance companies actively deny people coverage to increase their profits, but what has been done about it?

The day before the underwear bomb incident, Christmas Eve, the U.S. Senate passed the Patient Protection and Affordable Care Act by a vote of 60 to 39. Obama described the bill as "the most important piece of social legislation since the Social Security Act passed in the 1930s." Yet in order to get to that magic number of sixty Senate votes, the already weak Senate bill had to be brought to its knees by the likes of Sen. Joe Lieberman, from the health insurance state of Connecticut, and conservative Democrat Ben Nelson of Nebraska. The Senate and House versions of health insurance reform now have to be reconciled in conference committee.

The conference committee process is one that is little understood in the U.S. In it major changes to legislation are often imposed, with little or no notice. That's why C-SPAN CEO Brian Lamb sent a letter to congressional leaders December 30 requesting access to televise the process. He wrote, "[W]e respectfully request that you allow the public full access, through television, to legislation that will affect the lives of every single American." Rather than simply grant access, House Speaker Nancy Pelosi asserted that "there has never been a more open process."

Yet Pelosi and the Democrats are now saying that the bills won't even go through a formal conference committee, but rather through informal, closed-door sessions with key committee chairs. While this would circumvent Republican opportunities to filibuster, it would also grant a very few individuals enormous power to cut deals in much the same way that Sens. Nelson and Lieberman did. Since the health insurance, medical equipment, and pharmaceutical industries spent close to $1.4 million per day to influence the health care debate, we have to ask: Who will have access to those few legislators behind those closed doors?

Wendell Potter, the former CIGNA insurance spokesperson turned whistleblower, says he knows "where the bodies are buried." Let's be consistent. If we care about saving American lives, let's take action now.

May 25, 2011

Single-Payer Health Care: Vermont's Gentle Revolution

Vermont is a land of proud firsts. This small New England state was the first to join the thirteen colonies. Its constitution was the first to ban slavery. It was the first to establish the right to free education for all—public education.

This week, Vermont will boast another first: the first state in the nation to offer single-payer health care, which eliminates the costly insurance companies that many believe are the root cause of our spiraling health care costs. In a single-payer system, both private and public health care providers are allowed to operate, as they always have. But instead of the patient or the patient's private health insurance company paying the bill, the state does. It's basically Medicare for all—just lower the age of eligibility to the day you're born. The state, buying these health care services for the entire population, can negotiate favorable rates, and can eliminate the massive overhead that the for-profit insurers impose.

Vermont hired Harvard economist William Hsiao to come up with three alternatives to the current system. The single-payer system, Hsiao wrote, "will produce savings of 24.3% of total health expenditure between 2015 and 2024." An analysis by Don McCanne, MD, of Physicians for a National Health Program pointed out that: "[T]hese plans would cover everyone without any increase in spending since the single payer efficiencies would be enough to pay for those currently uninsured or under-insured. So this is the really good news— single payer works."

Vermont Gov. Peter Shumlin explained to me his intention to sign the bill into law: "Here's our challenge. Our premiums go up 10, 15, 20 percent a year. This is true in the rest of the country as well. They are killing small business. They're killing middle-class Americans, who have been kicked in the teeth over the last several years. What our plan will do is create a single pool, get the insurance company profits, the pharmaceutical company profits, the other folks that are mining the system to make a lot of money on the backs of our illnesses, and ensure that we're using those dollars to make Vermonters healthy."

Speaking of healthy firsts, Vermont may become the first state to shutter a nuclear power plant. The Vermont legislature is the first to empower itself with the right to determine its nuclear future, to put environmental policy in the hands of the people.

Another Vermont first was the legalization of same-sex civil unions. Then the state trumped itself and became the first legislature in the nation to legalize gay marriage. After being passed by the Vermont House and Senate, then Gov. Jim Douglas vetoed the bill. The next day, April 7, 2009, the House and the Senate overrode the governor's veto, making the Vermont Freedom to Marry Act the law of the land.

Vermont has become an incubator for innovative public policy. Canada's single-payer health care system started as an experiment in one province, Saskatchewan. It was pushed through in the early 1960s by Saskatchewan's premier, Tommy Douglas, considered by many to be the greatest Canadian. It was so successful, it was rapidly adopted by all of Canada. (Douglas is the grandfather of actor Kiefer Sutherland.) Perhaps Vermont's health care law will start a similar, national transformation.

The anthropologist Margaret Mead famously said: "Never doubt that a small group of thoughtful, committed citizens can change the world. Indeed, it is the only thing that ever has."

Just replace "group" with "state," and you've got Vermont.

• •

March 3, 2010

Domestic Violence: A Pre-Existing Condition?

March is Women's History Month, recognizing women's central role in society. Unfortunately, violence against women is epidemic in the United States and around the world.

Domestic violence is on the minds of many now, as reports published by the *New York Times* implicate New York Gov. David Paterson in an alleged attempt to influence a domestic violence case against one of his top aides. The *Times* reports, based in part on unnamed sources, say that the Paterson aide, David W. Johnson, attacked his girlfriend on Halloween night, October 31, 2009, "choking her, smashing her into a mirrored dresser and preventing her from calling for help." New York state police from the governor's personal protection detail contacted the victim, despite having no jurisdiction. Then the governor himself intervened, the *Times* alleges, asking two aides to contact the victim and to arrange a phone call between him and the victim. The call occurred on February 7 of this year, the night before the victim was to appear in court to request an order of protection from Johnson. She did not appear in court, and the case was dismissed. After the exposé, the governor ended his bid for election and suspended Johnson without pay.

Denise O'Donnell, Paterson's deputy secretary for public safety and commissioner of the state's Division of Criminal Justice Services, resigned last week, saying, "The behavior alleged here is the antithesis of what many of us have spent our entire careers working to build—a legal system that protects victims of domestic violence and brings offenders to justice." The National Organization for Women, a longtime ally of Paterson, has called on him to resign.

The Paterson scandal follows that of New York state Sen. Hiram Monserrate, who was charged with assaulting a female companion with the jagged edge of a broken glass in December 2008. She later altered her story to conform to Monserrate's version of events, but the weakened criminal case proceeded against him, without her cooperation, and he was found guilty of misdemeanor assault. He was expelled from the New York Senate last month.

These high-profile cases are sadly symptomatic of a massive problem. The Family Violence Prevention Fund offers this chilling summary of domestic violence in the U.S.: One in four women report violence at the hands of a current or former spouse or boyfriend at some point in their lives; three women per day are murdered by their husbands or boyfriends; women suffer 2 million injuries from intimate-partner violence each year; and there were 248,300 rapes / sexual assaults in 2007, more than 500 per day, up from 190,600 in 2005.

President Barack Obama has reaffirmed October as National Domestic Violence Awareness Month, and stressed the link between the economy and domestic violence: "In the best of economic times, victims worry about finding a job and housing, and providing for their children; these problems only intensify during periods of financial stress." Sen. Harry Reid said about domestic abuse last week: "It has gotten out of hand. Why? Men don't have jobs. Women don't have jobs either, but women aren't abusive, most of the time. Men, when they're out of work, tend to become abusive. Our domestic crisis shelters in Nevada are jammed. It's the way it is all over the country." Given the severity of the problem of domestic violence, and its likely exacerbation by the economic crisis, it is hard to believe that so-called health insurance companies actually label a woman's victimization by domestic violence as a "pre-existing condition." The term has long been used by health insurance corporations to deny coverage to applicants or, perhaps worse, to retroactively deny coverage to people who suffered from a condition before they were insured.

At Obama's bipartisan health care summit last week, New York Rep. Louise Slaughter pointed out, "Eight states in this country right now have declared that domestic violence is a pre-existing condition, on the grounds, I assume, that if you've been unlucky enough to get yourself beaten up once, you might go round and do it again."

March 8 is recognized by the United Nations and many countries around the world (but not the U.S.) as International Women's Day. March is Women's History Month. Thousands of events are being held around the world to honor women. Let's start here in the U.S. by making violence against women history.

• •

November 4, 2010

Rich Media, Poor Democracy

As the 2010 elections come to a close, the biggest winner of all remains undeclared: the broadcasters. The biggest loser: democracy. These were the most expensive midterm elections in U.S. history, costing close to $4 billion, $3 billion of which went to advertising. What if ad time were free? We hear no debate about this, because the media corporations are making such a killing by selling campaign ads. Yet the broadcasters are using public airwaves.

I am reminded of the 1999 book by media scholar Robert McChesney, *Rich Media, Poor Democracy*. In it, he writes, "Broadcasters have little incentive to cover candidates, because it is in their interest to force them to publicize their campaigns."

The Wesleyan Media Project, at Wesleyan University, tracks political advertising. Following the recent Supreme Court ruling, Citizens United v. FEC, the project notes, "The airwaves are being saturated with more House and Senate advertising, up 20 percent and 79 percent respectively in total airings." Evan Tracey, the founder and president of Campaign Media Analysis Group, predicted in *USA Today* in July, "There is going to be more money than there is airtime to buy." John Nichols of *The Nation* commented that in the genteel, earlier days of television political advertising, the broadcasters would never juxtapose an ad for a candidate with an ad opposed to that candidate. But they are running out of broadcast real estate. Welcome to the brave, new world of the multi-billion-dollar campaigns.

There have been efforts in the past to regulate the airwaves to better serve the public during elections. The most ambitious in recent years was what became known as McCain-Feingold campaign-finance reform. During the debate on that landmark legislation, the problem of exorbitant television advertising rates was brought up, by Democrats and Republicans alike. Nevada Sen. John Ensign, a Republican, lamented: "The broadcasters used to dread campaigns because that was the time of year they made the least amount of money because of this lowest unit rate. Now it is one of their favorite times of the year because it is actually one of their highest profit-margin times of the year." Ultimately, to get the bill passed, the public airtime provisions were dropped.

The Citizens United ruling effectively neutralizes McCain-Feingold campaign-finance reform. One can only imagine what the cost of the 2012 presidential election will be. Sen. Russ Feingold, D-Wis., lost his re-election bid to the largely self-financed multimillionaire Ron Johnson. The *Wall Street Journal* editorial page celebrated Feingold's expected loss. The *Journal* is owned by Rupert Murdoch's News Corp., which also owns the Fox television network and which gave close to $2 million to Republican campaign efforts.

"The elections have become a commodity, a profit center for these radio and TV stations," Ralph Nader, consumer advocate and former presidential candidate, told me on Election Day. He went on: "The public airwaves, as we know, belong to the people, and they're the landlords, and the radio and TV stations are the licensees. They're the tenants, so to speak. They pay no money to the

FCC for their annual license. And therefore, it's really quite persuasive, were we to have a public policy to condition modestly the license to this enormously lucrative control of the public airwaves twenty-four hours a day by these TV and radio stations and say, as part of the reciprocity for controlling this commons, so to speak, you have to allow a certain amount of time, free time, on radio and TV for ballot-qualified candidates."

The place where we should debate this is in the major media, where most Americans get their news. But the television and radio broadcasters have a profound conflict of interest. Their profits take precedence over our democratic process. You very likely won't hear this discussed on the Sunday-morning talk shows.

* *

March 9, 2011

Don't Ice Out Public Media

The aspen grove on Kebler Pass in Colorado is one of the largest organisms in the world. Thousands of aspen share the same, interconnected root system. Last weekend, I snowmobiled over the pass, 10,000 feet above sea level, between the towns of Paonia and Crested Butte. I was racing through Colorado to help community radio stations raise funds, squeezing in nine benefits in two days. The program director of public radio station KVNF in Paonia dropped us at the trailhead, where the program director of KBUT public radio in Crested Butte and a crew of station DJs picked us up on snowmobiles to whisk us thirty miles over the pass.

Now that the Republicans have taken over the House of Representatives, one of their first acts was to "zero out" current funding for the Corporation for Public Broadcasting (CPB). Furthermore, Rep. Doug Lamborn from Colorado Springs has offered a bill to permanently strip CPB funding. Lamborn told NPR, "We live in a day of 150 cable channels—99 percent of Americans own a TV, we get Internet on our cell phones, we are in a day and age when we no longer need to subsidize broadcasting."

But public broadcasting was established precisely because of the dangers of the commercial media. When we are discussing war, we need a media not brought to us by weapons manufacturers. When discussing health care reform, we need a media not sponsored by insurance companies or Big Pharma.

In Senate testimony last week, Secretary of State Hillary Clinton fiercely criticized the commercial media, saying: "We are in an information war, and we are losing that war.... Viewership of Al-Jazeera is going up in the United States because it's real news. You may not agree with it, but you feel like you're getting real news around the clock instead of a million commercials and, you know, arguments between talking heads and the kind of stuff that we do on our news." Clinton was asking for more funding for the overseas propaganda organs of the U.S. government, like Voice of America, Radio Marti, and the Arabic-language TV channel that is produced in Virginia for broadcast to the Middle East, Al-Hurra. That arm of the State Department is slated to receive $769 million, almost twice the funding of the CPB. The U.S. military's media operation has an annual budget exceeding $150 million and distributes entertainment programming to overseas bases, and propagandistic content on its full-time U.S. television platform, the Pentagon Channel.

While Clinton's description of the failed U.S. commercial media is correct, her prescription is all wrong. We need more genuine news and less propaganda. Media studies professor Robert McChesney echoed that, telling me: "The smart thing to do is to take most of that $750 million, add it onto what's being spent currently in the United States, and create a really dynamic, strong, competitive public and community broadcasting system that treats the U.S. government the same way it treats other governments, the same standard of journalism, then broadcast that to the world, make that fully accessible to the world. And I think that would show the United States at its very best."

In rural Colorado, as in rural regions across the country, and on Native American reservations, public radio stations rely on CPB grants for anywhere from 25 percent to 50 percent of their operating budgets. At the standing-room-only benefit in Paonia, KVNF General Manager Sally Kane explained the crisis: "The Communications Act of 1934 set aside a small spectrum of the airwaves to serve the public interest and to be free of commercial influence.... Once again, it's cutting services to those who need it most, while protecting those groups who can afford a posse of lobbyists to defend their interests. I refuse to imagine my region without my community radio station."

The response was the same, from Idaho Springs to Carbondale, Paonia via snowmobile to Crested Butte, then over Monarch Pass to Salida (at the western edge of Lamborn's district), to Telluride, then Rico, and on to Durango. In the packed town halls, auditoriums and theaters, the passion among the local residents for their stations demonstrates that, like the aspen groves of the Rocky Mountains, these small stations are resilient, strong, and deeply rooted in their communities. Their funding is an investment that should be preserved.

LUMINARIES

June 13, 2012

John Lewis: Across That Bridge, Again

As the election season heats up, an increasing number of states are working to limit the number of people who are allowed to vote. Already we have a shamefully low percentage of those eligible to vote actually participating. Florida, a key swing state, is preparing for the Republican National Convention, five days of pomp promoted as a celebration of democracy. While throwing this party, Florida Republican Gov. Rick Scott, along with his secretary of state, Ken Detzner, are systematically throwing people off the voter rolls, based on flawed, outdated Florida state databases.

Many eligible Florida voters recently received a letter saying they were removed and had limited time to prove their citizenship. Hundreds of cases emerged where people with longstanding U.S. citizenship were being purged. According to the American Civil Liberties Union of Florida, "of those singled out to prove their citizenship, 61 percent are Hispanic when only 14 percent of registered Florida voters are Hispanic," suggesting an attempt to purge Latinos, who tend to vote Democratic. Recall the year 2000, when then Florida Secretary of State Katherine Harris systematically purged African-Americans from voter rolls. The U.S. Justice Department has ordered Detzner to stop the purge, but he and Gov. Scott promise to continue. The Justice Department has sued the state in federal court, as have the ACLU and other groups.

For Georgia Congressman John Lewis, efforts to limit access to vote are not just bureaucratic. "It is unreal, it is unbelievable, that at this time in our history, 40 years after the Voting Rights Act was signed and passed into law, that we're trying to go backward. I think there is a systematic, deliberate attack on the part of so many of these states, not just Florida, but it's all across the country. . . . Some people were beaten, shot and murdered trying to help people become registered voters. I can never forget the three civil-rights workers that were murdered in the state of Mississippi on the night of June 21, 1964," he said, recalling the murder of James Chaney, Andrew Goodman, and Michael Schwerner, killed while registering African-Americans to vote.

Back in 1961, Lewis, just twenty-one years old, was a leader of the Freedom Rides, testing new federal laws banning segregation in interstate travel. He and many others were severely beaten when their buses crossed state lines into the Deep South. He sat down at segregated lunch counters, and joined the Student Nonviolent Coordinating Committee, soon rising to chair the organization. He told me about a pivotal moment in his life, and this nation's history, the march over the Edmund Pettus Bridge:

> On March 7, 1965, a group of us tried to march from Selma to Montgomery, Alabama, to dramatize to the nation that people wanted to vote. One young African-American man had been shot and killed a few days earlier, in an adjoining county, called Perry County. Because of what happened to him we made a decision to march. In Selma, Alabama, in 1965, only 2.1 percent of blacks of voting age were registered to vote. The only place you could attempt to register was to go down to the courthouse, you had to pass a so-called literacy test.

As Lewis and scores of others tried to cross the Pettus Bridge in Selma, at the beginning of their fifty-mile march to Montgomery, Lewis recalled, "we got to the top of the bridge, we saw a sea of blue, Alabama state troopers, and we continued to walk, we came within hearing distance of the state troopers. One said, 'I'm Major John Cloud of the Alabama State Troopers, this is an unlawful march, it will not be allowed to continue, I give you three minutes to disperse, return to your church.' ... You saw these guys putting on their gas masks, they came toward us beating us with nightsticks and bullwhips and trampling us with horses. I was hit in the head by a state trooper with a nightstick. I had a concussion at the bridge. My legs went out from under me. I felt like I was going to die. I thought I saw death."

When I asked Lewis what propelled him forward in the face of such violence, he said, "My mother, my father, my grandparents, my uncle and aunts, people all around me had never registered to vote." Universal suffrage, the right to vote, is never safe, never secure, never complete. This election season will be one where money from a few will have enormous influence, while the votes of many are being eliminated, their voices effectively silenced.

Unless people fight to dramatically expand voter participation, not just prevent the purges, our democracy is in serious danger.

November 11, 2009

The Man Who Put the Rainbow in *The Wizard of Oz*

Thanksgiving is around the corner, and families will be gathering to share a meal and, perhaps, enjoy another annual telecast of *The Wizard of Oz*. The seventy-year-old film classic bears close watching this year, perhaps more than in any other, for the message woven into the lyrics, written during the Great Depression by Oscar-winning lyricist E. Y. "Yip" Harburg. There's more to the Scarecrow and the Tin Man than meets the eye, and Harburg's message has renewed resonance today in the midst of the greatest financial collapse since the Depression.

Harburg grew up in New York's Lower East Side. In high school, he was seated alphabetically next to Ira Gershwin, and the two began a friendship that lasted a lifetime and helped shape twentieth-century American song and culture. Ernie Harburg, Yip's son and co-author of the biography *Who Put the Rainbow in The Wizard of Oz?* told me, "Yip knew poverty deeply . . . it was the basis of Yip's understanding of life as struggle."

Harburg was deep in debt after the 1929 Wall Street crash. Gershwin suggested that Harburg write song lyrics. Before long, he wrote the song that captured the essence of the Great Depression, "Brother, Can You Spare a Dime?" Ernie said of the music industry then: "They only wanted love songs or escape songs, so that in 1929 you had 'Happy Days Are Here Again.' . . . There wasn't one song that addressed the Depression, in which we were all living."

"Brother, Can You Spare a Dime?" became a national hit and remains a kind of anthem for hard times, corporate greed, and the dignity of working people:

> Once I built a railroad, I made it run, made it race against time.
> Once I built a railroad; now it's done. Brother, can you spare a dime?

In the 1930s, Harburg became the lyricist for *The Wizard of Oz*. He also added the rainbow to the story, which doesn't appear in L. Frank Baum's original 1900 book, *The Wonderful Wizard of Oz*. This led Harburg to write the famous song "Over the Rainbow," sung by the then unknown Judy Garland.

While academic debate persists over whether Baum intended the story as a political allegory about the rise of industrial monopolists like John D. Rockefeller and the subsequent populist backlash, there is no doubt that Harburg's influence made the 1939 film version more political.

The film, says Ernie Harburg, is about common people confronting and defeating seemingly insurmountable and violent oppression: The Scarecrow represented farmers, the Tin Man stood for the factory workers, and the Munchkins of the "Lollipop Guild" were the union members. Ernie recalled: "There was at least 30 percent unemployment at those times. And among blacks and minorities, it was 50, 60 percent. And there were bread lines, and the rich kept living their lifestyle."

The Wizard of Oz was to be "MGM's answer to [Disney's] Snow White and the Seven Dwarfs," Ernie recounts. It was initially a critical success, but a commercial flop. Yip Harburg went on to write Finian's Rainbow for Broadway. It addresses racial bigotry, hatred of immigrants, easy credit, and mortgage foreclosures. In 1947, Finian's Rainbow was the first Broadway musical with an integrated cast. It was a hit, running for a year and a half. When Harburg's unabashed political expression made him a target during the McCarthy era, he was blacklisted, and was banned from TV and film work from 1951 to 1962. Ironically, in the middle of his blacklist period, CBS broadcast The Wizard of Oz on television. It broke all viewership records, and has been airing since, gaining global renown and adulation.

This October, Finian's Rainbow began its first full Broadway revival—the first since it was originally produced six decades ago—to rave reviews. Yip Harburg would be especially proud, no doubt, to know that one of the actors, Terri White, who plays a black sharecropper in Finian's Rainbow, is back on Broadway despite having recently been homeless. From sleeping on park benches to starring on Broadway once again, this is just the kind of tale that inspired Harburg.

In response to his blacklisting, Harburg wrote a satiric poem, which reads in part:

> Lives of great men all remind us
> Greatness takes no easy way,
> All the heroes of tomorrow
> Are the heretics of today.
> ...
> Why do great men all remind us

We can write our names on high
And departing leave behind us
Thumbprints in the FBI.

Let's give thanks to Yip Harburg and all heretical artists, past and present, who have withstood censorship and banishment just for talking turkey.

* *

December 31, 2009

The Poetic Justice of Dennis Brutus

Dennis Brutus broke rocks next to Nelson Mandela when they were imprisoned together on notorious Robben Island. His crime, like Mandela's, was fighting the injustice of racism, challenging South Africa's apartheid regime. Brutus' weapons were his words: soaring, searing, poetic. He was banned, he was censored, he was shot. But this poet's commitment and activism, his advocacy on behalf of the poor, never flagged. Brutus died in his sleep early on December 26 in Cape Town, at the age of eighty-five, but he lived with his eyes wide open. His life encapsulated the twentieth century, and even up until his final days, he inspired, guided, and rallied people toward the fight for justice in the twenty-first century.

Oddly, for this elfin poet and intellectual, it was rugby that early on nagged him about the racial injustice of his homeland. Brutus recalled being sarcastically referred to by a white man as a "future Springbok."

The Springboks were the national rugby team, and Brutus knew that nonwhites could never be on the team. "It stuck with me, until years later, when I began to challenge the whole barrier—questioning why blacks can't be on the team." This issue is depicted in Clint Eastwood's new feature film, *Invictus*. President Mandela, played by Morgan Freeman, embraces the Springboks during the 1995 World Cup, admitting that until then blacks always knew whom to root for: any team playing against the Springboks.

In the late 1950s, Brutus was penning a sports column under the pseudonym "A. de Bruin"—meaning "A brown" in Afrikaans. Brutus wrote, "The column . . .

was ostensibly about sports results, but also about the politics of race and sports." He was banned, an apartheid practice that imposed restrictions on movement, meeting, publishing, and more. In 1963, while attempting to flee police custody, he was shot. He almost died on a Johannesburg street while waiting for an ambulance restricted to blacks.

Brutus spent eighteen months in prison, in the same section of Robben Island as Nelson Mandela, where he wrote his first collection of poems, *Sirens, Knuckles, Boots.* His poem "Sharpeville" described the March 21, 1960, massacre in which South African police opened fire, killing sixty-nine civilians, an event which radicalized him:

> Remember Sharpeville
> bullet-in-the-back day
> Because it epitomized oppression
> and the nature of society
> more clearly than anything else;
> it was the classic event

After prison, Brutus began life as a political refugee. He formed the South African Non-Racial Olympic Committee to leverage sports into a high-profile, global anti-apartheid campaign. He succeeded in getting South Africa banned from the Olympic Games in 1970. Brutus moved to the United States, where he remained as a university professor and anti-apartheid leader, despite efforts by the Reagan administration to deny him continued status as a political refugee and deport him.

After the fall of apartheid and ascension to power of the African National Congress, Brutus remained true to his calling. He told me, "As water is privatized, as electricity is privatized, as people are evicted even from their shacks because they can't afford to pay the rent of the shacks, the situation becomes worse. . . . The South African government, under the ANC . . . has chosen to adopt a corporate solution."

He went on: "We come out of apartheid into global apartheid. We're in a world now where, in fact, wealth is concentrated in the hands of a few; the mass of the people are still poor . . . a society which is geared to protect the rich and the corporations and actually is hammering the poor, increasing their burden, this is the reverse of what we thought was going to happen under the ANC government."

Many young activists know Dennis Brutus not for his anti-apartheid work but as a campaigner for global justice, ever present at mass mobilizations against the World Trade Organization, the World Bank, and the International Monetary Fund—and, most recently, although not present, giving inspiration to the protesters at the U.N. climate summit in Copenhagen. He said, on his eighty-fifth birthday, days before the climate talks were to commence: "We are in serious difficulty all over the planet. We are going to say to the world: There's too much of profit, too much of greed, too much of suffering by the poor. . . . The people of the planet must be in action."

* *

February 3, 2010

Howard Zinn: The People's Historian

Howard Zinn, legendary historian, author and activist, died last week at the age of eighty-seven. His most famous book is *A People's History of the United States*. Zinn told me last May, "The idea of *A People's History* is to go beyond what people have learned in school . . . history through the eyes of the presidents and the generals in the battles fought in the Civil War, [to] the voices of ordinary people, of rebels, of dissidents, of women, of black people, of Asian-Americans, of immigrants, of socialists and anarchists and troublemakers of all kinds."

It is fitting to write of Zinn's life at the start of Black History Month. Although he was white, he wrote eloquently of the civil rights struggle and was a part of that movement as well. Fifty years ago, on February 1, 1960, four black students entered the F.W. Woolworth store in Greensboro, North Carolina, and sat down at the "whites only" lunch counter. They were refused service, and returned day after day. Each day, more and more people came with them. The lunch-counter desegregation movement spread to other Southern cities. By July, the Greensboro Woolworth lunch counter was desegregated. This week, the International Civil Rights Center and Museum opened at the site of that original lunch-counter protest.

At the time of the sit-ins, Zinn was a professor at Spelman College, a historically black women's college in Atlanta. He told me why, after seven years there, he was fired: "The students at Spelman College rose up out of that very tranquil and controlled atmosphere at the college during the sit-ins and went into town, got arrested, they came back fired up and determined to change the conditions of their lives on campus. . . . I supported them in their rebellion, and I was too much for the administration of the college." Zinn wrote in the afterword of *A People's History*: "It was not until I joined the faculty of Spelman College . . . that I began to read the African-American historians who never appeared in my reading lists in graduate school. Nowhere in my history education had I learned about the massacres of black people that took place again and again, amid the silence of a national government pledged, by the Constitution, to protect equal rights for all."

One of his students at Spelman was Pulitzer Prize–winning author Alice Walker. Soon after she learned of Zinn's death, Walker explained: "He was thrown out because he loved us, and he showed that love by just being with us. He loved his students. He didn't see why we should be second-class citizens." Just a few years ago, Zinn was invited back to Spelman to give the commencement address and receive an honorary degree.

World-renowned linguist and dissident Noam Chomsky, a longtime friend of Zinn's, reflected on Zinn's "reverence for and his detailed study of what he called 'the countless small actions of unknown people' that lead to those great moments that enter the historical record." Zinn co-wrote, with Anthony Arnove, *Voices of a People's History of the United States*, with speeches, letters, and other original source material from those "unknown people" who have shaped this country. It was made into a star-studded documentary, which premiered on the History Channel just weeks before Zinn died. Matt Damon, its executive producer, gave *A People's History* enormous popular exposure in the hit movie *Good Will Hunting* when his character Will recommended the book to his psychiatrist. Damon was Zinn's neighbor in Newton, Massachusetts, and knew him since he was ten years old.

Last May, when I interviewed Zinn, he reflected on Barack Obama's first months in office: "I wish President Obama would listen carefully to Martin Luther King. I'm sure he pays verbal homage, as everyone does, to Martin Luther King, but he ought to think before he sends missiles over Pakistan, before he agrees to this bloated military budget, before he sends troops to Afghanistan, before he opposes the single-payer system. "He ought to ask: 'What would Martin Luther King do? And what would Martin Luther King say?' And if he only listened to King, he would be a very different president than he's turning out to be so far. I think we ought to hold Obama to his promise to be different and bold and to make change. So far, he hasn't come through on that promise."

• •

March 10, 2010

Rachel Corrie's (Posthumous) Day in Court

An unusual trial begins in Israel this week, and people around the world will be watching closely. It involves the tragic death of a twenty-three-year-old American student named Rachel Corrie. On March 16, 2003, she was crushed to death by an Israeli military bulldozer.

Corrie was volunteering with the group International Solidarity Movement (ISM), which formed after Israel and the United States rejected a proposal by then United Nations High Commissioner for Human Rights Mary Robinson to place international human rights monitors in the occupied territories. The ISM defines itself as "a Palestinian-led movement committed to resisting the Israeli occupation of Palestinian land using nonviolent, direct-action methods and principles." Israel was building a large steel wall to separate Rafah from Egypt, and was bulldozing homes and gardens to create a "buffer zone." Corrie and seven other ISM activists responded to a call on that March day to protect the home of the Nasrallah family, which was being threatened with demolition by two of the armored Israeli military bulldozers made by the U.S. company Caterpillar.

Cindy Corrie, Rachel's mother, related what happened: "The bulldozer proceeded toward Rachel.... She was in her orange jacket. When it kept coming, she rose on the mound, and the eyewitnesses testified that her head rose above the top of the blade of the bulldozer, so she could clearly be seen, but the bulldozer continued and proceeded over her, and so that it was covering her body.

It stopped and then reversed, according to the eyewitness testimonies, without lifting its blade, so backed over her once again. "Her friends were screaming at the bulldozer drivers through this to stop. They rushed to her, and she said to them, 'I think my back is broken.' And those were her final words."

Shortly after Rachel's death, the Corries met with the Bush State Department. It was there that the idea of a civil lawsuit was first presented, by Secretary of State Colin Powell's own chief of staff, Lawrence B. Wilkerson. Craig Corrie, Rachel's father, recalled: "He said: 'If it was my daughter, I'd sue them. I don't care about money. I wouldn't care about anything. I would sue the state of Israel.'" Ultimately, this is what the Corrie family did.

Just before heading to JFK Airport in New York to attend the trial, Craig Corrie told me about the lawsuit: "We're accusing the state of Israel of either intentionally killing Rachel or of gross negligence in her killing seven years ago." The day after Rachel was killed, Israeli Prime Minister Ariel Sharon promised President George W. Bush a "thorough, credible and transparent investigation." Yet according to a Human Rights Watch report from 2005, Israel's "investigations into Corrie's killing . . . fell far short of the transparency, impartiality, and thoroughness required by international law."

The civil trial, Craig Corrie says, is not about the monetary damages, but discovering information, and "like [South African Archbishop] Desmond Tutu talks about, of mending the tear in society." The Corries never speak solely about their daughter, but about the plight of the Palestinians and the Israeli siege of Gaza. According to the latest figures of the Israeli Committee Against House Demolitions, 24,145 houses have been demolished in the occupied territories since 1967, including the 4,247 that the United Nations estimated were destroyed during Operation Cast Lead, the name Israel gave to its military assault on Gaza in December 2008 and January 2009.

Of course, more than houses were destroyed there. More than 1,400 Palestinians and thirteen Israelis were killed. The Corries also express concern about the psychological toll exacted on Israeli soldiers. Craig Corrie said, "We lost Rachel, and that hurts every day, but that bulldozer driver lost a lot of his humanity when he crushed Rachel."

The trial begins during the same week that Joe Biden makes his first trip to Israel as vice president. As chair of the Senate Foreign Relations Committee, Biden sought answers on the death of Rachel Corrie during the confirmation hearings for U.S. Ambassador to Israel James Cunningham.

Biden knows the pain of losing a daughter. His daughter was killed with his first wife in a car accident in 1972. The Corries are calling on people around the world to stand with them on March 16, the anniversary of Rachel's death, for truth, accountability, and justice, "to raise and highlight many of the critical issues to which Rachel's case is linked."

• •

May 12, 2010

Singing Lena Horne's Praises

Lena Horne died this week at the age of ninety-two. More than just a brilliant singer and actress, she was a pioneering civil rights activist, breaking racial barriers for generations of African-Americans who have followed her. She fought segregation and McCarthyism, was blacklisted, yet persisted to gain worldwide fame and success. Her grandmother signed her up as the youngest member of the NAACP as a fourteen-month-old.

Hers is the story of the twentieth century, of the slow march to racial equality, and of remarkable perseverance.

Horne's career began in Harlem's renowned Cotton Club, where African-Americans performed for an exclusively white audience. She joined several orchestras, including one of the first integrated bands, and then landed the first meaningful, long-term contract for an African-American actor with a major Hollywood film studio, MGM. Her contract included provisions that she would not be cast in the stereotypical role of a maid. She was never given full acting roles, though, only stand-alone singing scenes. "I looked good and I stood up against a wall and sang and sang. But I had no relationship with anybody else," she told the *New York Times* in 1957. "Mississippi wanted its movies without me. It was an accepted fact that any scene I did was going to be cut when the movie played the South." During the World War II years, she toured with the USO, entertaining troops. At Camp Joseph T. Robinson in Arkansas, she learned she would be performing for a segregated whites-only audience. Afterward, she gave an impromptu performance for the African-American troops and was again angered when German POWs imprisoned at the base were allowed to crowd into the mess hall. She insisted they be thrown out.

Horne, in a 1966 Pacifica Radio interview, recalled a watershed moment in Cincinnati. She was touring with a band, and on the night of the boxing match between Joe Louis and Max Schmeling of Nazi Germany, Horne, who didn't care for boxing, found herself backstage with the band members, around the radio, rooting for Louis: "I said, 'He's mine.' And I didn't want him to be beaten. 'He's ours.' I think that's the first I remember ever identifying with another Negro in that way before. I was identifying with the symbol that we had, of a powerful man, an impregnable fortress. And I didn't realize that we drew strength from these symbols."

Paul Robeson, the great African-American singer and activist, had a profound influence on Lena Horne. In the Pacifica interview, she recalled, "Paul taught me about being proud because I was Negro . . . he sat down for hours, and he told me about Negro people. . . . And he didn't talk to me as a symbol of a pretty Negro chick singing in a club. He talked to me about my heritage. And that's why I always loved him." The association with Robeson, a proud, outspoken activist, contributed to Horne's blacklisting during the McCarthy era.

James Gavin, who wrote the definitive biography of Lena Horne, *Stormy Weather*, told me: "Lena Horne was a very brave woman and is not given credit for the activism that she did in the 1940s, at a time when a lot of the black performers that she knew were simply accepting the conditions of the day as the way things were and were afraid of rocking the boat and losing their jobs. And Lena never hesitated to speak her mind." Gavin described Horne's appearance at the 1963 March on Washington, where she took the microphone and unleashed one word, "Freedom!" She appeared with the great civil rights leader Medgar Evers at an NAACP rally, just days before he was assassinated. She worked with Eleanor Roosevelt on anti-lynching legislation, and supported SNCC, the Student Nonviolent Coordinating Committee, and the National Council of Negro Women (led by Dorothy Height, another civil rights leader, who died last month at the age of ninety-eight).

Horne's biographer Gavin says she was filled with anguish for not doing enough. But Halle Berry thinks otherwise. When Berry became the first

African-American woman to win the Academy Award for best actress in 2001, she sobbed as she held up her Oscar in her acceptance speech: "This moment is so much bigger than me. This moment is for Dorothy Dandridge, Lena Horne, Diahann Carroll. . . . And it's for every nameless, faceless woman of color that now has a chance because this door tonight has been opened."

● ●

September 1, 2010

Eve Ensler: Bald, Brave, and Beautiful

Bald, brave, and beautiful: Those words can't begin to capture the remarkable Eve Ensler. She sat down with me last week, in the midst of her battle with uterine cancer, to talk about New Orleans and the Democratic Republic of Congo. Eve, the author of the hit play *The Vagina Monologues* and the creator of V-Day, a global activist movement to stop violence against women and girls, told me how "cancer has been a huge gift."

Eve's moving essay "Congo Cancer" begins, "Some people may think that being diagnosed with uterine cancer, followed by extensive surgery that led to a month of debilitating infections, rounded off by months of chemotherapy, might get a girl down. But, in truth, this has not been my poison." The poison, she went on, was the epidemic of rape, torture, and violence against women and girls in the eastern Democratic Republic of Congo.

Eve wrote *The Vagina Monologues* in 1996 as a celebration of women's bodies and women's empowerment. "When I did the play initially," she told me, "everywhere I went on the planet, women would literally line up after the show . . . 90 to 95 percent of the women were lining up to tell me how they had been raped or battered or incested or abused. . . . I had no idea that one out of three women on the planet will be raped or beaten in their lifetime. Suddenly this door opened for me."

Eve began producing the play to raise funds for rape crisis hot lines and women's organizations across the U.S. "We came up with this idea of V-Day," she told me, "which was Ending Violence Day, Vagina Day—reclaiming Valentine's

Day as a day of kindness and good will to women. . . . We are now in 130 countries. Last year, there were 5,000 events in 1,500 or 1,600 places. It's raised close to $80 million, that has all gone into local communities."

The V-Day movement brought Eve to some of the most desperate places on earth—Haiti, the Democratic Republic of Congo, and post-Katrina New Orleans. She spent a year with women in New Orleans, compiling their descriptions of their lives and the impact of Hurricane Katrina into a series of monologues. It's called "Swimming Upstream." Unbelievably, in the middle of her chemotherapy, Eve is directing two special performances in mid-September, in New Orleans and at the Apollo Theater in Harlem.

Eastern Congo, a war-ravaged region of the world's most impoverished country, is where Eve and V-Day have been devoting most of their recent efforts. Since 1996, hundreds of thousands of women and girls have been raped in the eastern Democratic Republic of Congo, victims of what V-Day calls femicide. Last month, Rwandan and Congolese rebels took over villages in the eastern Democratic Republic of Congo and gang-raped almost 200 women and five young boys. The rapes occurred between July 30 and August 3 within miles of a U.N. peacekeeping base, and went unreported for three weeks.

These rapes are brutal, leaving the victims with deep wounds and fistulae that require surgery. V-Day has been working with Panzi Hospital in Bukavu, the only facility in the region where the women can receive adequate treatment. V-Day is also building a woman-controlled safe zone attached to the hospital called "The City of Joy."

Eve said the women themselves developed the plans for the City of Joy, "a place where they could heal, where they could be trained, where they could become leaders, where they had time and a respite to rebuild themselves and redirect their energies towards their communities." If all goes well with her own treatment, she will be joining them to open the City of Joy in February.

The work, Eve told me, defines what she calls a "kind of three-way V between Haiti, the Congo, and New Orleans."

With a scarf on her head, having lost her hair during cancer treatments, she was days away from starting her fourth round of chemotherapy. I asked her how she does it.

"The women of Congo saved my life," she said. "Every day I get up, and I think to myself, I can keep going. If a woman in Congo gets up this morning after she's had her insides eviscerated, what problem do I really have? And I think of how they dance. Every time I go to the Congo, they dance and they sing and they keep going, in spite of being forgotten and forsaken by the world. And I think to myself, I have to get better. I have to live to see the day when the women of Congo are free, because if those women are free, women throughout the world will be free and will get to continue."

• •

November 24, 2010

The Health Insurance Industry's Vendetta Against Michael Moore

Michael Moore, the Oscar-winning documentary filmmaker, makes great movies but they are not generally considered "cliff-hangers." All that might change since a whistle-blower on the *Democracy Now!* news hour revealed that health insurance executives thought they may have to implement a plan "to push Moore off a cliff." The whistle-blower: Wendell Potter, the former chief spokesman for health insurance giant CIGNA. He was quoting from an industry strategy session on how to respond to Moore's 2007 documentary *Sicko*, a film critical of the U.S. health insurance industry. Potter told me that he is not sure how serious the threat was but he added, ominously, "These companies play to win."

Moore won an Oscar in 2002 for his film about gun violence, *Bowling for Columbine*. He followed that with *Fahrenheit 9/11*, a documentary on the presidency of George W. Bush that became the top-grossing documentary film in U.S. history. So when Moore told a reporter that his next film would be about the U.S. health care system, the insurance industry took notice.

AHIP (America's Health Insurance Plans), the major lobbying group of the for-profit health insurance corporations, secretly sent someone to the world premiere of *Sicko* at the Cannes Film Festival in France. Its agent rushed from the screening to a conference call with industry executives, including Potter. "We were very scared," Potter said, "and we knew that we would have to develop a very sophisticated and expensive campaign to turn people away from the idea of universal care. ... We were told by our pollsters [that] a majority of people were in favor of much greater government involvement in our health care system."

AHIP hired a public-relations firm, APCO Worldwide, founded by the powerful law firm Arnold & Porter, to coordinate the response. APCO formed the fake grassroots consumer group "Health Care America" to counter the expected popularity of Moore's *Sicko* and to promote fear of "government run health care."

Potter writes in his new book, *Deadly Spin: An Insurance Company Insider Speaks Out on How Corporate PR Is Killing Health Care and Deceiving Americans,* that he "found the film very moving and very effective in its condemnation of the practices of private health insurance companies. There were many times when I had to fight to hold back tears. Moore had gotten it right."

The insurance industry declared its campaign against *Sicko* a resounding success. Potter wrote, "AHIP and APCO Worldwide had succeeded in getting their talking points into most of the stories about the movie, and not a single reporter had done enough investigative work to find out that insurers had provided the lion's share of funding to set up Health Care America." Indeed, everyone from CNN to *USA Today* cited Health Care America as if it were a legitimate group.

Moore concedes, "Their smear campaign was effective and did create the dent they were hoping for—single payer and the public option never even made it into the real discussion on the floor of Congress."

Moore has called Potter the "Daniel Ellsberg of corporate America," invoking the famous Pentagon whistle-blower whose revelations helped end the Vietnam War. Potter's courageous stand made an impact on the debate, but the insurance industry, the hospitals, and the American Medical Association prevailed in blunting the elements of the plan that threatened their profits.

A recent Harvard Medical School study found that nearly 45,000 Americans die each year—one every twelve minutes—largely because they lack health insurance. But for the insurance lobby, the only tragedy is the prospect of true health care reform. In 2009, the nation's largest health insurance corporations funneled more than $86 million to the U.S. Chamber of Commerce to oppose health care reform. This year, the nation's five largest insurers contributed three times as much money to Republican candidates as to Democrats, in an effort to further roll back insurance industry reform. Rep. Anthony Weiner, D-N.Y., an advocate of single-payer health care, declared in Congress that "the Republican Party is a wholly owned subsidiary of the insurance industry." Potter agrees, saying the Republican Party has "been almost bought and paid for."

The health insurance industry is getting its money's worth. Moore said that the industry was willing to attack his film because it was afraid it "could trigger a populist uprising against a sick system that will allow companies to profit off of us when we fall ill." Now that is truly sick.

* *

October 13, 2010

John le Carré: Calling Out the Traitors

John le Carré, the former British spy turned spy novelist, has some grave words for Tony Blair. More than seven years after the invasion of Iraq, the former British prime minister, now out of office and touring the world pushing his political memoir, is encountering serious protests at his book signings.

"I can't understand that Blair has an afterlife at all. It seems to me that any politician who takes his country to war under false pretenses has committed the ultimate sin," le Carré told me when I sat down with him recently in London. "We've caused irreparable damage in the Middle East. I think we shall pay for it for a long time."

We sat in a television studio across the River Thames overlooking two of his former places of employment: MI5, the domestic security service, and MI6, the secret intelligence service, which operates internationally (the equivalents of the U.S.'s FBI and CIA). John le Carré is the pen name of David Cornwell, who was a spy from the late 1950s into the early 1960s. He began to write novels and had to assume a pen name due to his work as a spy. He was stationed in Germany when, in 1961, he saw the Berlin Wall go up, motivating him to write his third novel, *The Spy Who Came in from the Cold*.

The novel came out as another British spy novelist, Ian Fleming, was enjoying success with his series about the notorious fictional British spy James Bond.

Unlike the flamboyant characters and endless action of the Bond books and films, the subjects of le Carré's novels were bleak characters engaged in unsavory acts of deception and calculated violence. With the world focused on the Berlin Wall and the Cuban missile crisis, le Carré captured a global audience, depicting the raw reality of the spy on the front lines of the Cold War.

As the Cold War ended, le Carré continued his prolific writing, shifting focus, increasingly, to the inequities of globalization, unchecked multinational corporate power, and the frequent confluence of corporate interests and the activities of national spy services.

Perhaps best known among his later novels is *The Constant Gardener*, about a pharmaceutical company using unwitting people in Kenya for dangerous, sometimes fatal, tests of an experimental drug. He explained, "The things that are done in the name of the shareholder are, to me, as terrifying as the things that are done—dare I say it—in the name of God." Like many of his novels, *The Constant Gardener* was made into a popular feature film, starring Ralph Fiennes and Rachel Weisz.

Le Carré has written often of Africa: "It's where I have seen globalization at work on the ground. It's a pretty ugly sight. It's a boardroom fantasy. What it actually means is the exploitation of very cheap labor, very often the ecological disaster that comes with it, the creation of mega-cities, the depletion of agrarian cultures and tribal cultures."

His latest book (his twenty-second), just out this week, is called *Our Kind of Traitor*. It targets a fictional array of London bankers and their protectors in Parliament, who collude with Russian Mafiosi to prop up the collapsed world economy by laundering hundreds of billions of dollars in criminal profits.

Back in 2003, before the invasion of Iraq, le Carré marched against the war with, by many estimates, more than 1 million people: "We were all wedged together and looking into Downing Street, where the prime minister's residency is . . . a kind of feral roar of popular will rose. I tried to imagine what it must have been like for Blair sitting inside that building and hearing that sound. . . . I think it will always be remembered of him that he took us to war on the strength of lies."

He said he wouldn't buy Blair's book, but he does have some questions for him: "Have you ever seen what happens when a grenade goes off in a school? Do you really know what you're doing when you order 'shock and awe'? Are you prepared to kneel beside a dying soldier and tell him why he went to Iraq, or why he went to any war?"

Le Carré summed up what he sees as a central problem for global powers, especially Britain and the U.S.: "Victims never forget, and the winners do. And they forget very quickly." Because of that, John le Carré continues writing, into his eightieth year, engaging people as he seeks what he calls "the big truth."

* *

January 26, 2011

Sundance and the Art of Democracy

PARK CITY, Utah—This small, alpine mountain town is transformed every winter during the Sundance Film Festival into a buzzing hive of the movie industry. While much of the attention is focused on the celebrities, Sundance has actually become a key intersection of art, film, politics, and dissent. It is where many of the most powerful documentaries premiere, films about genuine grassroots struggles, covering the sweep of social justice history and the burning issues of today. They educate and inspire a growing audience about the true nature, and cost, of direct democracy.

The Last Mountain is a documentary about the threat to Coal River Mountain in West Virginia, which is slated for destruction by mountaintop-removal coal mining, one of the most environmentally devastating forms of mining being practiced today. The worst offender is the coal giant Massey Energy and its former CEO, Don Blankenship. A broad coalition of activists from around the world has been active in trying to stop Massey, led by regular, working-class people from the surrounding towns and hamlets of Appalachia. Robert F. Kennedy Jr., a longtime environmentalist and lawyer, joined them in the fight and is featured in the film. I asked him about the struggle:

> This film is about the subversion of American democracy. Last year, the Supreme Court overruled a hundred years of ironclad American precedent with the Citizens United case, and got rid of a law that was passed by Teddy

Roosevelt in 1907 that saved democracy from the huge concentrations of wealth that had created essentially a corporate kleptocracy during the Gilded Age, and Americans had forfeited their democracy during that time. . . . For the first time since the Gilded Age, we're seeing those kinds of economic concentrations return to our country.

Kennedy describes the subversion by corporate power of the press, the courts, and Congress and state legislatures: "The erosion of all these institutions, I think, of American democracy have forced people who care about our country, and who care about civic health, into this box of civil disobedience and local action."

This is a historic month for Robert Kennedy Jr.: It is the fiftieth anniversary of his uncle John Kennedy's inauguration as president, and also of his father Robert Kennedy's inauguration as U.S. attorney general. I asked him about those two, felled by assassins' bullets:

To me, the most important thing that John Kennedy did, and my father was trying to do, was to stand up to the military-industrial complex, which . . . President Eisenhower, in his final speech just before my uncle took the reins of power, said this is the greatest threat to American democracy in the history of our republic, ever: the growth of an uncontrolled military-industrial complex in combination with large corporations and with influential members of Congress, who would slowly but systematically deprive Americans of the civil rights and the constitutional rights that made this country an exemplary nation.

In a moving moment here at Sundance, Kennedy, who had just flown in from the funeral of his uncle, Sargent Shriver (founder of the Peace Corps), came out after a screening of *The Last Mountain*, and was embraced by Harry Belafonte, himself the subject of the film that opened this year's festival, the breathtaking biopic of the singer and activist called *Sing Your Song*, which is really a chronicle of the movements for racial and economic justice of the twentieth century.

Belafonte was one of Dr. Martin Luther King Jr.'s closest confidants. I spoke with Harry about his lifetime of activism, and about his feelings about President Barack Obama. He told me, "During his campaign for the presidency, he was talking before businessmen on Wall Street in New York. I said, 'Well, you know, I hope you bring the challenge more forcefully to the table.' And he said, 'Well, when are you and Cornel West going to cut me some slack?' I said, 'What makes you think we haven't?'"

Belafonte was a friend of Eleanor Roosevelt, who told him of an exchange between her late husband, President Franklin Roosevelt, and A. Philip Randolph, a key organizer of the 1963 March on Washington, and before that the major force behind the black train conductors' union, the Brotherhood of Sleeping Car Porters. Randolph described what needed to happen to improve the condition of black and working people in the country. Roosevelt said he did not disagree with anything Randolph said. Retelling the story here to me at Sundance, Harry leaned back in his chair and repeated what Roosevelt told Randolph: "Go out and make me do it."

. . . .

September 7, 2011

9/11 Victim 0001: Father Mychal's Message

The body bag marked "Victim 0001" on September 11, 2001, contained the corpse of Father Mychal Judge, a Catholic chaplain with the Fire Department of New York. When he heard about the disaster at the World Trade Center, he donned his Catholic collar and firefighter garb and raced downtown. He saw people jump to their deaths to avoid the inferno more than 1,000 feet above. At 9:59 a.m., the South Tower collapsed, and the force and debris from that mass of steel, concrete, glass, and humanity as it hit the ground is likely what killed Father Mychal. His was the first recorded death from the attacks that morning. His life's work should be central to the tenth anniversary commemorations of the September 11 attacks: peace, tolerance, and reconciliation.

One of the first vigils held this year was in honor of Father Mychal. About 300 people gathered Sunday in front of the St. Francis Church where Judge lived and worked, just down the block from the Ladder 24 / Engine 1 Firehouse. The march followed Father Mychal's final path to Ground Zero. The man behind the annual remembrance is Steven McDonald, the former New York police detective who was shot in 1986. He was questioning fifteen-year-old Shavod Jones in Central Park. Jones shot McDonald, leaving him paralyzed for life.

I caught up with McDonald as he led the procession, rolling down Seventh Avenue in his wheelchair. He talked about what Father Mychal meant to him: "He, more than anything... reaffirmed my faith in God, and that it was important to me to forgive the boy who shot me. And I'm alive today because of that."

Father Mychal had managed to get Jones on the phone with McDonald and his wife. He apologized from prison. Taking the lessons of reconciliation, McDonald joined Judge in a trip to Northern Ireland, where they worked together to try to help end the violence there.

Father Mychal was well known to the poor and afflicted of New York City and New Jersey. He helped the homeless, and people with HIV/AIDS. As a member of the Franciscan order, he would often wear the traditional brown robe and sandals. But there was a half-known secret about him: He was gay. In his private diaries, the revered Catholic priest wrote, "I thought of my gay self and how the people I meet never get to know me fully." The diaries were given to journalist Michael Daly by Judge's twin sister, Dympna, and appear in Daly's book *The Book of Mychal: The Surprising Life and Heroic Death of Father Mychal Judge*.

Brendan Fay is a longtime Irish-American gay activist who was a friend of Judge's. He produced a film about the Franciscan friar in 2006 called *Saint of 9/11* and is finishing up another one called *Remembering Mychal*. Fay told me this week: "He was one of the priests at Dignity New York, an organization for gay and lesbian Catholics. . . . He ministered to [us] during the AIDS crisis, when there were few priests available to our community."

I first interviewed Fay in October 2001, after an Associated Press photo appeared showing a U.S. bomb before being dropped on Afghanistan, with the words scrawled in chalk, "High Jack This, Fags." The offensive slogan forced the military to order its sailors to pen more "positive" messages on their bombs.

On September 20, 2001, President George W. Bush addressed a joint session of Congress. He declared, famously, "They hate our freedoms." He welcomed Lisa Beamer to the Capitol, the widow of Todd Beamer, the passenger on board United Flight 93 who was heard to say, "Let's roll" before attacking the hijackers.

Beamer's fellow passenger, Mark Bingham, a rugby player and public relations consultant who also joined in the fight to prevent the hijackers from using the plane as a weapon, was openly gay. As was David Charlebois, the co-pilot of American Airlines Flight 77, which hit the Pentagon.

A decade later, Brendan Fay reflects on the life of his friend: "On 9/11, the one thing we can take from Mychal Judge is, in the midst of this hell and war and evil and violence, here is this man who directs us to another possible path as human beings: We can choose the path of compassion and nonviolence and reconciliation. Mychal Judge had a heart as big as New York. There was room for everybody. And I think that's the lesson."

STOP THE VIOLENCE

August 9, 2012

Sikh Killings: On Gun Laws, It's Bipartisan Consensus, Not Gridlock, That's the Problem

Another mass murder, another shooting spree, leaving bodies bullet-riddled by a legally obtained weapon. This time, it was Oak Creek, Wisconsin, at a Sikh temple, as people gathered for their weekly worship. President Barack Obama said Monday, "I think all of us recognize that these kinds of terrible, tragic events are happening with too much regularity for us not to do some soul-searching." Amidst the carnage, platitudes. With an average of thirty-two people killed by guns in this country every day—the equivalent of five Wisconsin massacres per day—both major parties refuse to deal with gun control. It's the consensus, not the gridlock, that's the problem.

The president's press secretary, Jay Carney, said, "We need to take common-sense measures that protect Second Amendment rights and make it harder for those who should not have weapons under existing law from obtaining weapons." It's important to note where Jay Carney made that point, reiterating the phrase "common sense" five times in relation to the president's intransigence against strengthening gun laws and invoking "Second Amendment" a stunning eight times. He spoke from the James S. Brady Press Briefing Room in the White House, named after one of Mr. Carney's predecessors, who was shot in the head by John Hinckley during the attempted assassination of President Ronald Reagan in 1981. Brady survived and co-founded with his wife the Brady Campaign to Prevent Gun Violence. After each of these massacres, the Brady Campaign has called for strengthened gun control.

This latest mass killing was very likely a hate crime, perpetrated by Wade Michael Page, a white, 40-year-old U.S. Army veteran with links to white supremacist groups and membership in skinhead rock bands. Page grew up in Littleton, Colorado, the same town where, in 1999, Eric Harris and Dylan Klebold plotted and executed their mass-murder plan at Columbine High School. Page was in the U.S. Army from 1992 to 1998. He did missile-system repairs and later was a "psychological operations" specialist, although it is not clear in what capacity, based first at Fort Bliss, Texas, then at Fort Bragg, North Carolina.

Page received a "general discharge" from the U.S. Army: lower than an honorable discharge, but not as bad as a dishonorable one. Reports suggest he had a problem with alcohol, with several arrests for drunken driving. He recently lost a truck-driving job for the same reason, which may have precipitated the loss of his home to foreclosure. Page may have been troubled, but he was by no means unknown. After the shooting, FBI special agent Teresa Carlson of Milwaukee told the press, "There may be references to him in various files, and those are things that are being analyzed right now, but we had no reason to believe, and as far as we know, no law-enforcement agency had any reason to believe that he was planning or plotting or capable of such violence."

Page was a prominent member of the neo-Nazi skinhead music scene, was known to the Southern Poverty Law Center, which tracks right-wing hate groups, and was also personally interviewed, between 2001 and 2003, by Pete Simi, associate professor of criminology at the University of Nebraska at Omaha. Despite the arrests, despite the history of membership in hate groups, Page was able to walk into a gun shop and buy the 9 mm pistol legally, according to the shop owner. The fact that it was legal is the problem.

As if on cue, two days after Page's murderous rampage in Wisconsin, Jared Loughner appeared in court to plead guilty to the shooting spree in Tucson, Arizona, that left six dead and many injured, including former member of Congress Gabrielle Giffords. Loughner has been diagnosed with schizophrenia and will spend the rest of his life behind bars. Patricia Maisch survived the shooting. As Loughner was tackled that day in January 2011, Maisch grabbed the high-capacity magazine that Loughner was using to reload his gun. Maisch and two other survivors of that shooting have launched an advertisement with the group Mayors Against Illegal Guns, demanding that both President Obama and Governor Mitt Romney come up with a plan to deal with guns in this country.

The day after the Wisconsin shooting, I spoke with Gurcharan Grewal, president of the Sikh Religious Society of Wisconsin. He told me: "Ultimately, the problem comes to gun control. I don't know when we're going to get serious about all this, and I don't know how many more lives it will take before something will be done."

Neither Obama nor Romney agrees that gun control is the answer. It will take a movement to make it happen.

August 2, 2012

The Obama Administration
Torpedoes the Arms Trade Treaty

Quick: What is more heavily regulated, global trade of bananas or battleships? In late June, activists gathered in New York's Times Square to make the absurd point, that, unbelievably, "there are more rules governing your ability to trade a banana from one country to the next than governing your ability to trade an AK-47 or a military helicopter." So said Amnesty International USA's Suzanne Nossel at the protest, just before the start of the United Nations Conference on the Arms Trade Treaty (ATT), which ran from July 2 to July 27. Thanks to a last-minute declaration by the United States that it "needed more time" to review the short, eleven-page treaty text, the conference ended last week in failure.

There isn't much that could be considered controversial in the treaty. Signatory governments agree not to export weapons to countries that are under an arms embargo or to export weapons that would facilitate "the commission of genocide, crimes against humanity, war crimes" or other violations of international humanitarian law. Exports of arms are banned if they will facilitate "gender-based violence or violence against children" or be used for "transnational organized crime." Why does the United States need more time than the more than ninety other countries that had sufficient time to read and approve the text? The answer lies in the power of the gun lobby, the arms industry, and the apparent inability of President Barack Obama to do the right thing, especially if it contradicts a cold, political calculation.

The Obama administration torpedoed the treaty exactly one week after the massacre in Aurora, Colorado. In Colorado, Obama offered promises of "prayer and reflection." As New York City mayor Michael Bloomberg said, commenting on Obama and Mitt Romney both avoiding a discussion of gun control, "Soothing words are nice, but maybe it's time the two people who want to be president of the United States stand up and tell us what they're going to do about it." Gun violence is a massive problem in the U.S., and it only seems to pierce the public consciousness when there is a massacre. Gun-rights advocates attack people who suggest more gun control is needed, accusing them of politicizing the massacre. Yet some elected officials are taking a stand. Governor Pat

Quinn of Illinois is seeking a ban on assault weapons, much like the ones in place in California, Connecticut, Massachusetts, New Jersey, and New York.

The National Rifle Association's executive vice president, Wayne LaPierre, issued the threat before the U.N. conference that "Without apology, the NRA wants no part of any treaty that infringes on the precious right of lawful Americans to keep and bear arms." The NRA organized letters opposing the treaty, signed by fifty-one U.S. senators and 130 members of the House. After the conference ended in failure, the NRA took credit for killing it.

Of course, there is nothing in the treaty that would impact U.S. domestic gun laws. The rights protected by the cherished Second Amendment ("a well regulated militia being necessary to the security of a free state, the right of the people to keep and bear arms shall not be infringed") would remain intact. The NRA's interest lies not only with individual gun owners, but also with the U.S. weapons manufacturers and exporters. The United States is the world's largest weapons producer, exporter, and importer. It is the regulation of this global flow of weaponry that most likely alarms the NRA, not the imagined prospect of the U.N. taking away the legally owned guns inside the U.S.

Protesters outside the U.N. during the ATT conference erected a mock graveyard, with each headstone reading, "2,000 people killed by arms every day." That's one person killed every minute. In many places around the world, massacres on the order of Aurora are all too common. Days after Aurora, at least nine people were killed in a U.S. drone strike in northwest Pakistan. Pakistani officials said the victims were suspected militants, but the Obama administration deems all adult-male drone targets to be militants unless proven otherwise, posthumously.

After the conference wrapped without success, Suzanne Nossel said, "This was stunning cowardice by the Obama administration, which at the last minute did an about-face and scuttled progress toward a global arms treaty, just as it reached the finish line." These words were doubly strong, as she criticized the very State Department where she worked previously under Hillary Clinton.

The U.N. has pledged to resume the effort to pass an arms trade treaty, despite the intransigence of the country that Martin Luther King Jr. called "the greatest purveyor of violence in the world." Until then, bananas will remain more heavily regulated than battleships and bazookas.

July 25, 2012

Aurora Massacre: U.S. Gun Laws Guilty by Reason of Insanity

James Holmes, the alleged shooter in the massacre in Aurora, Colorado, reportedly amassed his huge arsenal with relative ease. Some of these weapons were illegal as recently as eight years ago. Legislation now before Congress would once again make illegal, if not the guns themselves, at least the high-capacity magazines that allow bullets to be fired rapidly without stopping to reload. Holmes bought most of his weaponry within recent months, we are told. Perhaps if sane laws on gun control, including the ban on high-capacity magazines, were in place, many in Aurora who are now dead or seriously injured would be alive and well today.

The facts of the assault are generally well known. Holmes allegedly burst into the packed theater during the 12:30 am premier of the Batman sequel *The Dark Knight Rises*, threw one or two canisters of some gas or irritant, which exploded, then began to methodically shoot people, killing twelve and wounding fifty-eight.

"Everybody sort of started screaming, and that's when the gunman opened fire on the crowd, and pandemonium just broke out," Omar Esparza told me. He was in the third row, with five friends out for a birthday celebration: "He started opening fire on the audience pretty freely, just started shooting in every direction, that's when everybody started screaming, started panicking. A lot of people had been hit at that point at those initial few rounds, and that's when everybody sort of hit the floor and started to exit."

Esparza continued: "It sounded like the bullets had stopped, and it sounded like he was either switching guns or reloading his rifle. At that very second when we sort of heard the silence, we realized that that was our only opportunity of getting out or of dying. So, at that split second, we had to react and had to exit as quickly as possible. And we barely made it, too, because approximately a second after we had exited, we heard him starting to shoot again."

That moment of silence may have been when one of the weapons jammed. CNN reported that "the semiautomatic rifle used in the Colorado theater killings jammed during the rampage . . . a law enforcement source with direct knowledge of the investigation said Sunday."

Holmes allegedly had an AR-15 equipped with a 100-round drum magazine, as well as one or two Glock pistols with 40-round extended magazines and a Remington 870 shotgun that can fire up to seven shells without reloading. The AR-15 can fire from fifty to sixty rounds per minute. Holmes had a massive arsenal, easily acquired at retail stores and online.

Carolyn McCarthy is a member of Congress from Long Island, New York. Her husband was shot in the head and among the six killed in the 1993 Long Island Rail Road massacre. Her son also was shot in the head, but survived and remains partially paralyzed. She was a nurse back then, but when her congressman voted against the assault-weapons ban, she ran against him. She won and has been in Congress ever since.

McCarthy has introduced H.R. 308, the Large Capacity Ammunition Feeding Device Act. It would ban the sale or transfer of these large-capacity clips that enabled the massive casualties in Aurora, and in Tucson, Arizona, in January 2011 when Rep. Gabrielle Giffords was shot and six were killed. McCarthy told me: "The problem is, politicians, legislators across this country are intimidated by the NRA and the gun manufacturers who put so much money out there to say that 'we will take you down in an election if you go against us.' Common sense will say we can take prudent gun-safety legislation and try to save people's lives. That is the bottom line."

One group pushing the large-magazine ban is the Brady Campaign to Prevent Gun Violence, named for Jim Brady, who was shot in the head and severely disabled during the 1981 attempted assassination of President Ronald Reagan. I spoke with Colin Goddard, who works for the group. He survived the 2007 Virginia Tech massacre, in which thirty-two people were killed. Goddard was shot four times. I asked him about the refrain so commonly uttered now on television, that it's too political to discuss gun control before the victims are even buried.

"This conversation should have happened before this shooting in the first place," Goddard told me. "This is when people are outraged. This is when people realize that this could happen to them. We cannot wait.... Now is the time for a change. We are better than this."

July 18, 2012

75 Years Later,
the Lessons of Guernica

Seventy-five years ago, the Spanish town of Guernica was bombed into rubble. The brutal act propelled one of the world's greatest artists into a three-week painting frenzy. Pablo Picasso's *Guernica* starkly depicts the horrors of war, etched into the faces of the people and the animals on the 20-by-30-foot canvas. It would not prove to be the worst attack during the Spanish Civil War, but it became the most famous, through the power of art. The impact of the thousands of bombs dropped on Guernica, of the aircraft machine guns strafing civilians trying to flee the inferno, is still felt to this day—by the elderly survivors, who will eagerly share their vivid memories, as well as by Guernica's youth, who are struggling to forge a future for their town out of its painful history.

The German Luftwaffe's Condor Legion did the bombing at the request of General Francisco Franco, who led a military rebellion against Spain's democratically elected government. Franco enlisted the help of Adolf Hitler and Benito Mussolini, who were eager to practice modern techniques of warfare on the defenseless citizens of Spain. The bombing of Guernica was the first complete destruction by aerial bombardment of a civilian city in European history. While homes and shops were destroyed, several arms-manufacturing facilities, along with a key bridge and the rail line, were left intact.

Spry and alert at eighty-nine, Luis Iriondo Aurtenetxea sat down with me in the offices of Gernika Gogoratuz, which means "Remembering Gernika" in the Basque language. Basque is an ancient language and is central to the fierce independence of Basque-speaking people, who have lived for millennia in the region that straddles the border of Spain and France.

Luis was fourteen and working as an assistant at a local bank when Guernica was bombed. It was market day, so the town was full, the market square packed with people and animals. The bombing started at 4:30 p.m. on April 26, 1937. Luis recalled: "It went on and on for three and a half hours. When the bombing ended, I left the shelter and I saw all of the town burning. Everything was on fire."

Luis and others fled uphill to the nearby village of Lumo, where, as night fell, they saw their hometown burning, saw their homes collapse in the flames. They were given space to sleep in a barn. Luis continued: "I don't remember if it was at midnight or at another time, as I did not own a watch at the time. I heard someone calling me. . . . In the background, you could see Guernica on fire, and thanks to the light of the fire, I realized that it was my mother. She had found my other three siblings. I was the last one to be found." Luis and his family were war refugees for many years, eventually returning to Guernica, where he still lives and works—as did Picasso in Paris—as a painter.

Luis took me to his studio, its walls covered with paintings. Most prominent was the one he painted of that moment in Lumo when his mother found him. I asked him how he felt at that moment. His eyes welled. He apologized and said he couldn't speak of it. Just blocks away stands one of the arms factories that avoided destruction. It was the plant where chemical weapons and pistols were made. It is called the Astra building. While Astra has moved away, the weapons company maintains its connection to the town by naming is various automatic weapons the "Guernica," designed "by warriors, for warriors."

Several years ago, young people occupied the vacant plant, demanding it be turned into a cultural center. Oier Plaza is a young activist from Guernica who told me, "At first the police threw us out, and then we occupied it again, and finally, the town hall bought the building, then we started this process to recover the building and to create the Astra project."

The aim of the Astra project is to convert this weapons plant into a cultural center with classes in art, video, and other media production. "We have to look to the past to understand the present, to create a better future, and I think Astra is part of that process. It is the past, it is the present, and it is the future of this town."

From Picasso's *Guernica* to Luis Iriondo Aurtenetxea's self-portrait with his mother to the efforts of Oier Plaza and his young friends, the power of art to turn swords into plowshares, to resist war, is perennially renewed.

INDEX

DEMOCRACYNOW.ORG

Democracy Now! is a national, daily, independent, award-winning news hour hosted by journalists Amy Goodman and Juan González. Pioneering the largest public media collaboration in the United States, *Democracy Now!* broadcasts on over 1,000 stations, including PBS and public access TV stations; Pacifica, NPR, college and community radio stations; as well as satellite TV (Free Speech TV: DISH Network channel 9415, DIRECTV channel 348, and on Link TV: DISH Network channel 9410, DIRECTV channel 375); and on the Internet at democracynow.org. *Democracy Now!*'s headlines are available in Spanish in text and audio, free for radio stations to carry, as is done on over 300 stations globally. *Democracy Now!*'s video and audio podcasts are among the most popular on the web. *Democracy Now!* is listener, viewer, and reader supported non-profit journalism.

Other books by Amy Goodman:
Breaking the Sound Barrier, with Denis Moynihan

**Other books by Amy Goodman,
coauthored with her brother David Goodman:**

The Exception to the Rulers: Exposing Oily Politicians, War Profiteers and the Media That Love Them

Static: Government Liars, Media Cheerleaders, and the People Who Fight Back

Standing Up to the Madness: Ordinary Heroes in Extraordinary Times

Get signed books, as well as audiobooks, DVDs, and other gifts, or make a tax-deductible contribtion, at democracynow.org.

AMY GOODMAN is an internationally acclaimed journalist, and host and executive producer of *Democracy Now!*, a daily grass-roots global news hour that broadcasts on over 1,000 radio and television stations and at democracynow.org. She is a syndicated columnist with King Features. Amy has received numerous awards for her work, including the Robert F. Kennedy Prize for International Reporting, the George Polk Award, the Alfred I. duPont-Columbia University Awards for excellence in broadcast journalism, and the Radio/Television News Directors Award, as well as awards from the Associated Press and United Press International. She is the first journalist to receive the Right Livelihood Award, also referred to as "The Alternative Nobel Prize," presented in the Swedish parliament. Amy was co-winner of the first annual Izzy Award from the Park Center for Independent Media at Ithaca College, named after legendary journalist I. F. Stone. She is the author of several books, all *New York Times* best-sellers, including *Breaking the Sound Barrier*, with Denis Moynihan, and, co-authored with her brother, David Goodman: *The Exception to the Rulers, Static,* and *Standing Up to the Madness.* She lives in New York City.

DENIS MOYNIHAN met the *Democracy Now!* team as they covered protests against the World Trade Organization in Seattle in 1999. Since 2001, he has participated in the organization's growth and sustainability, focusing primarily on distribution, infrastructure development, and coordinating special projects, including live broadcasts from around the world. He lives in Denver, and is the founder of a new full-power noncommercial, community FM radio station in Colorado's high country, as well as an avid telemark skier and mountain biker. This is his first book.

ABOUT HAYMARKET BOOKS

Haymarket Books is a nonprofit, progressive book distributor and publisher, a project of the Center for Economic Research and Social Change. We believe that activists need to take ideas, history, and politics into the many struggles for social justice today. Learning the lessons of past victories, as well as defeats, can arm a new generation of fighters for a better world. As Karl Marx said, "The philosophers have merely interpreted the world; the point however is to change it."

We take inspiration and courage from our namesakes, the Haymarket Martyrs, who gave their lives fighting for a better world. Their 1886 struggle for the eight-hour day reminds workers around the world that ordinary people can organize and struggle for their own liberation.

For more information and to shop our complete catalog of titles, visit us online at www.haymarketbooks.org.

ALSO FROM HAYMARKET BOOKS

Breaking the Sound Barrier • Amy Goodman

Democracy at Work: A Cure for Capitalism • Richard Wolff

The Democrats: A Critical History (Revised and Updated Edition)
Lance Selfa

Howard Zinn Speaks: Collected Speeches 1963 to 2009 • Howard Zinn;
edited by Anthony Arnove

My People Are Rising: Memoir of a Black Panther Party Captain
Aaron Dixon

Islamophobia and the Politics of Empire • Deepa Kumar

The John Carlos Story: The Sports Moment That Changed the World
John Carlos with Dave Zirin

Detroit: I Do Mind Dying • Dan Georgakas and Marvin Surkin

A Time to Die: The Attica Prison Revolt • Tom Wicker